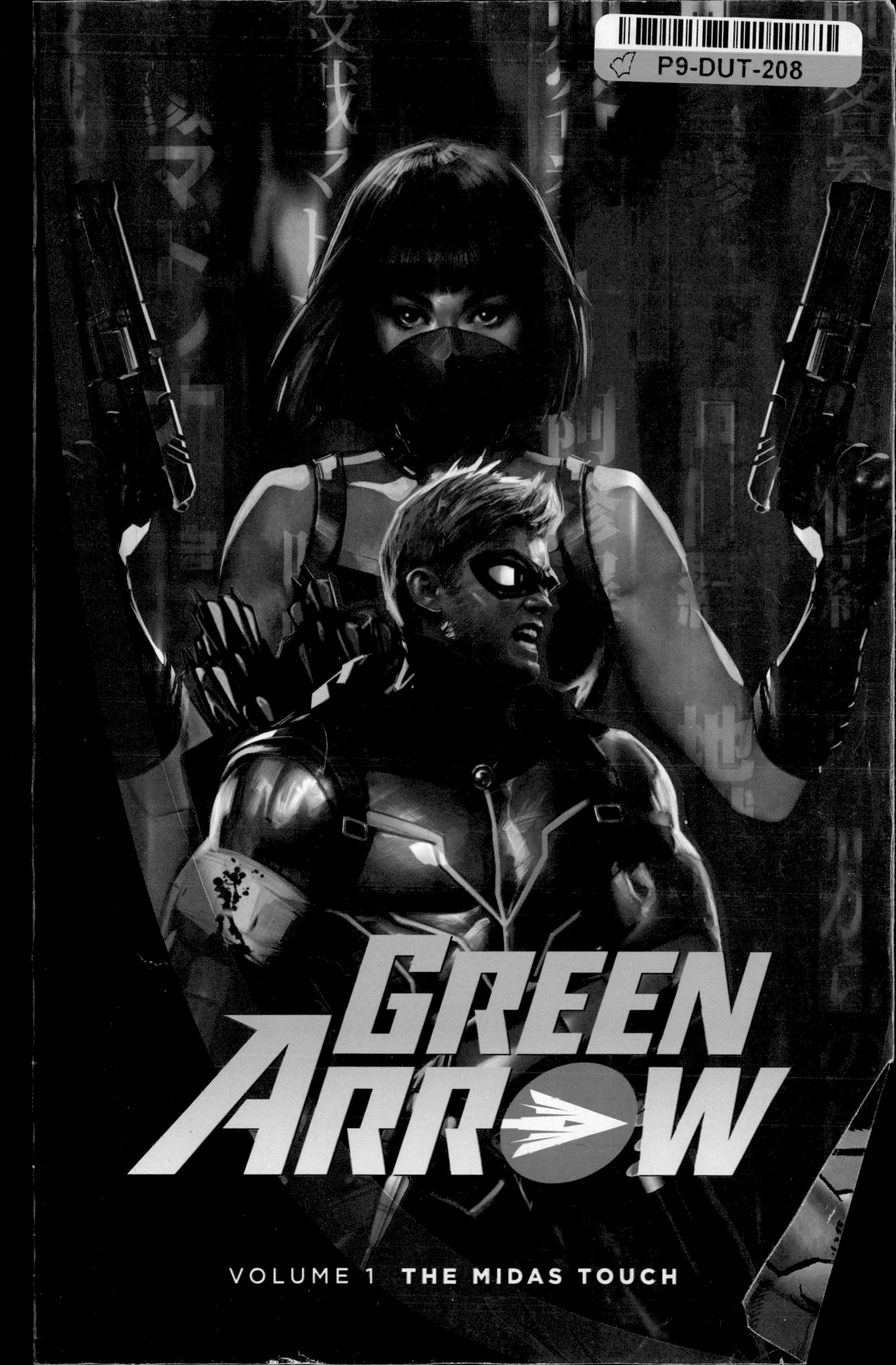
GREEN
ARROW
VOLUME 1 THE MIDAS TOUCH

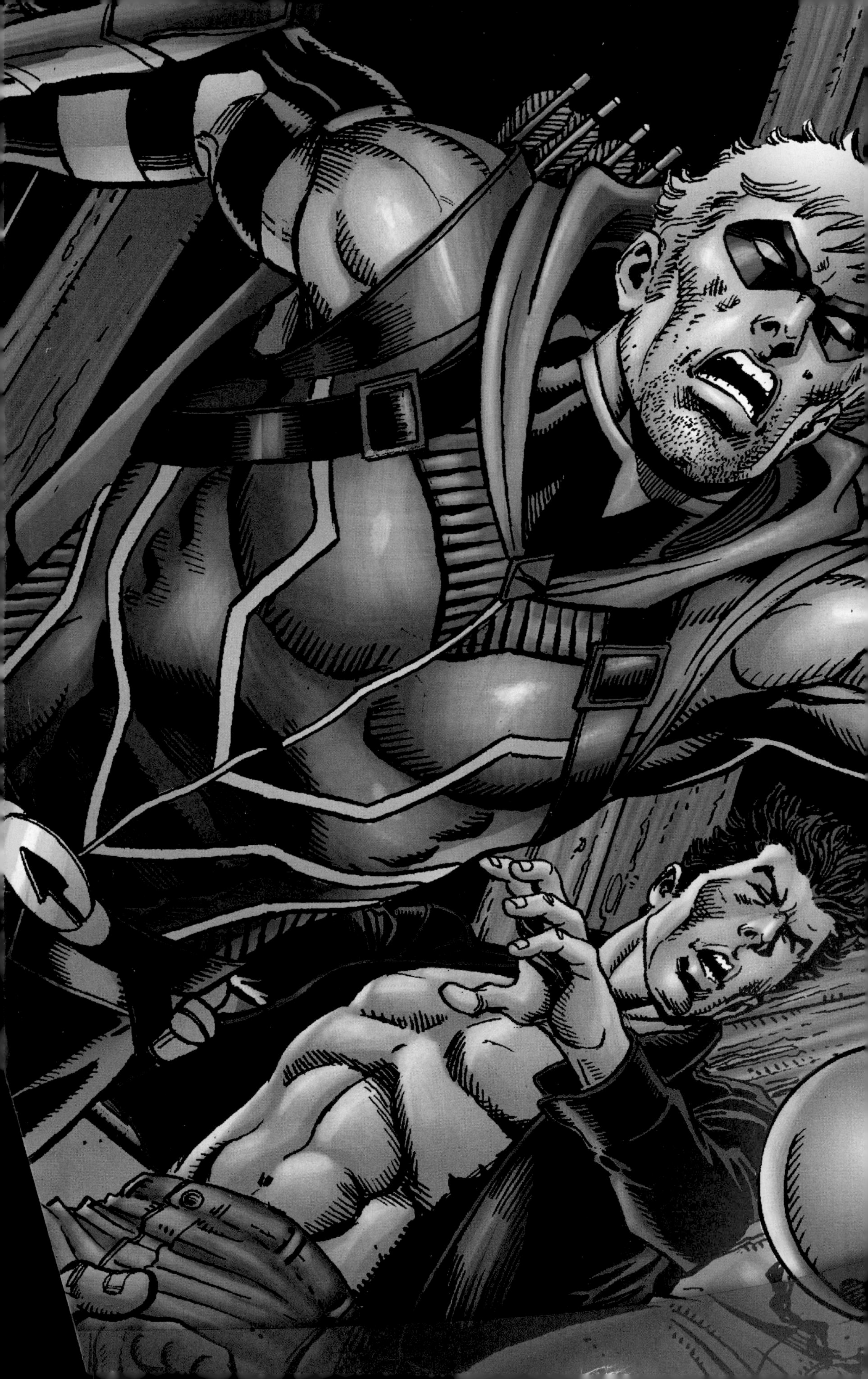

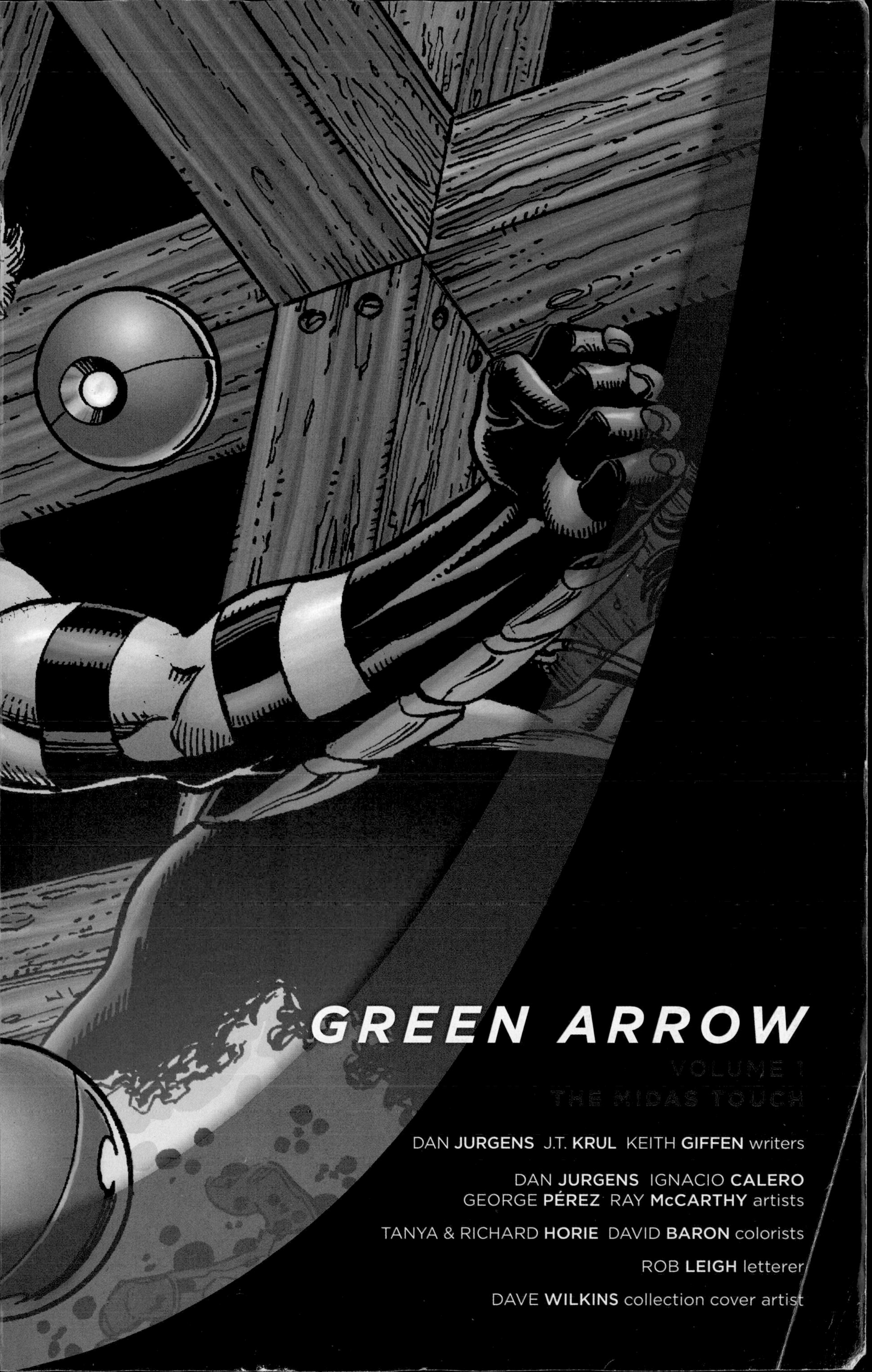

GREEN ARROW

VOLUME 1
THE MIDAS TOUCH

DAN **JURGENS** J.T. **KRUL** KEITH **GIFFEN** writers

DAN **JURGENS** IGNACIO **CALERO**
GEORGE **PÉREZ** RAY **McCARTHY** artists

TANYA & RICHARD **HORIE** DAVID **BARON** colorists

ROB **LEIGH** letterer

DAVE **WILKINS** collection cover artist

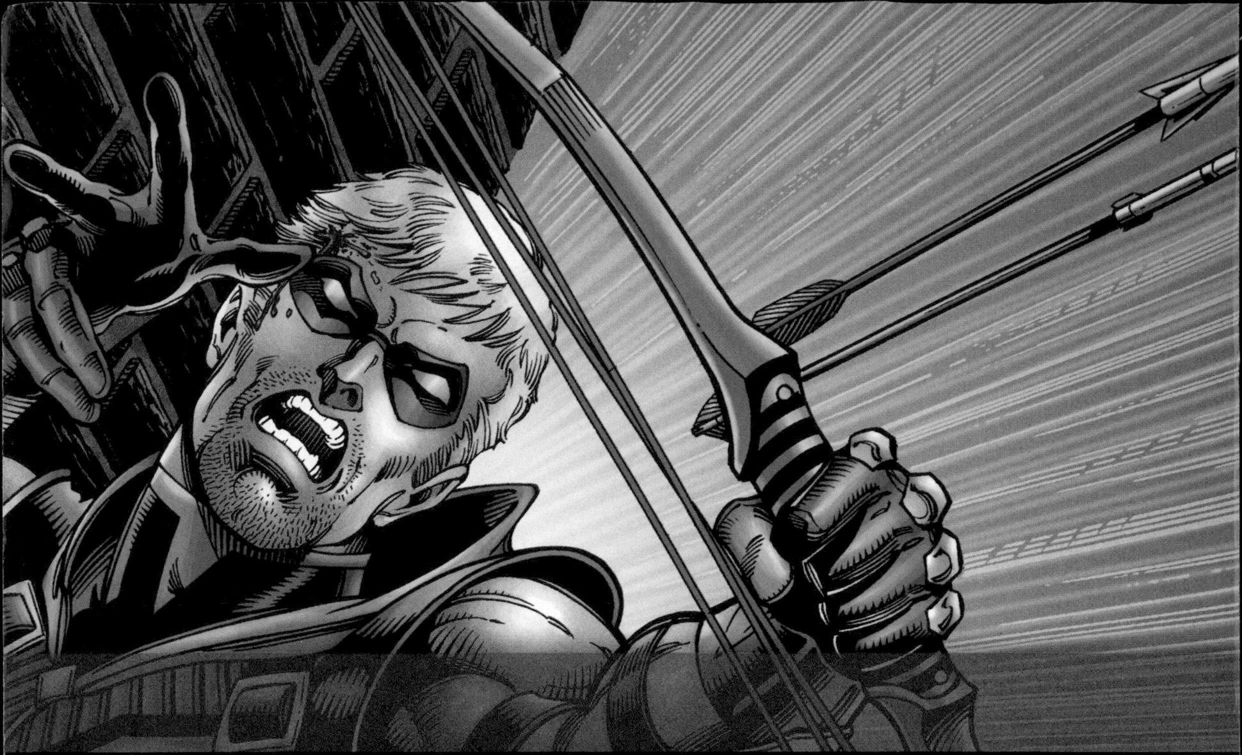

PAT McCALLUM Editor – Original Series SEAN MACKIEWICZ Assistant Editor – Original Series
ROBIN WILDMAN Editor ROBBIN BROSTERMAN Design Director – Books
ROBBIE BIEDERMAN Publication Design

BOB HARRAS Senior VP – Editor-in-Chief, DC Comics

DIANE NELSON President DAN DIDIO and JIM LEE Co-Publishers
GEOFF JOHNS Chief Creative Officer
AMIT DESAI Senior VP – Marketing & Franchise Management
AMY GENKINS Senior VP – Business & Legal Affairs NAIRI GARDINER Senior VP – Finance
JEFF BOISON VP – Publishing Planning MARK CHIARELLO VP – Art Direction & Design
JOHN CUNNINGHAM VP – Marketing TERRI CUNNINGHAM VP – Editorial Administration
LARRY GANEM VP – Talent Relations & Services ALISON GILL Senior VP – Manufacturing & Operations
HANK KANALZ Senior VP – Vertigo & Integrated Publishing JAY KOGAN VP – Business & Legal Affairs, Publishing
JACK MAHAN VP – Business Affairs, Talent NICK NAPOLITANO VP – Manufacturing Administration
SUE POHJA VP – Book Sales FRED RUIZ VP – Manufacturing Operations
COURTNEY SIMMONS Senior VP – Publicity BOB WAYNE Senior VP – Sales

GREEN ARROW VOLUME 1: THE MIDAS TOUCH

DC Comics, 1700 Broadway, New York, NY 10019
A Warner Bros. Entertainment Company
Printed by RR Donnelley, Owensville, MO, USA. 7/25/14. Fourth Printing.

ISBN: 978-1-4012-3486-7

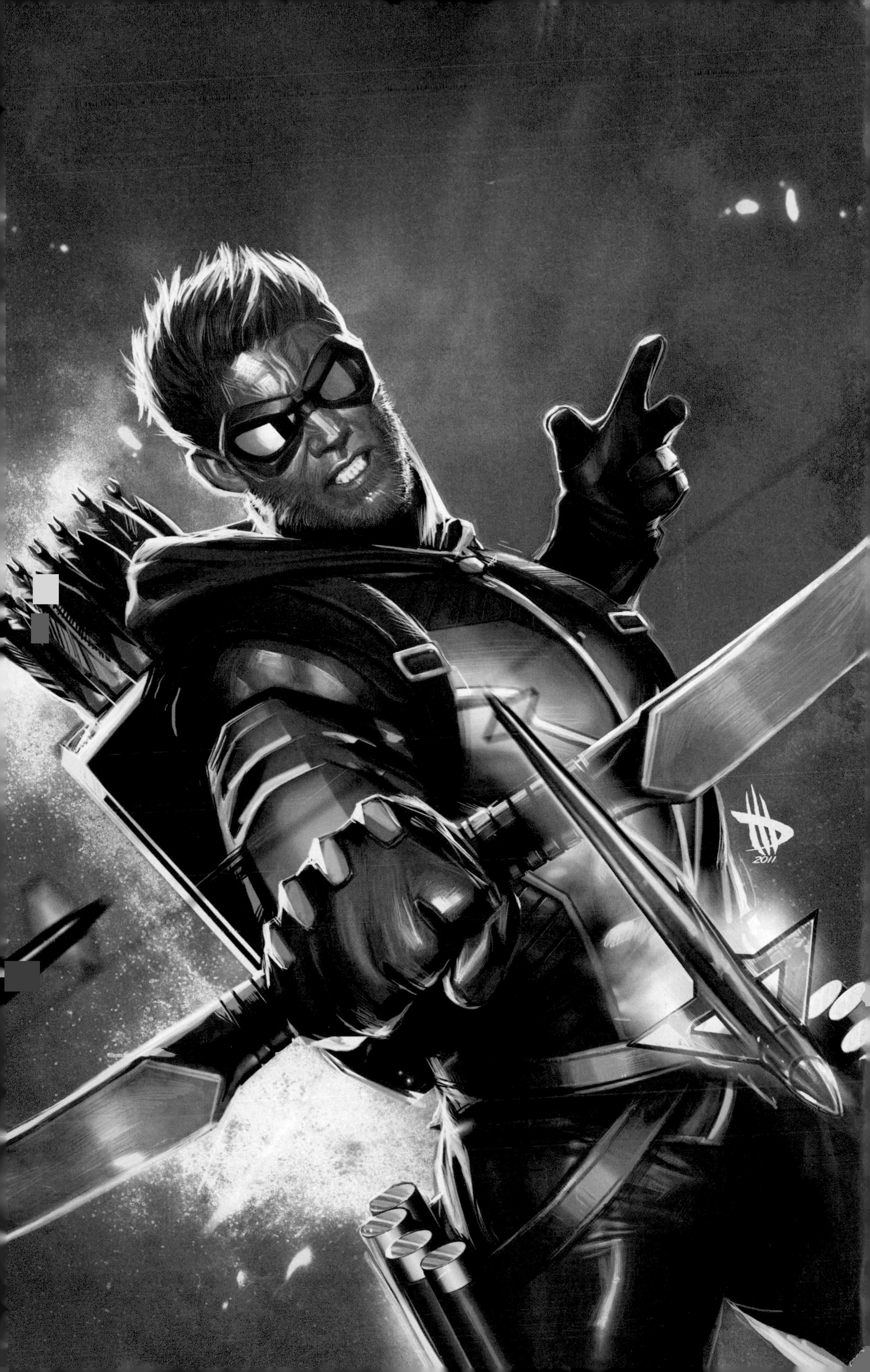

LIVING A LIFE OF PRIVILEGE

J.T. KRUL
writer

DAN JURGENS
layouts

GEORGE PÉREZ
finishes

cover by DAVE WILKINS

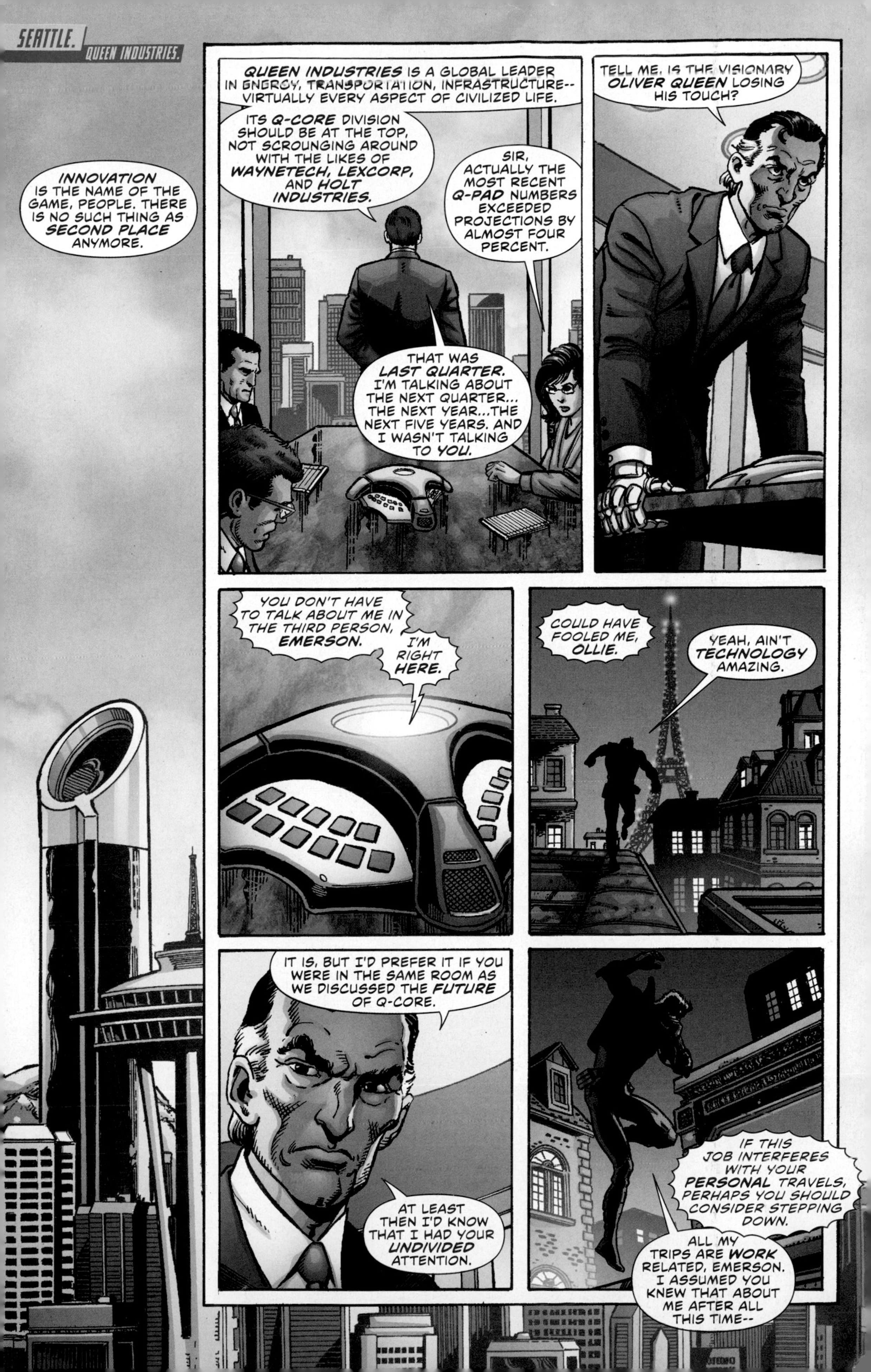
SEATTLE.
QUEEN INDUSTRIES.
INNOVATION IS THE NAME OF THE GAME, PEOPLE. THERE IS NO SUCH THING AS SECOND PLACE ANYMORE.
QUEEN INDUSTRIES IS A GLOBAL LEADER IN ENERGY, TRANSPORTATION, INFRASTRUCTURE-- VIRTUALLY EVERY ASPECT OF CIVILIZED LIFE.
ITS Q-CORE DIVISION SHOULD BE AT THE TOP, NOT SCROUNGING AROUND WITH THE LIKES OF WAYNETECH, LEXCORP, AND HOLT INDUSTRIES.
SIR, ACTUALLY THE MOST RECENT Q-PAD NUMBERS EXCEEDED PROJECTIONS BY ALMOST FOUR PERCENT.
THAT WAS LAST QUARTER. I'M TALKING ABOUT THE NEXT QUARTER... THE NEXT YEAR...THE NEXT FIVE YEARS. AND I WASN'T TALKING TO YOU.
TELL ME. IS THE VISIONARY OLIVER QUEEN LOSING HIS TOUCH?
YOU DON'T HAVE TO TALK ABOUT ME IN THE THIRD PERSON, EMERSON.
I'M RIGHT HERE.
COULD HAVE FOOLED ME, OLLIE.
YEAH, AIN'T TECHNOLOGY AMAZING.
IT IS, BUT I'D PREFER IT IF YOU WERE IN THE SAME ROOM AS WE DISCUSSED THE FUTURE OF Q-CORE.
AT LEAST THEN I'D KNOW THAT I HAD YOUR UNDIVIDED ATTENTION.
IF THIS JOB INTERFERES WITH YOUR PERSONAL TRAVELS, PERHAPS YOU SHOULD CONSIDER STEPPING DOWN.
ALL MY TRIPS ARE WORK RELATED, EMERSON. I ASSUMED YOU KNEW THAT ABOUT ME AFTER ALL THIS TIME--

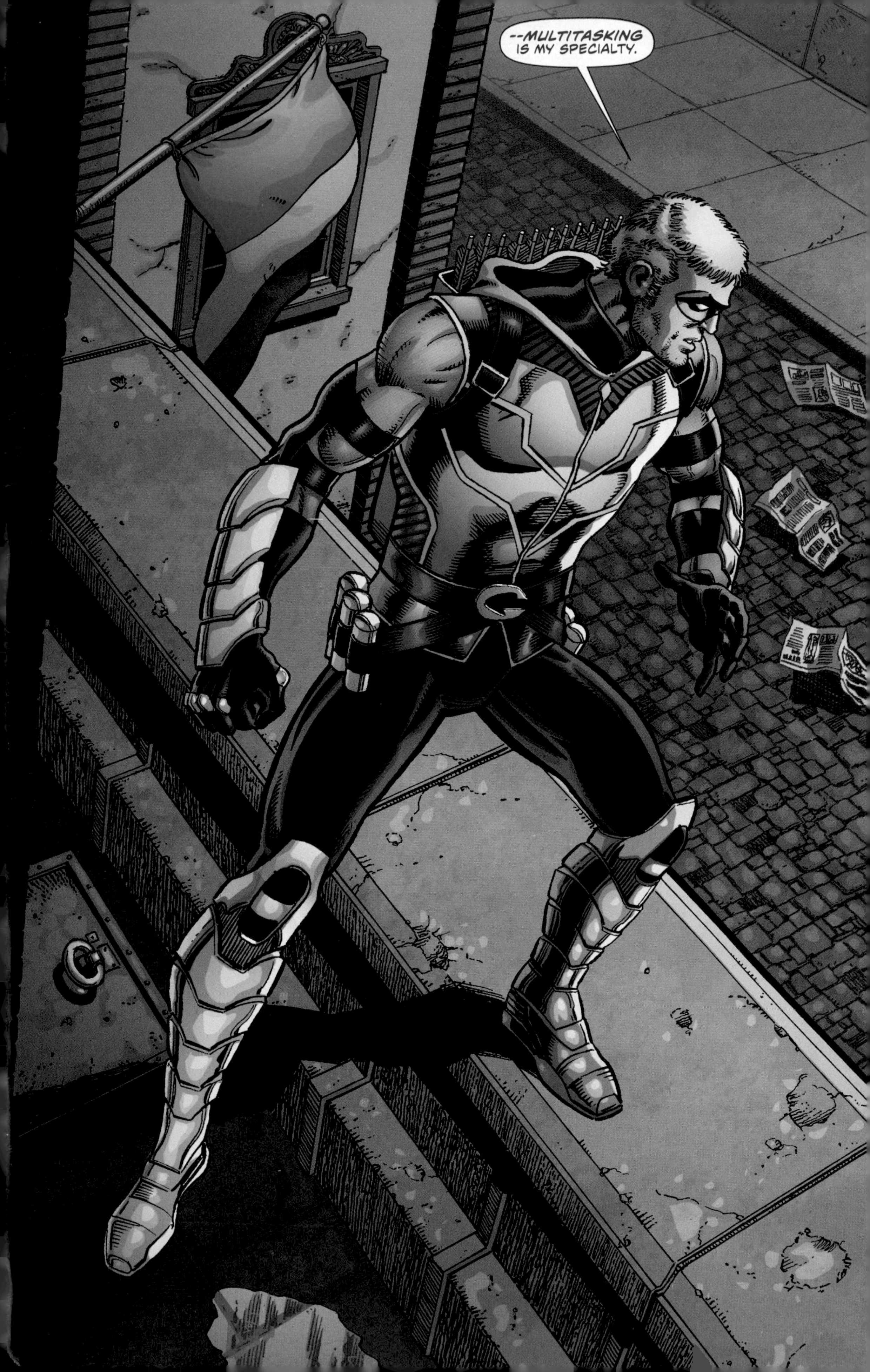
--MULTITASKING IS MY SPECIALTY.

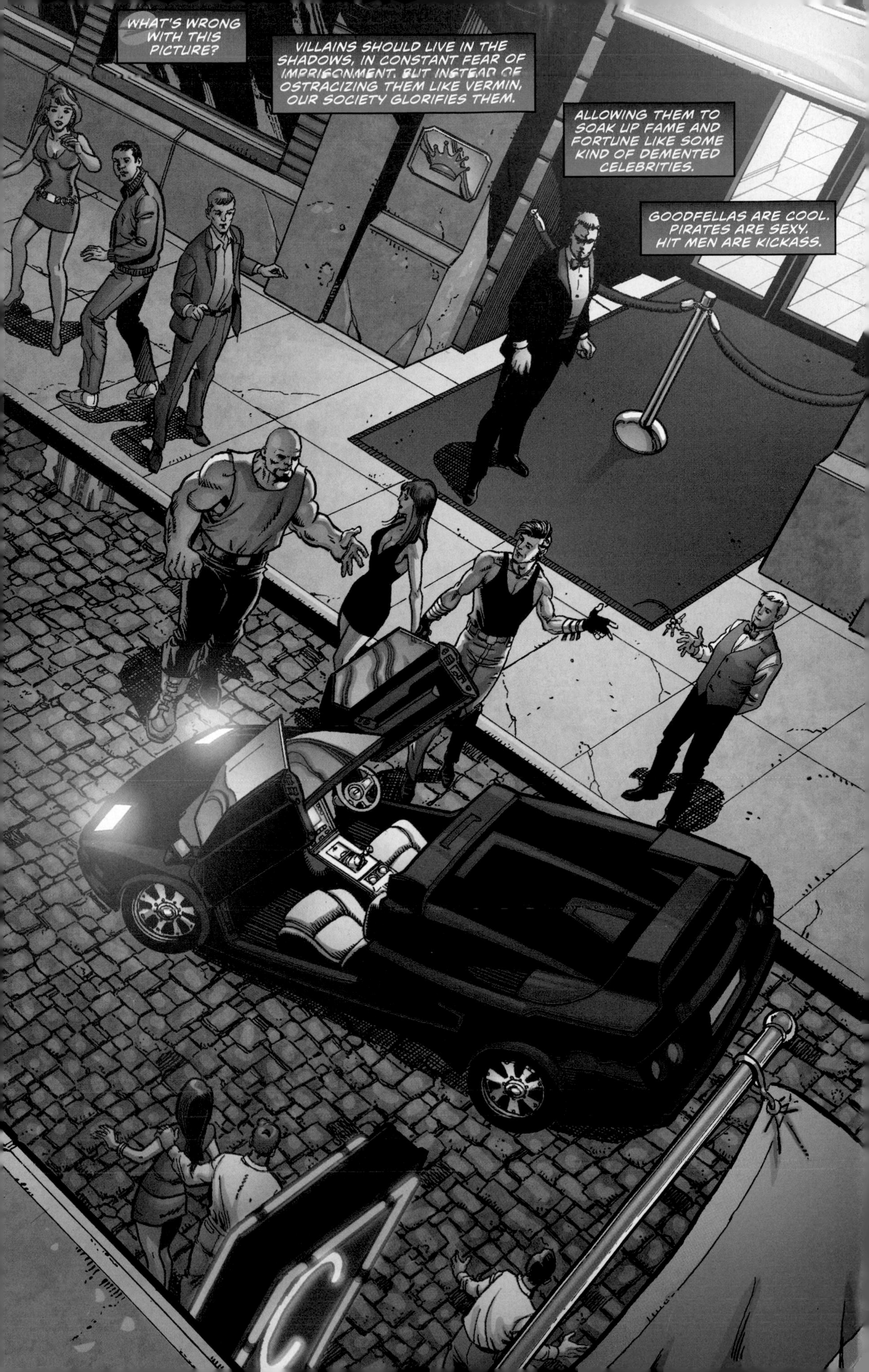
WHAT'S WRONG WITH THIS PICTURE?
VILLAINS SHOULD LIVE IN THE SHADOWS, IN CONSTANT FEAR OF IMPRISONMENT. BUT INSTEAD OF OSTRACIZING THEM LIKE VERMIN, OUR SOCIETY GLORIFIES THEM.
ALLOWING THEM TO SOAK UP FAME AND FORTUNE LIKE SOME KIND OF DEMENTED CELEBRITIES.
GOODFELLAS ARE COOL. PIRATES ARE SEXY. HIT MEN ARE KICKASS.

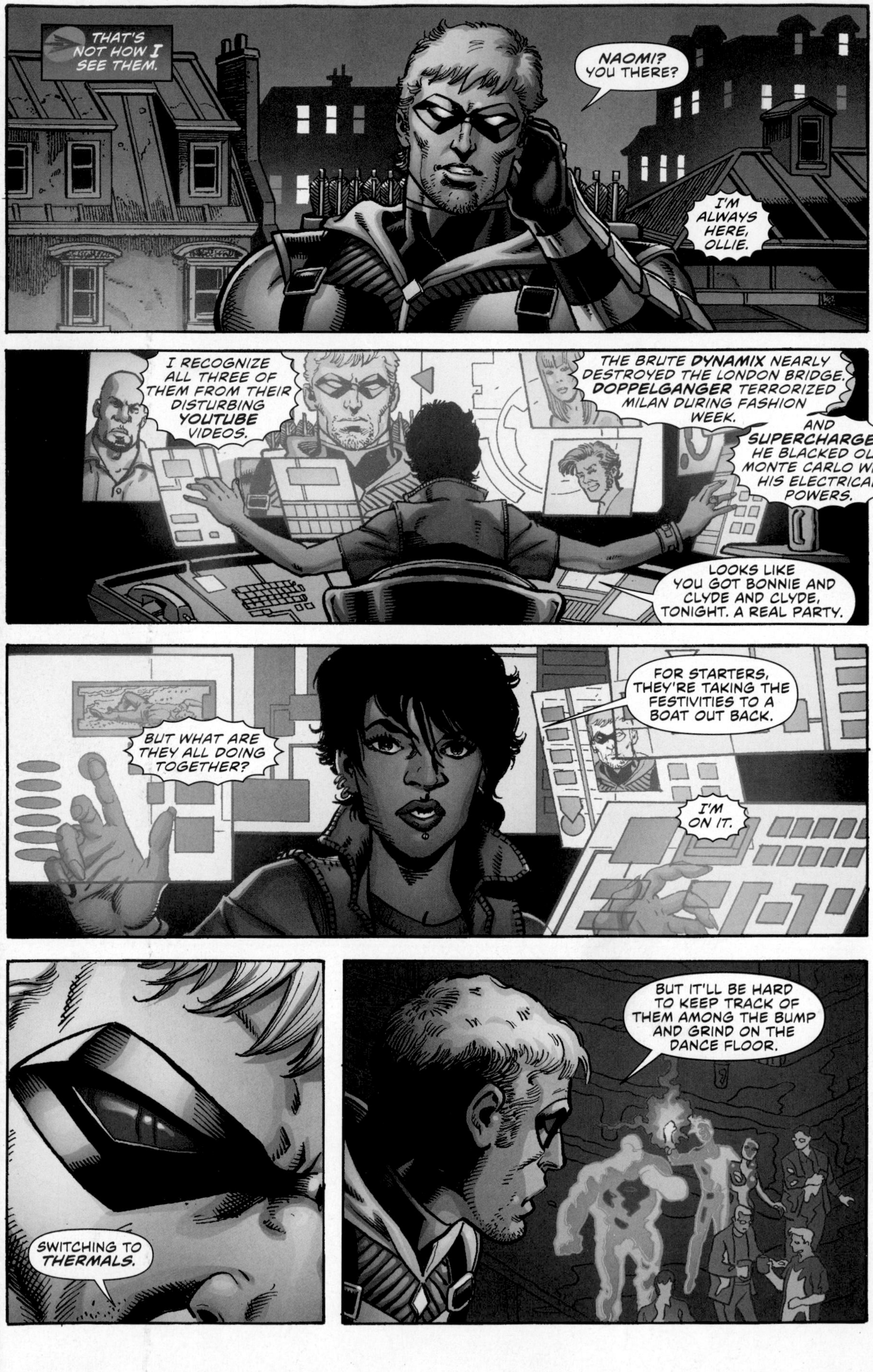

THAT'S NOT HOW I SEE THEM.
NAOMI? YOU THERE?
I'M ALWAYS HERE, OLLIE.
I RECOGNIZE ALL THREE OF THEM FROM THEIR DISTURBING YOUTUBE VIDEOS.
THE BRUTE DYNAMIX NEARLY DESTROYED THE LONDON BRIDGE. DOPPELGANGER TERRORIZED MILAN DURING FASHION WEEK.
AND SUPERCHARGE-- HE BLACKED OUT MONTE CARLO WITH HIS ELECTRICAL POWERS.
LOOKS LIKE YOU GOT BONNIE AND CLYDE AND CLYDE, TONIGHT. A REAL PARTY.
BUT WHAT ARE THEY ALL DOING TOGETHER?
FOR STARTERS, THEY'RE TAKING THE FESTIVITIES TO A BOAT OUT BACK.
I'M ON IT.
SWITCHING TO THERMALS.
BUT IT'LL BE HARD TO KEEP TRACK OF THEM AMONG THE BUMP AND GRIND ON THE DANCE FLOOR.

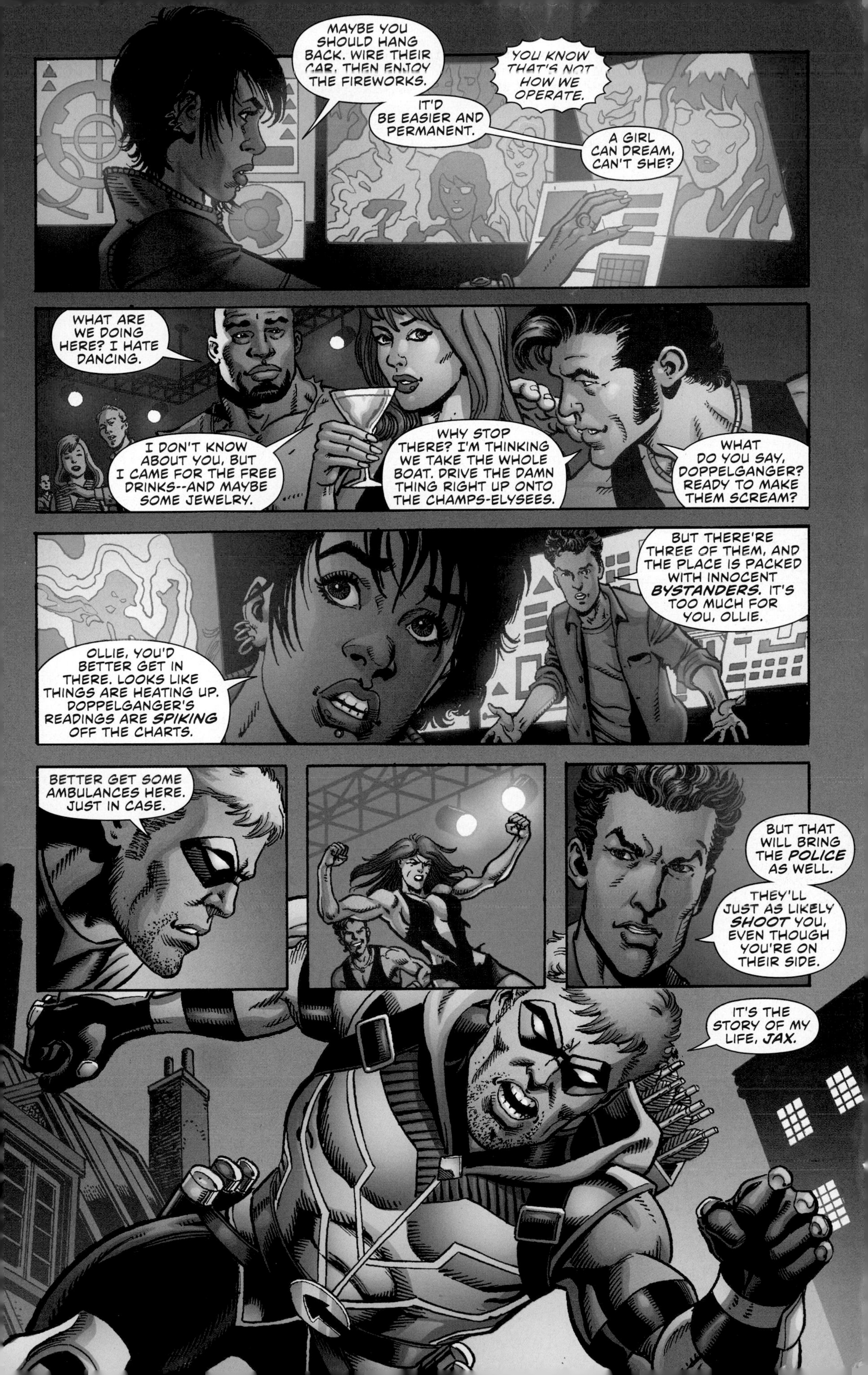
MAYBE YOU SHOULD HANG BACK. WIRE THEIR CAR, THEN ENJOY THE FIREWORKS.
YOU KNOW THAT'S NOT HOW WE OPERATE.
IT'D BE EASIER AND PERMANENT.
A GIRL CAN DREAM, CAN'T SHE?
WHAT ARE WE DOING HERE? I HATE DANCING.
I DON'T KNOW ABOUT YOU, BUT I CAME FOR THE FREE DRINKS--AND MAYBE SOME JEWELRY.
WHY STOP THERE? I'M THINKING WE TAKE THE WHOLE BOAT. DRIVE THE DAMN THING RIGHT UP ONTO THE CHAMPS-ELYSEES.
WHAT DO YOU SAY, DOPPELGANGER? READY TO MAKE THEM SCREAM?
OLLIE, YOU'D BETTER GET IN THERE. LOOKS LIKE THINGS ARE HEATING UP. DOPPELGANGER'S READINGS ARE SPIKING OFF THE CHARTS.
BUT THERE'RE THREE OF THEM, AND THE PLACE IS PACKED WITH INNOCENT BYSTANDERS. IT'S TOO MUCH FOR YOU, OLLIE.
BETTER GET SOME AMBULANCES HERE. JUST IN CASE.
BUT THAT WILL BRING THE POLICE AS WELL.
THEY'LL JUST AS LIKELY SHOOT YOU, EVEN THOUGH YOU'RE ON THEIR SIDE.
IT'S THE STORY OF MY LIFE, JAX.

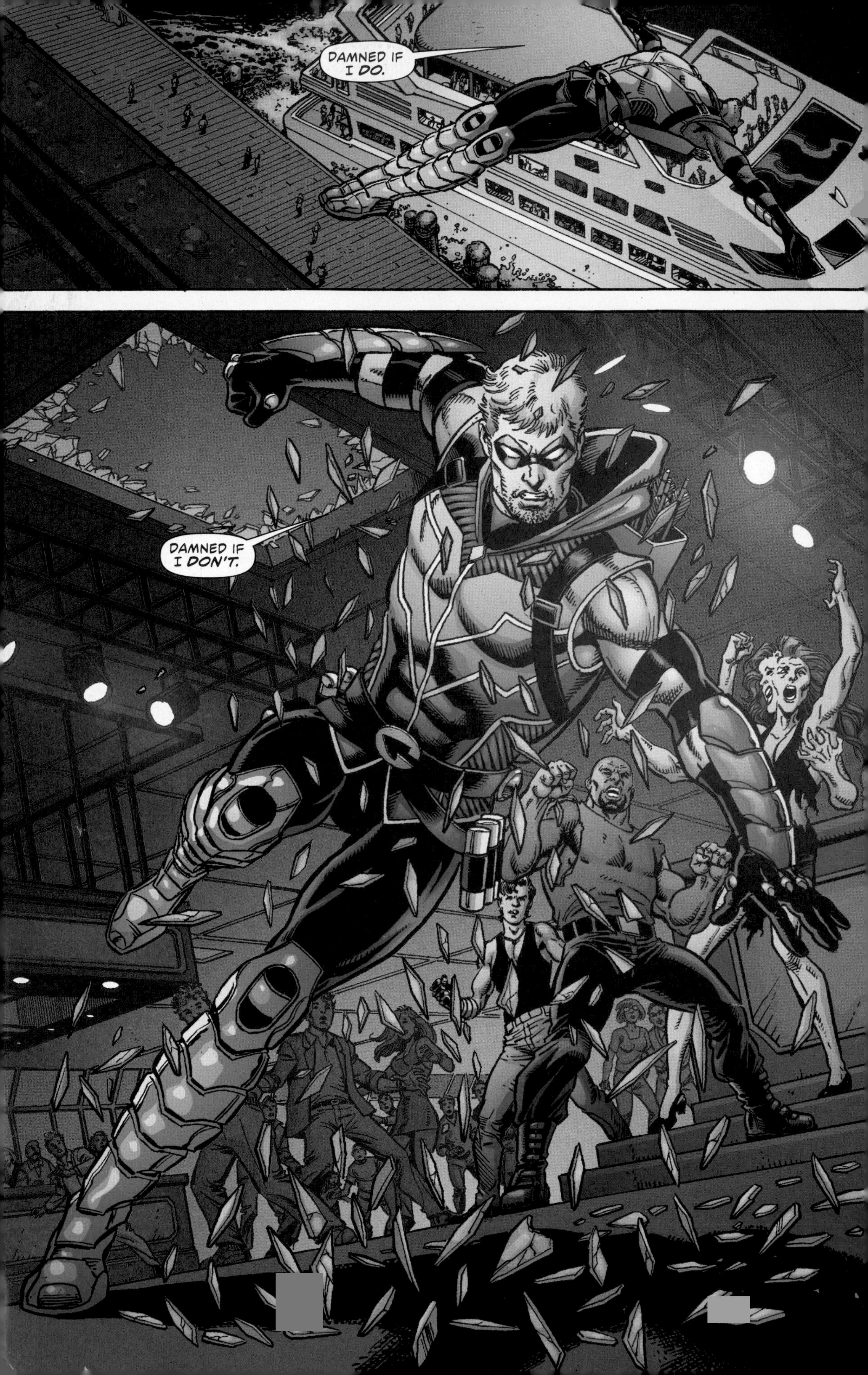
DAMNED IF I DO.
DAMNED IF I DON'T.

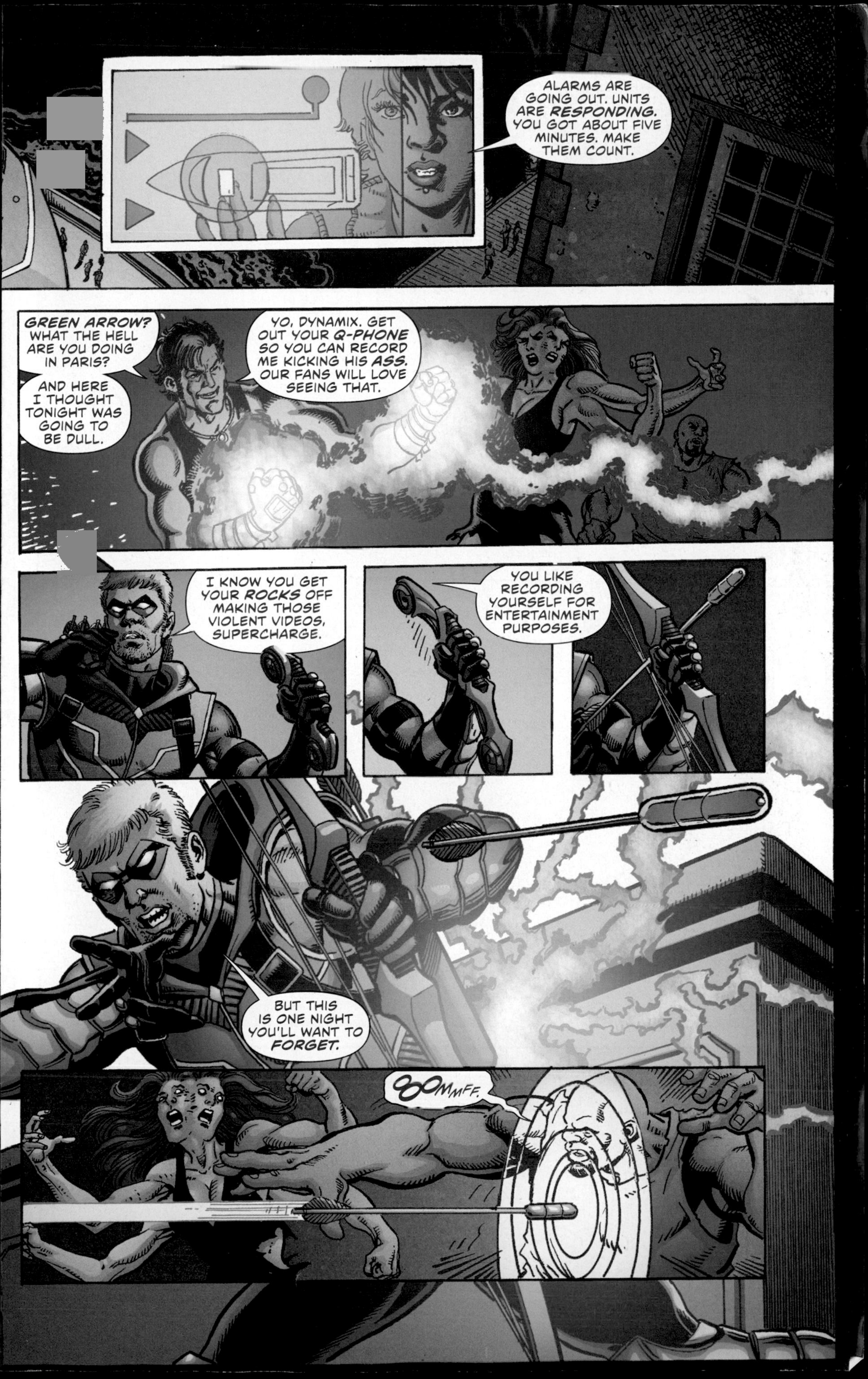
ALARMS ARE GOING OUT. UNITS ARE RESPONDING. YOU GOT ABOUT FIVE MINUTES. MAKE THEM COUNT.
GREEN ARROW? WHAT THE HELL ARE YOU DOING IN PARIS?
AND HERE I THOUGHT TONIGHT WAS GOING TO BE DULL.
YO, DYNAMIX. GET OUT YOUR Q-PHONE SO YOU CAN RECORD ME KICKING HIS ASS. OUR FANS WILL LOVE SEEING THAT.
I KNOW YOU GET YOUR ROCKS OFF MAKING THOSE VIOLENT VIDEOS, SUPERCHARGE.
YOU LIKE RECORDING YOURSELF FOR ENTERTAINMENT PURPOSES.
BUT THIS IS ONE NIGHT YOU'LL WANT TO FORGET.
OOOMMFF.

HEY, PARTY PEOPLE-- HOW ABOUT YOU STOP GAWKING AND GET THE HELL OUT OF HERE.

THIS AIN'T NO DISCO.

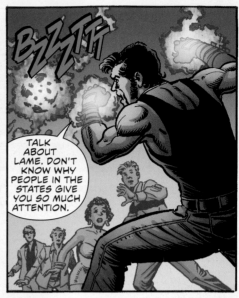

BZZTF

TALK ABOUT LAME. DON'T KNOW WHY PEOPLE IN THE STATES GIVE YOU SO MUCH ATTENTION.

YOU'RE NOTHING BUT A MAN IN A SUIT. RUNNING AROUND PLAYING SUPER HERO WITH A BUNCH OF TOYS.

I DON'T USE TOYS. THIS-- THIS IS REAL POWER!

YOU'RE RIGHT, I HAVE A LOT OF TOYS.

BUT I DON'T PLAY GAMES.

GAHH!

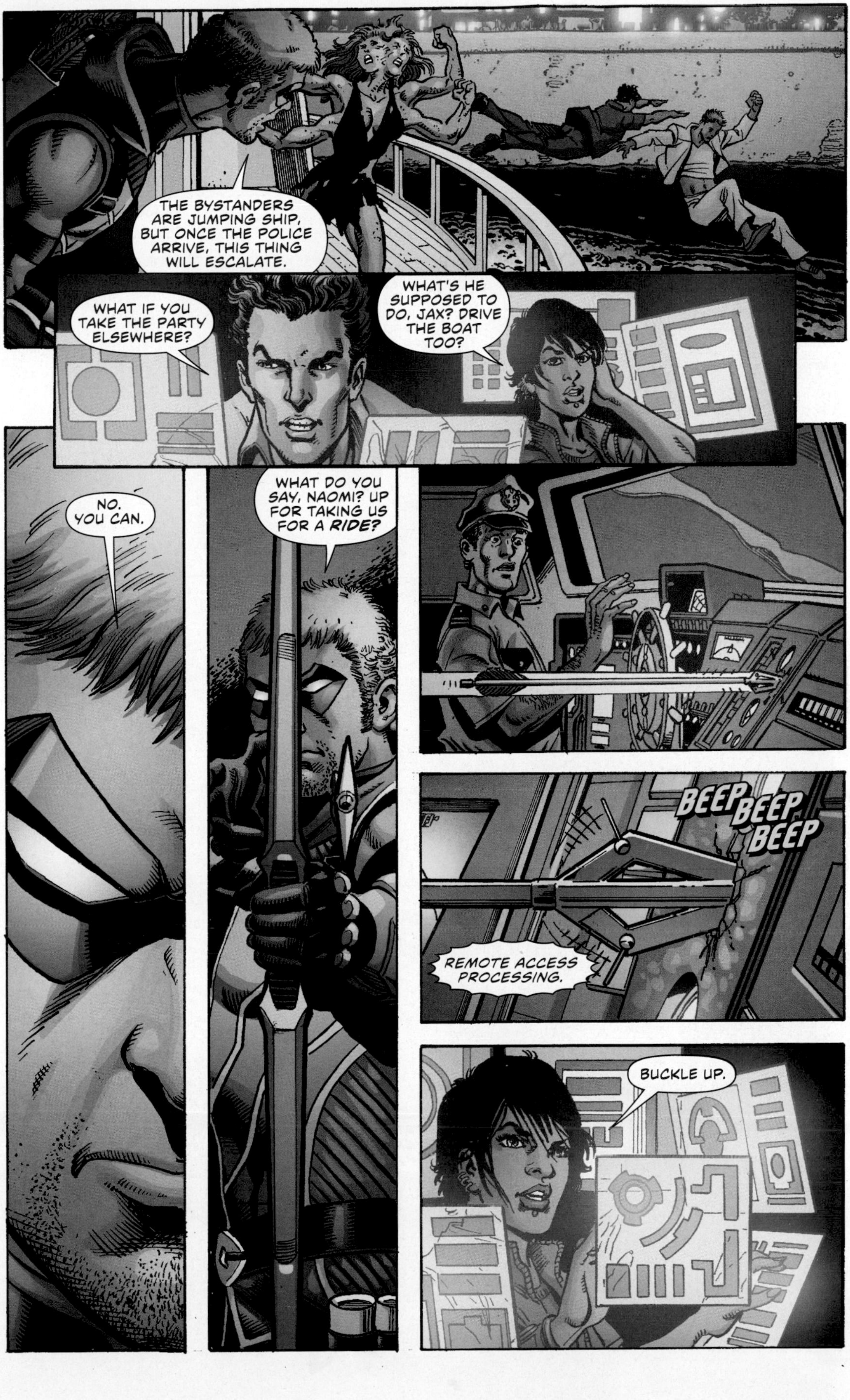
THE BYSTANDERS ARE JUMPING SHIP, BUT ONCE THE POLICE ARRIVE, THIS THING WILL ESCALATE.
WHAT IF YOU TAKE THE PARTY ELSEWHERE?
WHAT'S HE SUPPOSED TO DO, JAX? DRIVE THE BOAT TOO?
NO. YOU CAN.
WHAT DO YOU SAY, NAOMI? UP FOR TAKING US FOR A *RIDE?*
BEEP BEEP BEEP
REMOTE ACCESS PROCESSING.
BUCKLE UP.

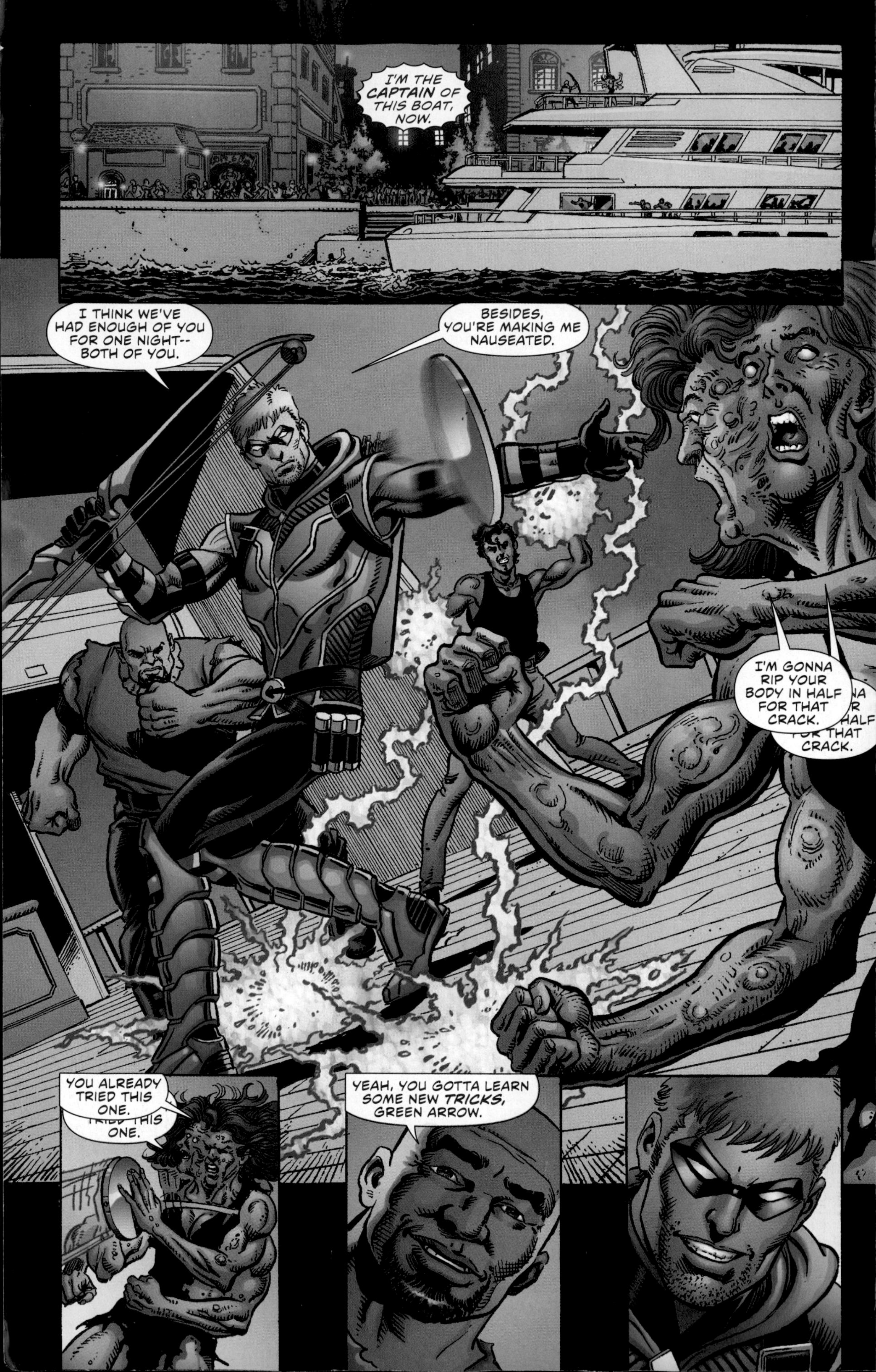
I'M THE CAPTAIN OF THIS BOAT, NOW.
I THINK WE'VE HAD ENOUGH OF YOU FOR ONE NIGHT-- BOTH OF YOU.
BESIDES, YOU'RE MAKING ME NAUSEATED.
I'M GONNA RIP YOUR BODY IN HALF FOR THAT CRACK.
YOU ALREADY TRIED THIS ONE.
YEAH, YOU GOTTA LEARN SOME NEW TRICKS, GREEN ARROW.

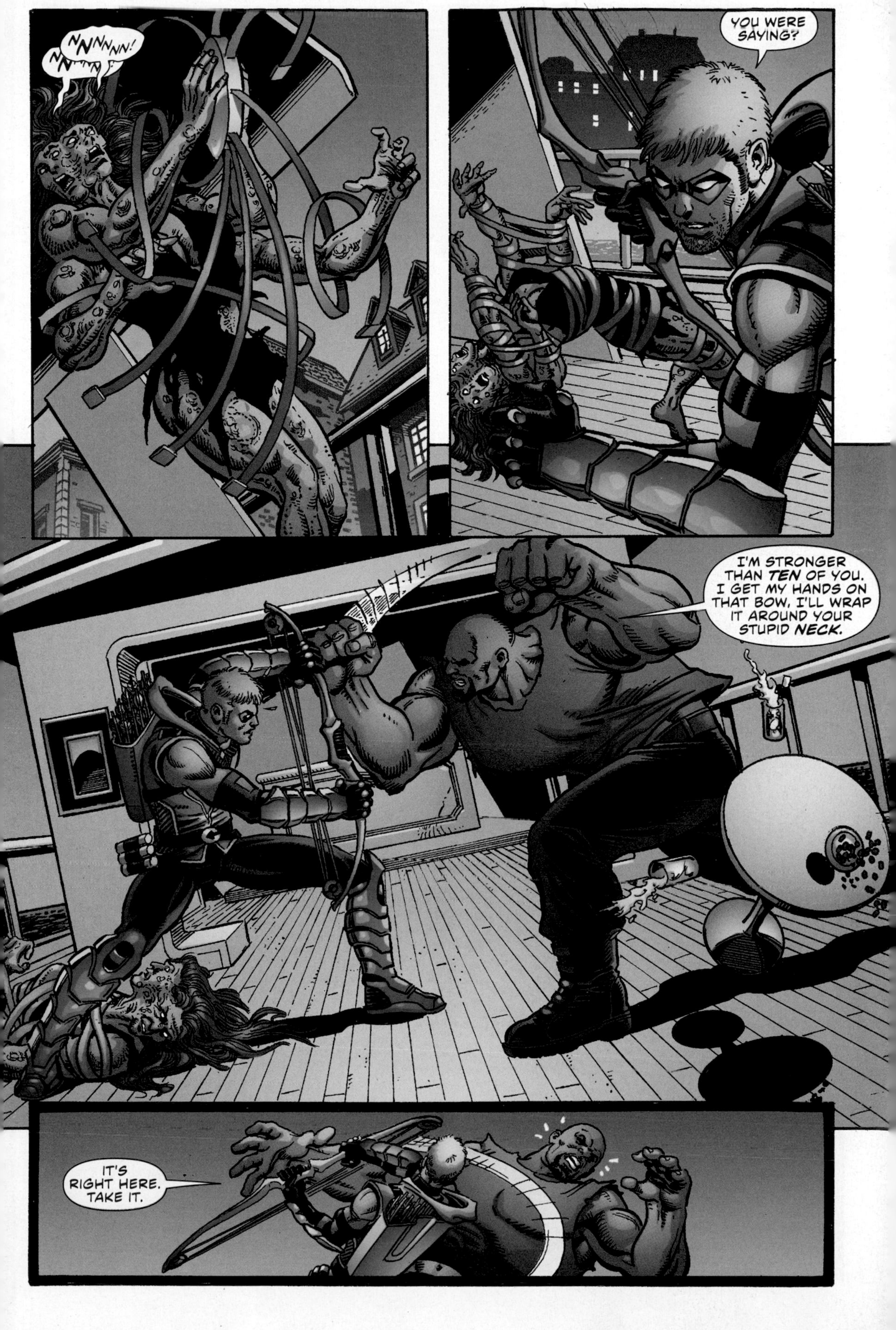
NNNNNN! NNNNN!
YOU WERE SAYING?
I'M STRONGER THAN TEN OF YOU. I GET MY HANDS ON THAT BOW, I'LL WRAP IT AROUND YOUR STUPID NECK.
IT'S RIGHT HERE. TAKE IT.

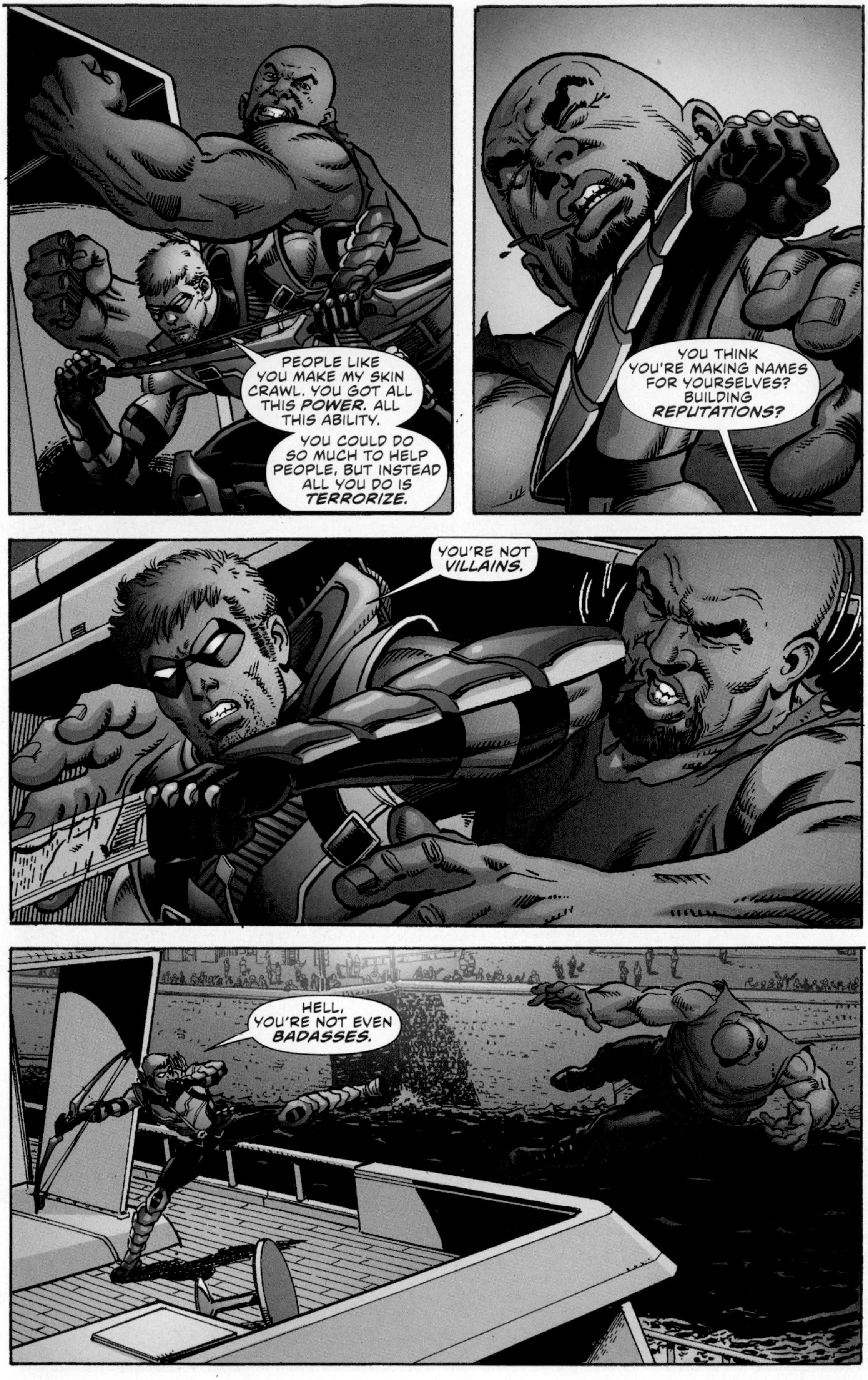
PEOPLE LIKE YOU MAKE MY SKIN CRAWL. YOU GOT ALL THIS POWER. ALL THIS ABILITY.
YOU COULD DO SO MUCH TO HELP PEOPLE, BUT INSTEAD ALL YOU DO IS TERRORIZE.
YOU THINK YOU'RE MAKING NAMES FOR YOURSELVES? BUILDING REPUTATIONS?
YOU'RE NOT VILLAINS.
HELL, YOU'RE NOT EVEN BADASSES.

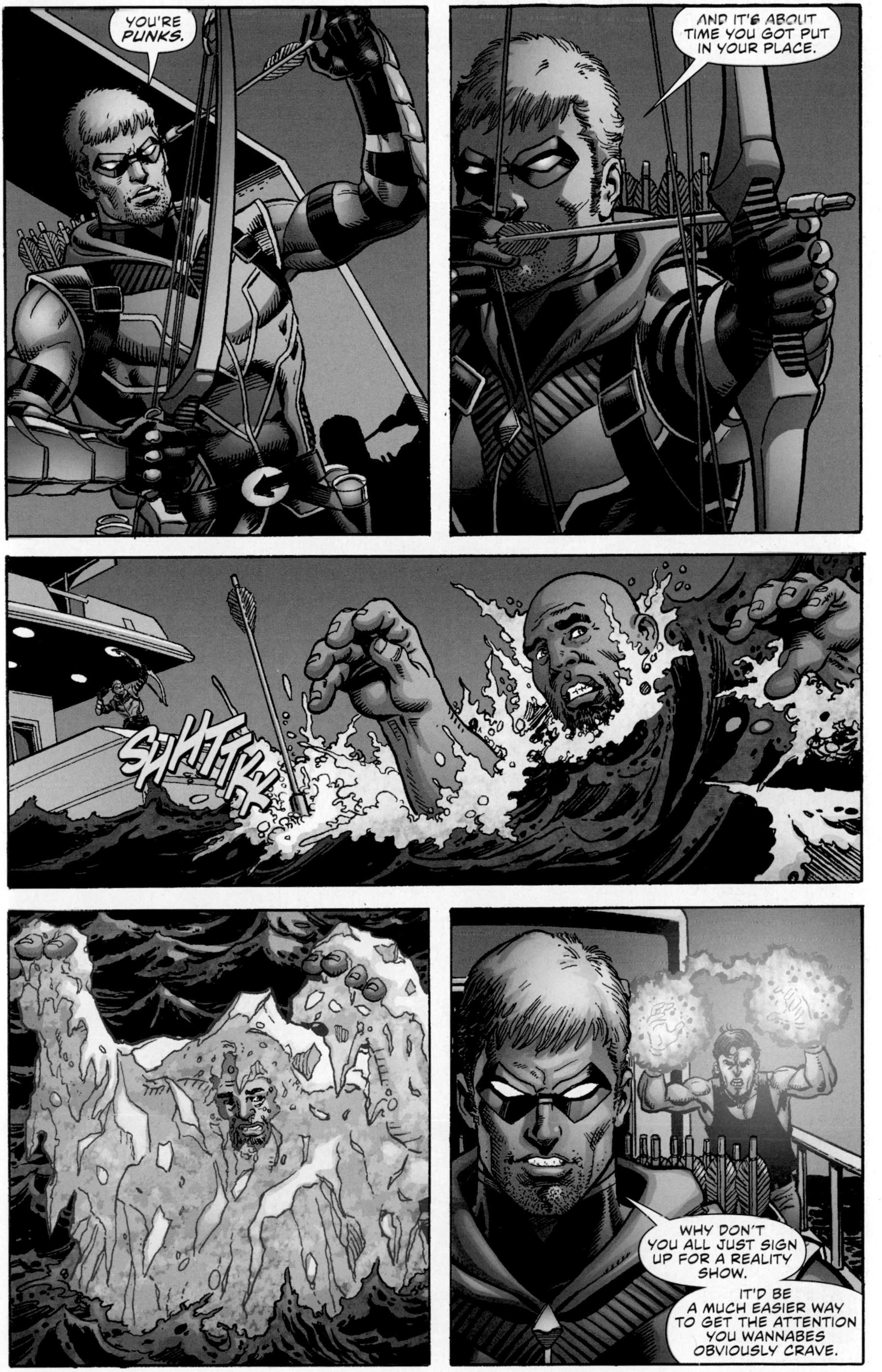
YOU'RE PUNKS.
AND IT'S ABOUT TIME YOU GOT PUT IN YOUR PLACE.
WHY DON'T YOU ALL JUST SIGN UP FOR A REALITY SHOW.
IT'D BE A MUCH EASIER WAY TO GET THE ATTENTION YOU WANNABES OBVIOUSLY CRAVE.

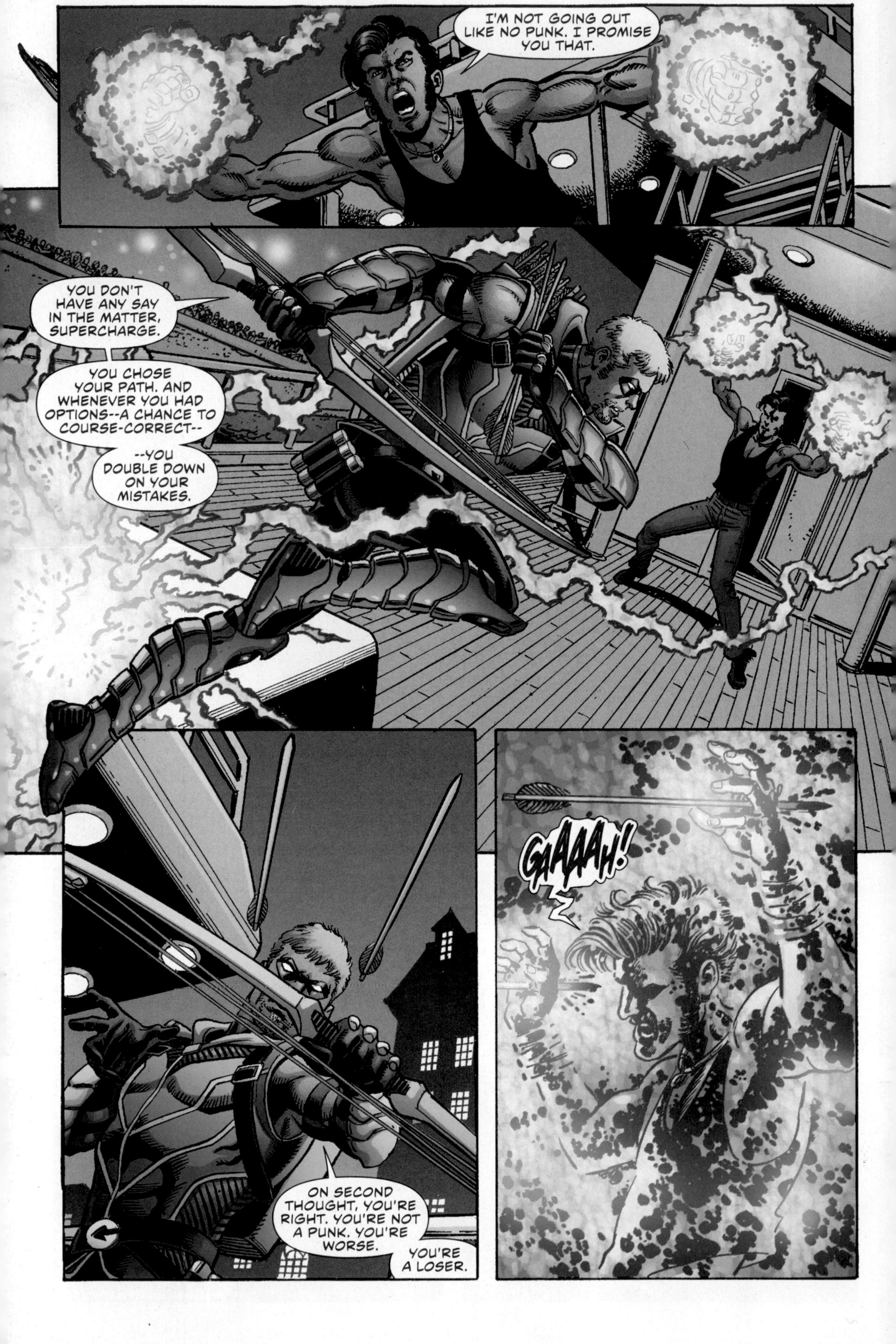

I'M NOT GOING OUT LIKE NO PUNK. I PROMISE YOU THAT.
YOU DON'T HAVE ANY SAY IN THE MATTER, SUPERCHARGE.
YOU CHOSE YOUR PATH. AND WHENEVER YOU HAD OPTIONS--A CHANCE TO COURSE-CORRECT--
--YOU DOUBLE DOWN ON YOUR MISTAKES.
ON SECOND THOUGHT, YOU'RE RIGHT. YOU'RE NOT A PUNK. YOU'RE WORSE.
YOU'RE A LOSER.
GAAAAH!

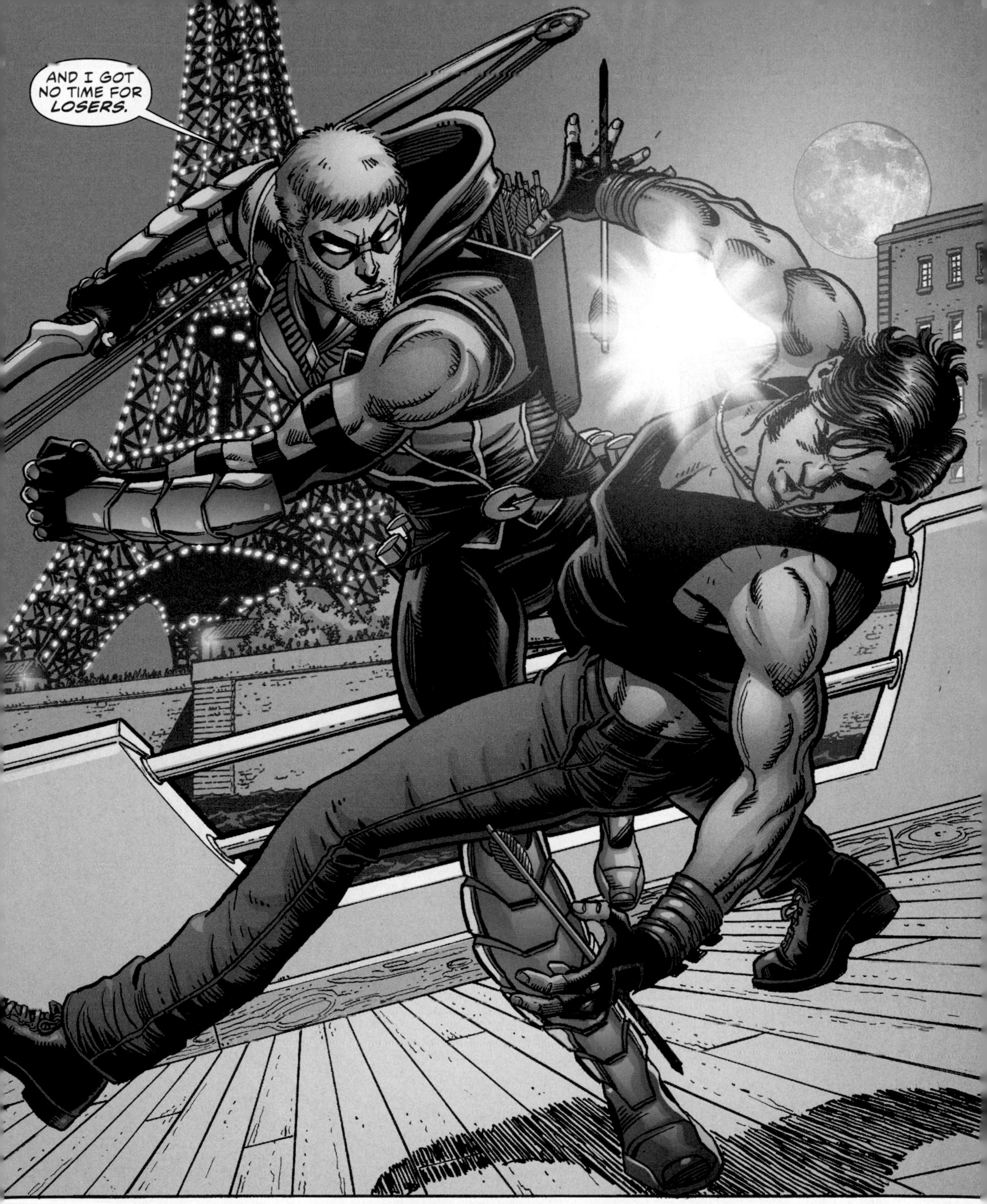
AND I GOT NO TIME FOR *LOSERS.*

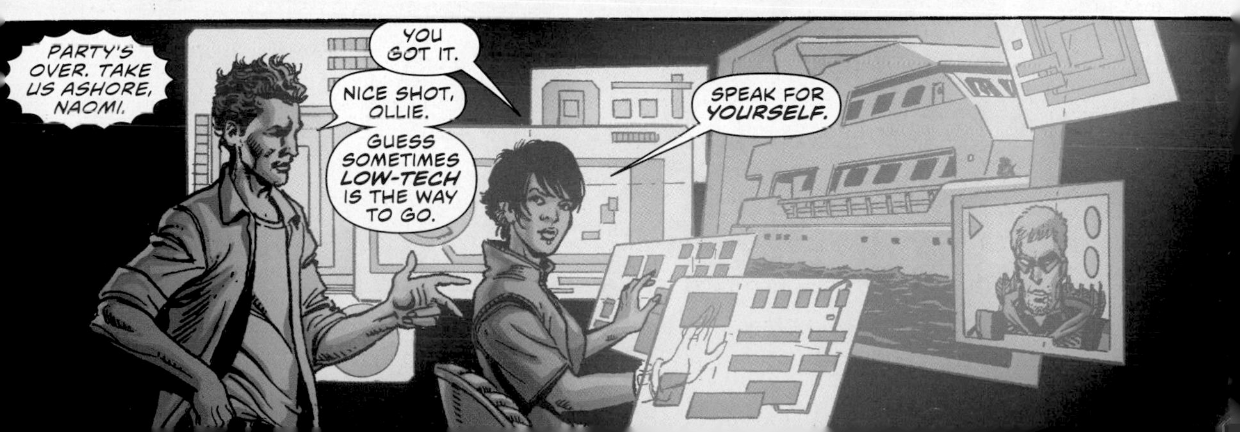
PARTY'S OVER. TAKE US ASHORE, NAOMI.
YOU GOT IT.
NICE SHOT, OLLIE.
GUESS SOMETIMES *LOW-TECH* IS THE WAY TO GO.
SPEAK FOR *YOURSELF.*

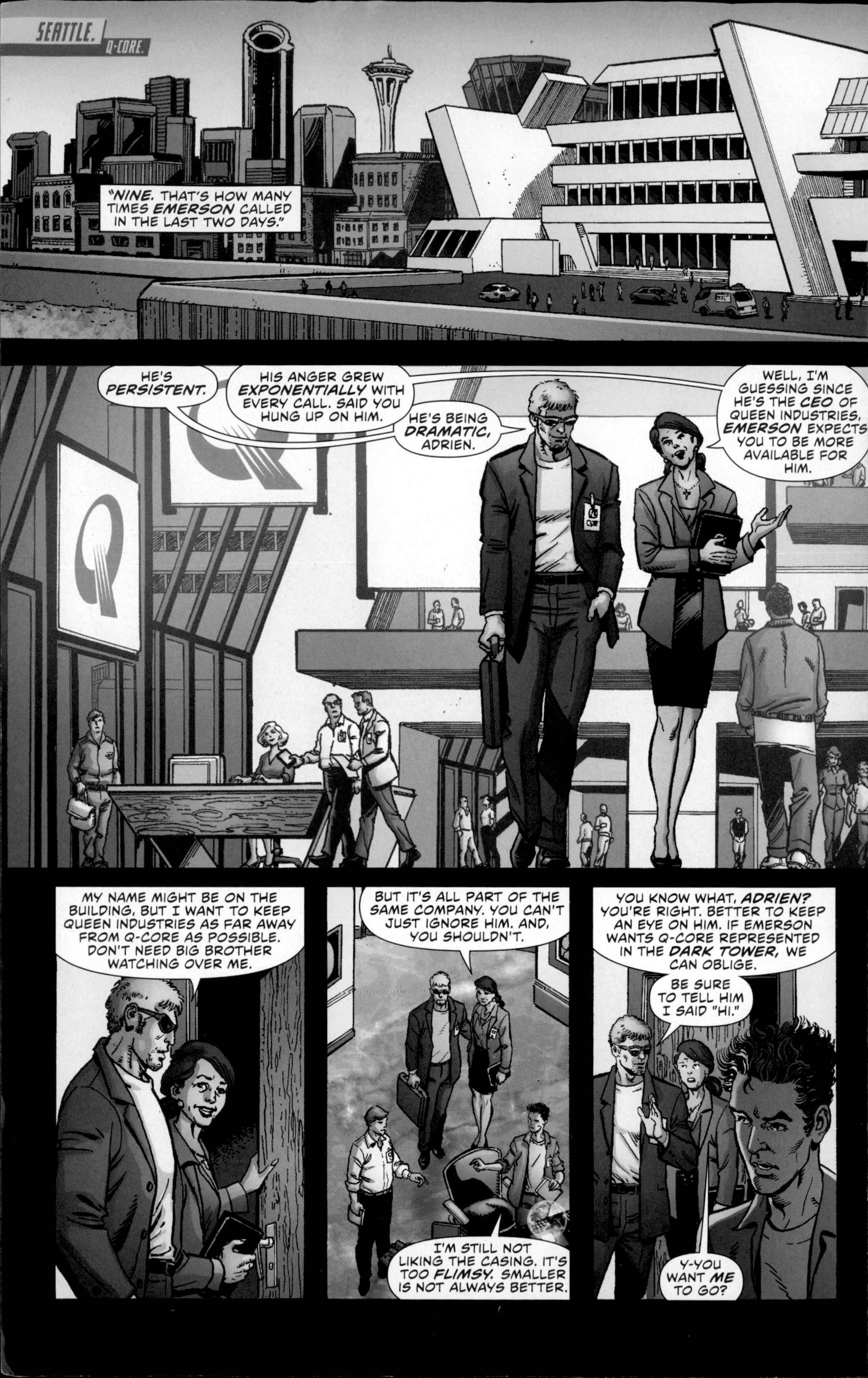
SEATTLE.
Q-CORE.
"NINE. THAT'S HOW MANY TIMES EMERSON CALLED IN THE LAST TWO DAYS."
HE'S PERSISTENT.
HIS ANGER GREW EXPONENTIALLY WITH EVERY CALL. SAID YOU HUNG UP ON HIM.
HE'S BEING DRAMATIC, ADRIEN.
WELL, I'M GUESSING SINCE HE'S THE CEO OF QUEEN INDUSTRIES, EMERSON EXPECTS YOU TO BE MORE AVAILABLE FOR HIM.
MY NAME MIGHT BE ON THE BUILDING, BUT I WANT TO KEEP QUEEN INDUSTRIES AS FAR AWAY FROM Q-CORE AS POSSIBLE. DON'T NEED BIG BROTHER WATCHING OVER ME.
BUT IT'S ALL PART OF THE SAME COMPANY. YOU CAN'T JUST IGNORE HIM. AND, YOU SHOULDN'T.
I'M STILL NOT LIKING THE CASING. IT'S TOO FLIMSY. SMALLER IS NOT ALWAYS BETTER.
YOU KNOW WHAT, ADRIEN? YOU'RE RIGHT. BETTER TO KEEP AN EYE ON HIM. IF EMERSON WANTS Q-CORE REPRESENTED IN THE DARK TOWER, WE CAN OBLIGE.
BE SURE TO TELL HIM I SAID "HI."
Y-YOU WANT ME TO GO?

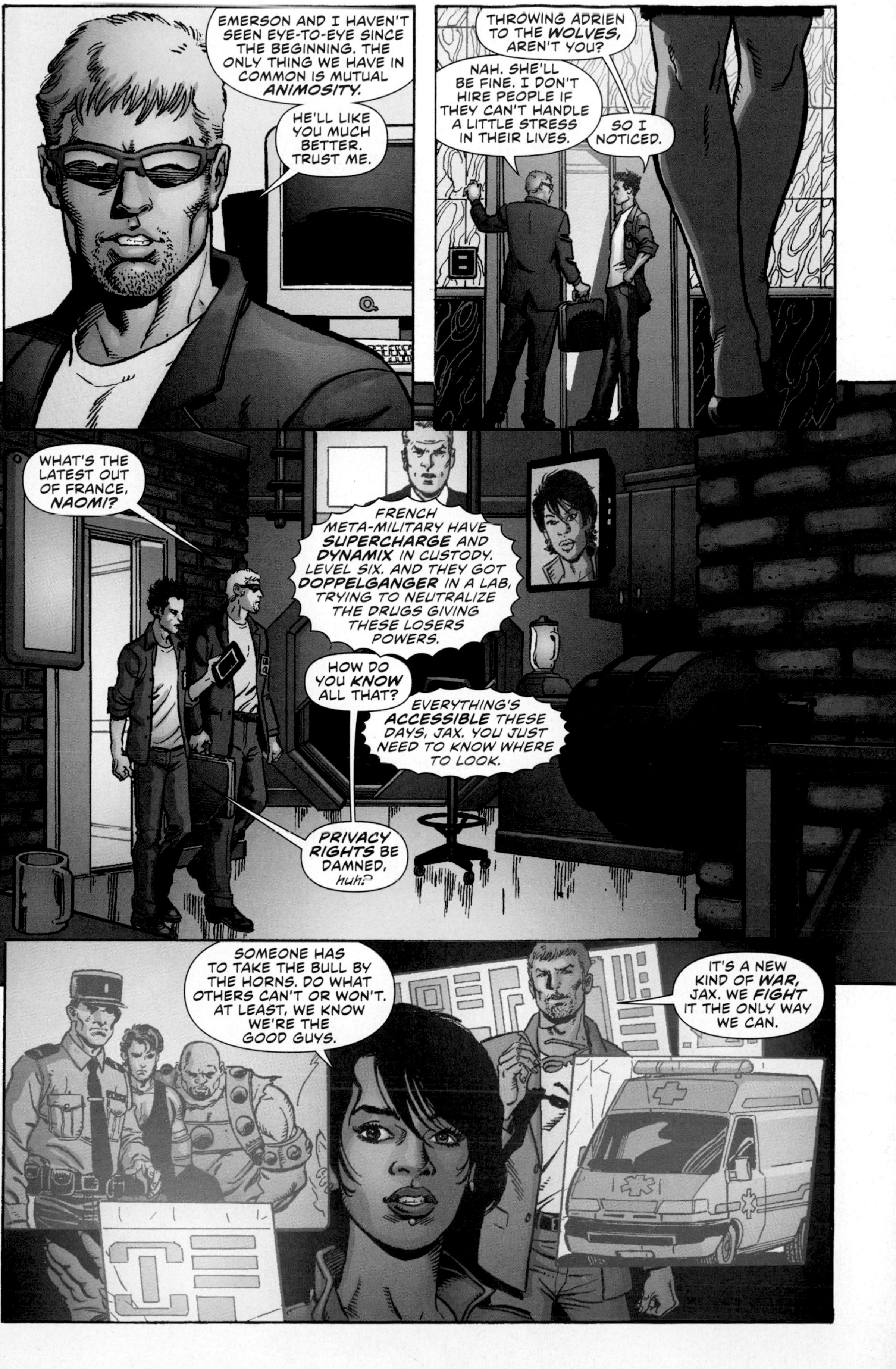
EMERSON AND I HAVEN'T SEEN EYE-TO-EYE SINCE THE BEGINNING. THE ONLY THING WE HAVE IN COMMON IS MUTUAL ANIMOSITY.
HE'LL LIKE YOU MUCH BETTER. TRUST ME.
THROWING ADRIEN TO THE WOLVES, AREN'T YOU?
NAH. SHE'LL BE FINE. I DON'T HIRE PEOPLE IF THEY CAN'T HANDLE A LITTLE STRESS IN THEIR LIVES.
SO I NOTICED.
WHAT'S THE LATEST OUT OF FRANCE, NAOMI?
FRENCH META-MILITARY HAVE SUPERCHARGE AND DYNAMIX IN CUSTODY. LEVEL SIX. AND THEY GOT DOPPELGANGER IN A LAB, TRYING TO NEUTRALIZE THE DRUGS GIVING THESE LOSERS POWERS.
HOW DO YOU KNOW ALL THAT?
EVERYTHING'S ACCESSIBLE THESE DAYS, JAX. YOU JUST NEED TO KNOW WHERE TO LOOK.
PRIVACY RIGHTS BE DAMNED, huh?
SOMEONE HAS TO TAKE THE BULL BY THE HORNS. DO WHAT OTHERS CAN'T OR WON'T. AT LEAST, WE KNOW WE'RE THE GOOD GUYS.
IT'S A NEW KIND OF WAR, JAX. WE FIGHT IT THE ONLY WAY WE CAN.

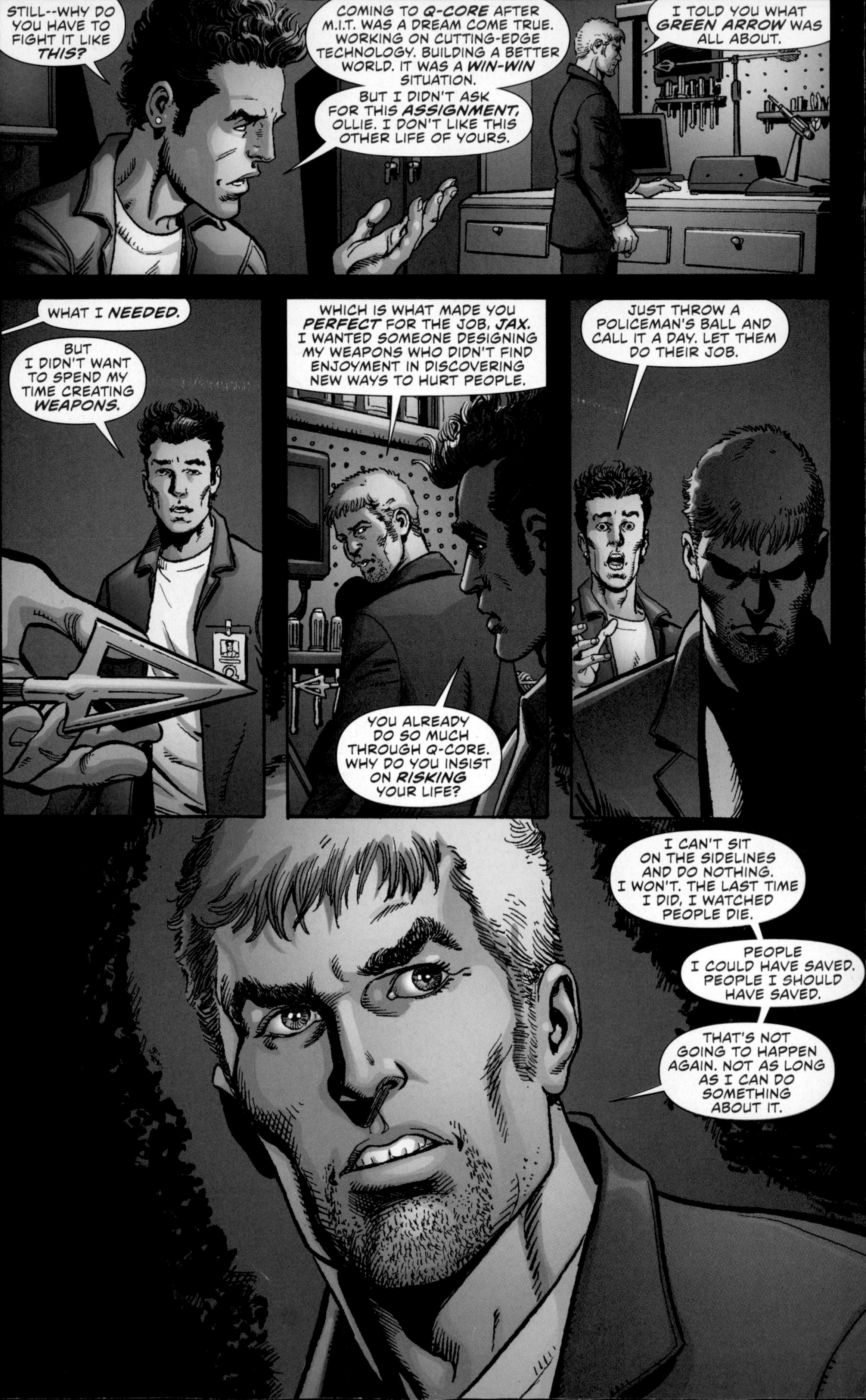
STILL--WHY DO YOU HAVE TO FIGHT IT LIKE THIS?
COMING TO Q-CORE AFTER M.I.T. WAS A DREAM COME TRUE. WORKING ON CUTTING-EDGE TECHNOLOGY. BUILDING A BETTER WORLD. IT WAS A WIN-WIN SITUATION.
BUT I DIDN'T ASK FOR THIS ASSIGNMENT, OLLIE. I DON'T LIKE THIS OTHER LIFE OF YOURS.
I TOLD YOU WHAT GREEN ARROW WAS ALL ABOUT.
WHAT I NEEDED.
BUT I DIDN'T WANT TO SPEND MY TIME CREATING WEAPONS.
WHICH IS WHAT MADE YOU PERFECT FOR THE JOB, JAX. I WANTED SOMEONE DESIGNING MY WEAPONS WHO DIDN'T FIND ENJOYMENT IN DISCOVERING NEW WAYS TO HURT PEOPLE.
YOU ALREADY DO SO MUCH THROUGH Q-CORE. WHY DO YOU INSIST ON RISKING YOUR LIFE?
JUST THROW A POLICEMAN'S BALL AND CALL IT A DAY. LET THEM DO THEIR JOB.
I CAN'T SIT ON THE SIDELINES AND DO NOTHING. I WON'T. THE LAST TIME I DID, I WATCHED PEOPLE DIE.
PEOPLE I COULD HAVE SAVED. PEOPLE I SHOULD HAVE SAVED.
THAT'S NOT GOING TO HAPPEN AGAIN. NOT AS LONG AS I CAN DO SOMETHING ABOUT IT.

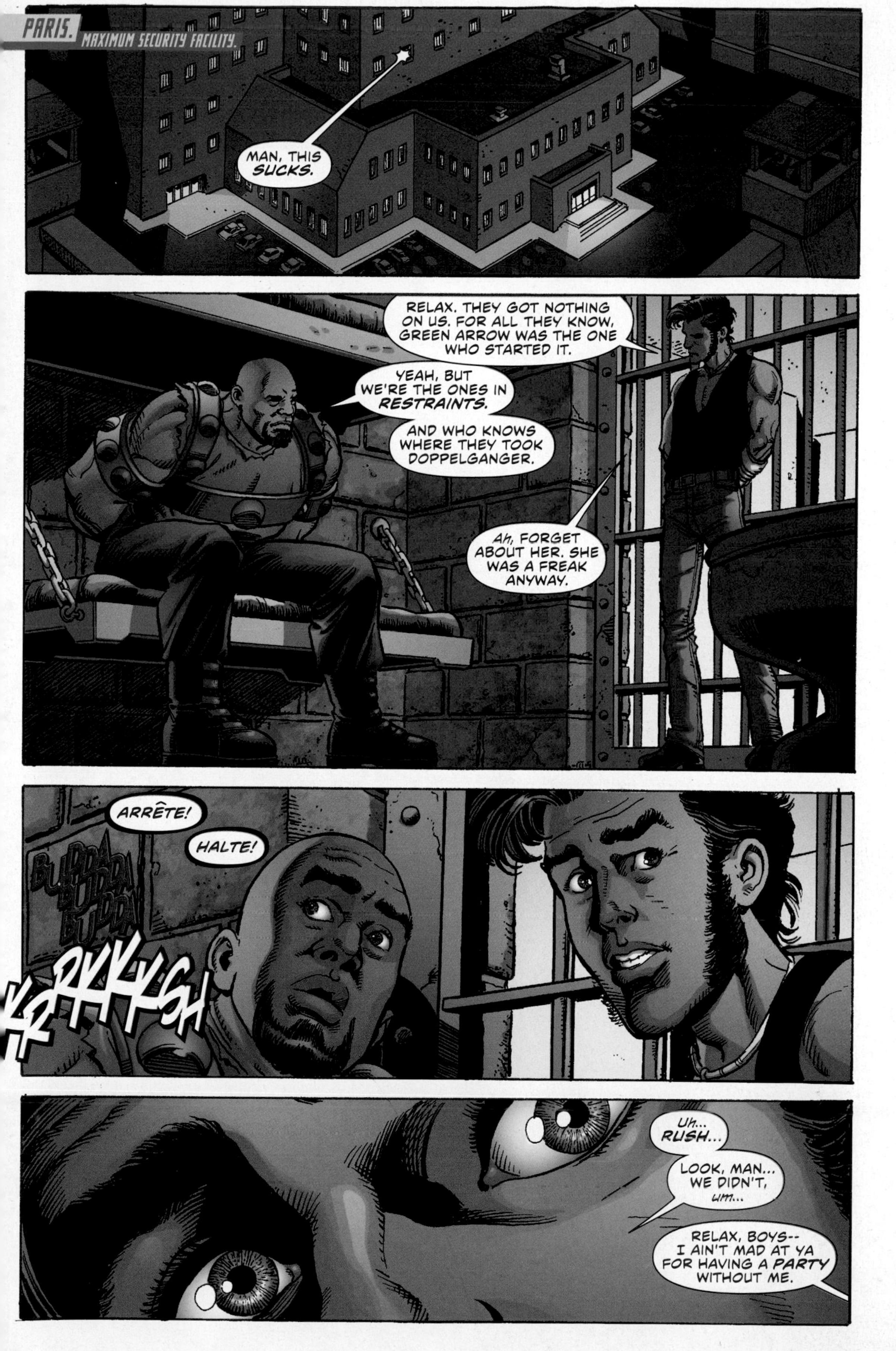
PARIS.
MAXIMUM SECURITY FACILITY.
MAN, THIS SUCKS.
RELAX. THEY GOT NOTHING ON US. FOR ALL THEY KNOW, GREEN ARROW WAS THE ONE WHO STARTED IT.
YEAH, BUT WE'RE THE ONES IN RESTRAINTS.
AND WHO KNOWS WHERE THEY TOOK DOPPELGANGER.
AH, FORGET ABOUT HER. SHE WAS A FREAK ANYWAY.
ARRÊTE!
HALTE!
BUDDA BUDDA BUDDA
KRRKKKSH
UH... RUSH...
LOOK, MAN... WE DIDN'T, UM...
RELAX, BOYS-- I AIN'T MAD AT YA FOR HAVING A PARTY WITHOUT ME.

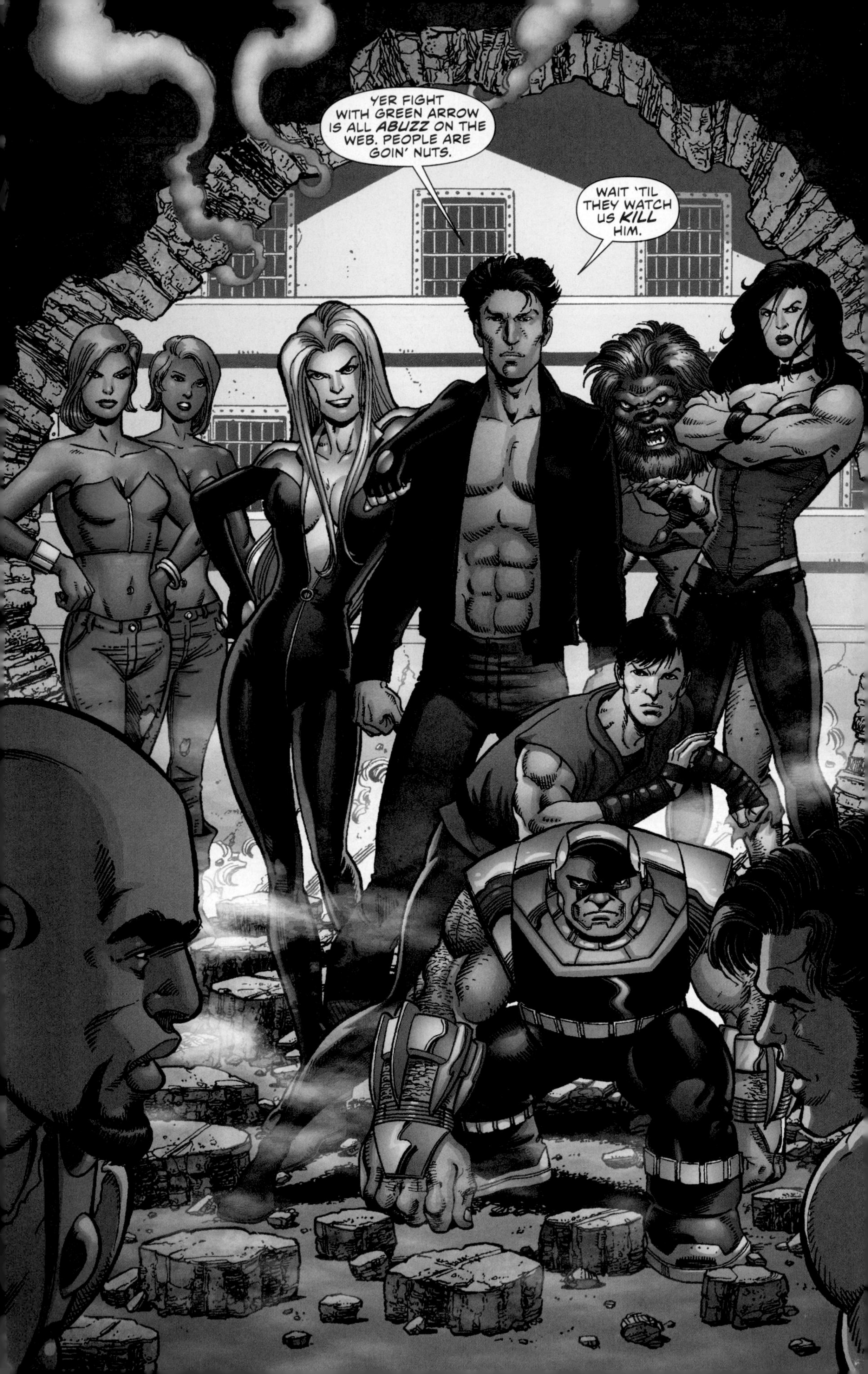
YER FIGHT WITH GREEN ARROW IS ALL ABUZZ ON THE WEB. PEOPLE ARE GOIN' NUTS.
WAIT 'TIL THEY WATCH US KILL HIM.

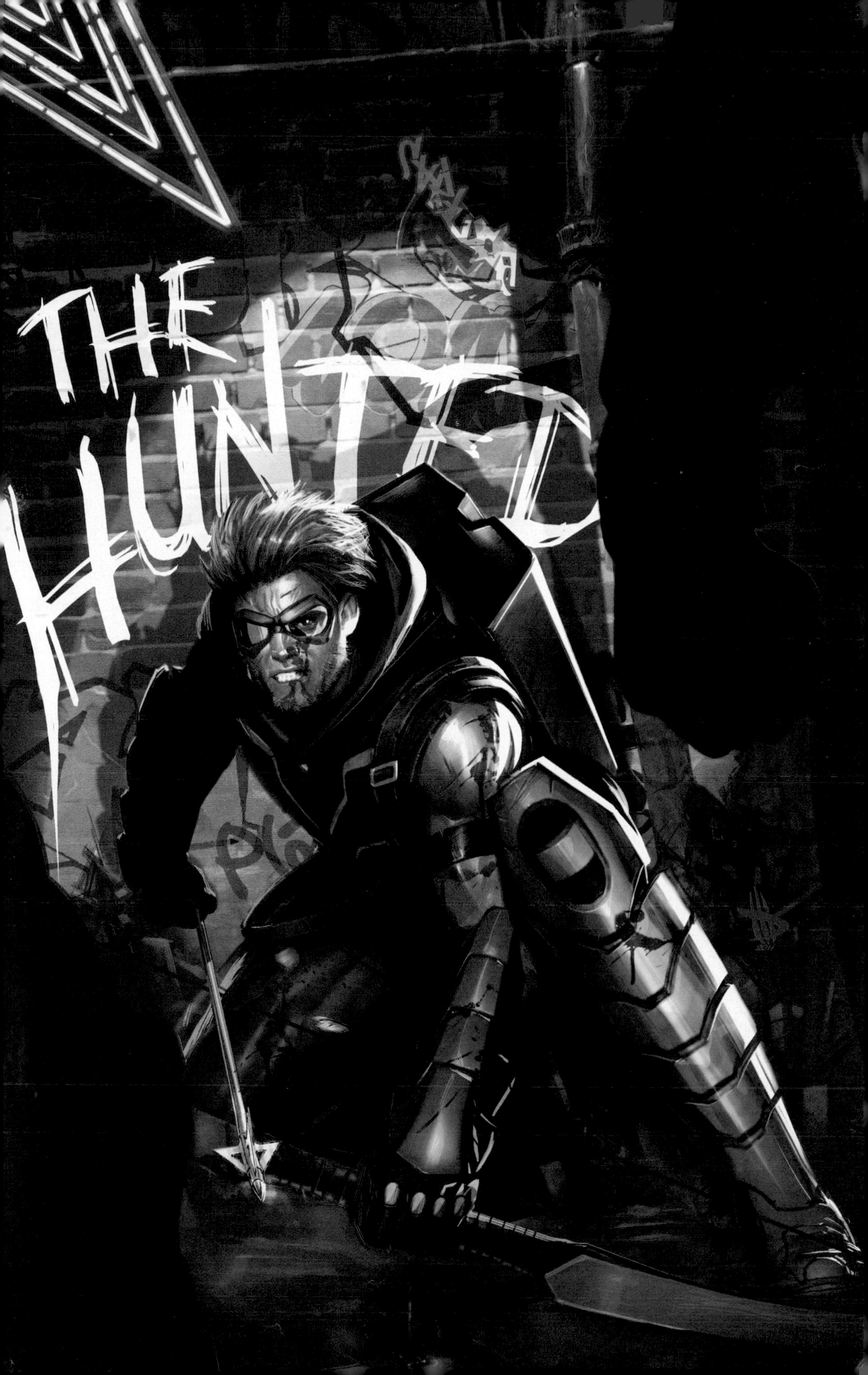
THE HUNTED

GOING VIRAL

J.T. KRUL
writer

DAN JURGENS
layouts

GEORGE PÉREZ
finishes

cover by DAVE WILKINS

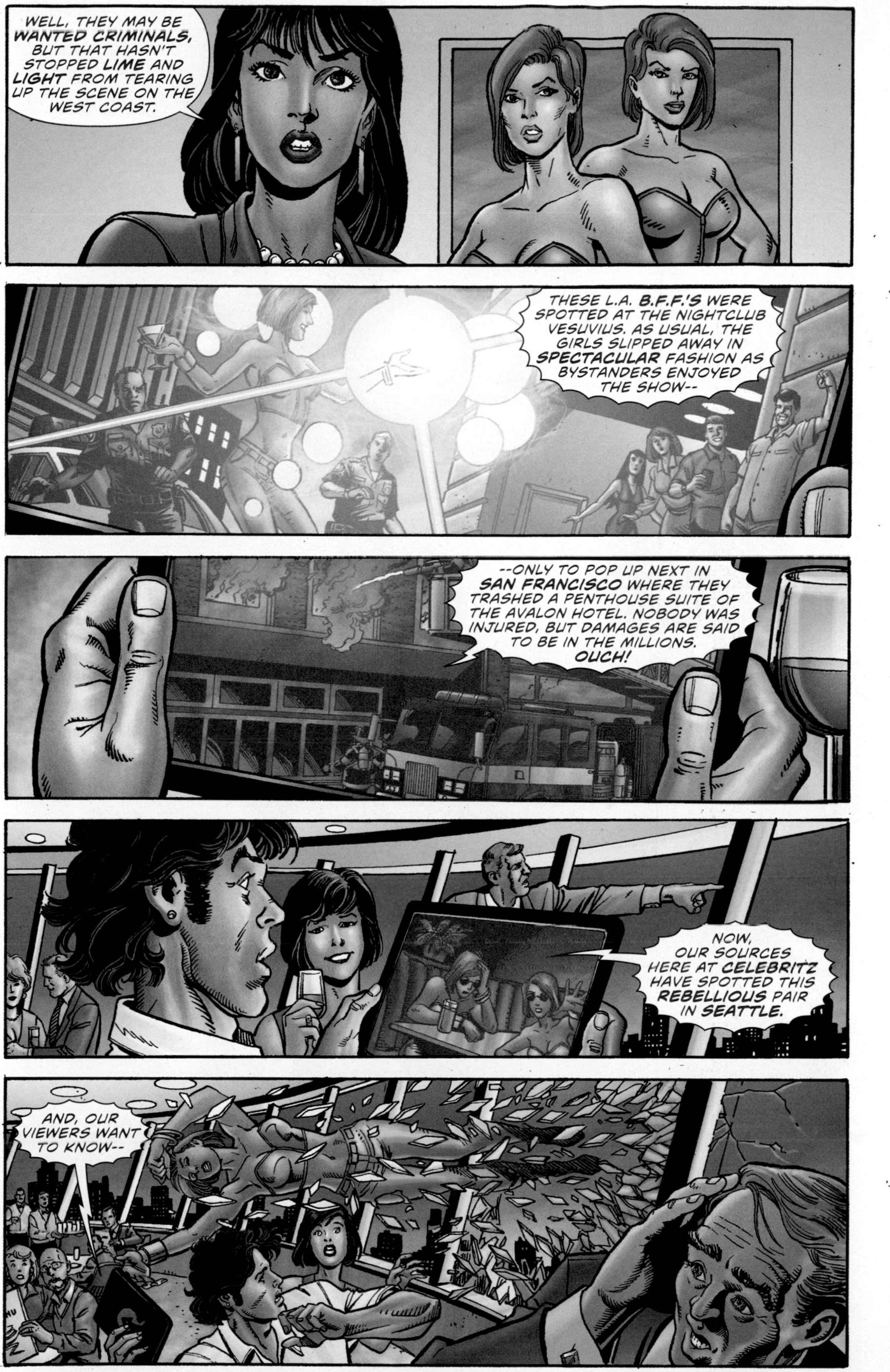
WELL, THEY MAY BE WANTED CRIMINALS, BUT THAT HASN'T STOPPED LIME AND LIGHT FROM TEARING UP THE SCENE ON THE WEST COAST.
THESE L.A. B.F.F.'S WERE SPOTTED AT THE NIGHTCLUB VESUVIUS. AS USUAL, THE GIRLS SLIPPED AWAY IN SPECTACULAR FASHION AS BYSTANDERS ENJOYED THE SHOW--
--ONLY TO POP UP NEXT IN SAN FRANCISCO WHERE THEY TRASHED A PENTHOUSE SUITE OF THE AVALON HOTEL. NOBODY WAS INJURED, BUT DAMAGES ARE SAID TO BE IN THE MILLIONS. OUCH!
NOW, OUR SOURCES HERE AT CELEBRITZ HAVE SPOTTED THIS REBELLIOUS PAIR IN SEATTLE.
AND, OUR VIEWERS WANT TO KNOW--

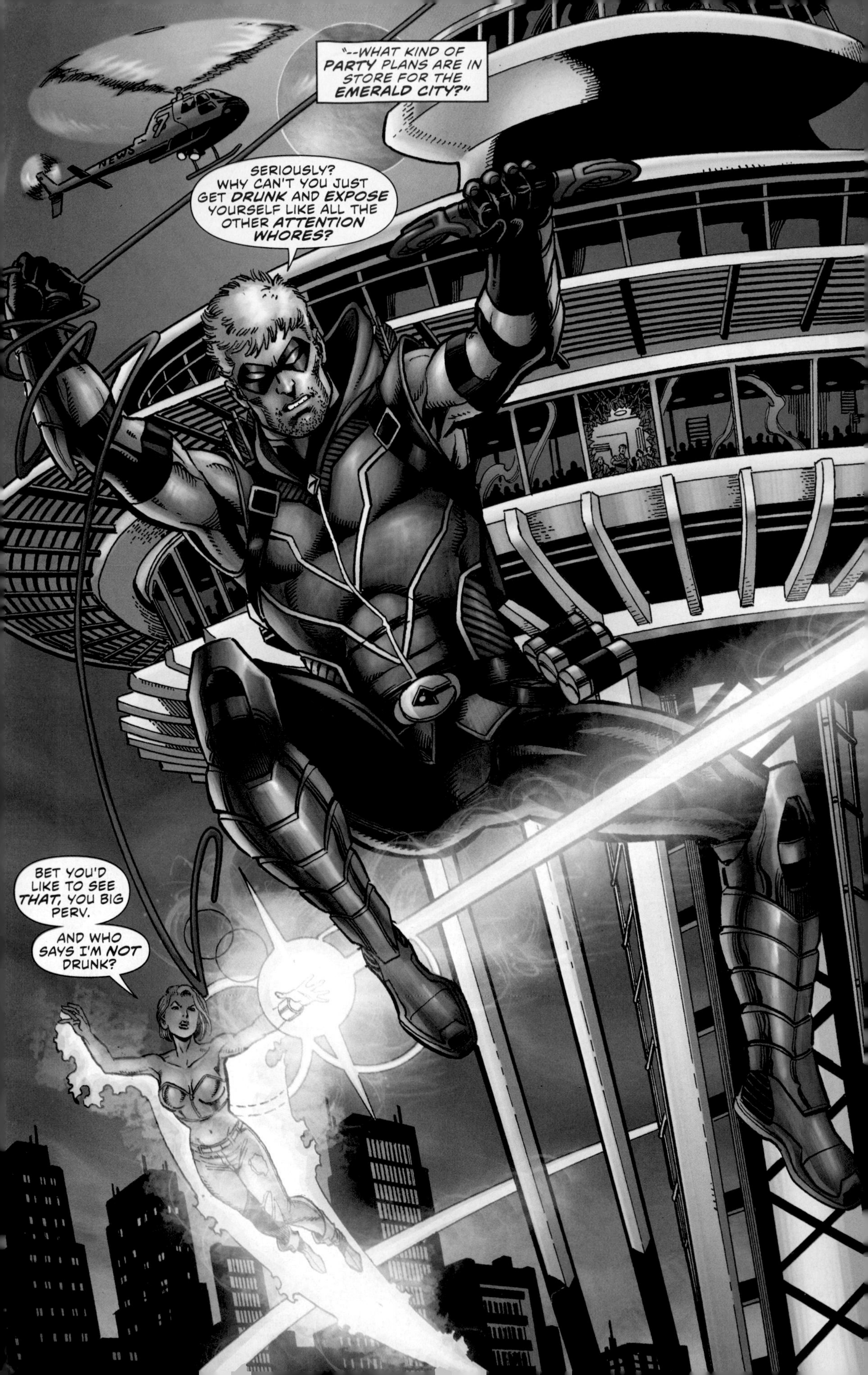
"--WHAT KIND OF PARTY PLANS ARE IN STORE FOR THE EMERALD CITY?"
SERIOUSLY? WHY CAN'T YOU JUST GET DRUNK AND EXPOSE YOURSELF LIKE ALL THE OTHER ATTENTION WHORES?
BET YOU'D LIKE TO SEE THAT, YOU BIG PERV.
AND WHO SAYS I'M NOT DRUNK?
NEWS

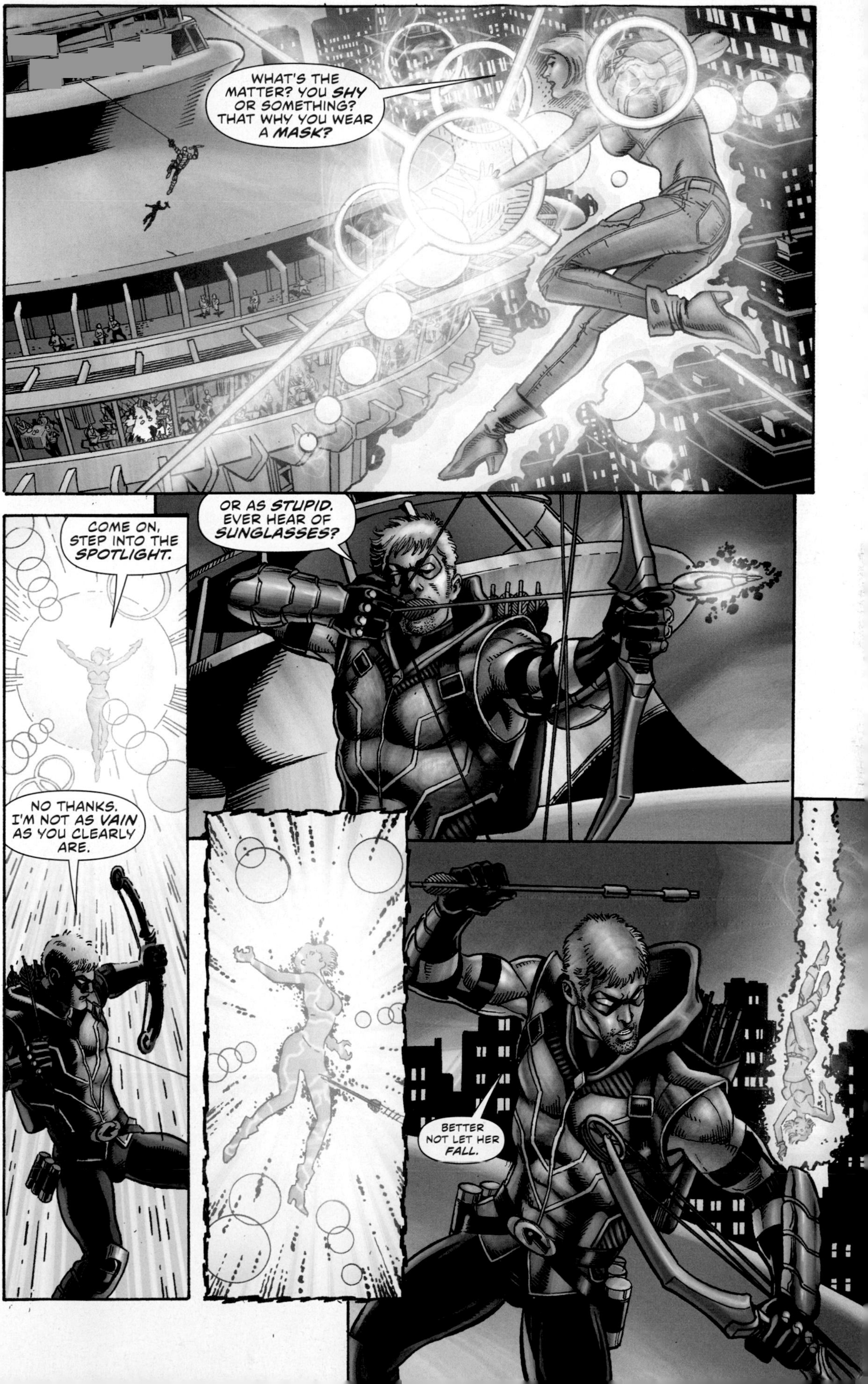
WHAT'S THE MATTER? YOU SHY OR SOMETHING? THAT WHY YOU WEAR A MASK?
COME ON, STEP INTO THE SPOTLIGHT.
NO THANKS. I'M NOT AS VAIN AS YOU CLEARLY ARE.
OR AS STUPID. EVER HEAR OF SUNGLASSES?
BETTER NOT LET HER FALL.

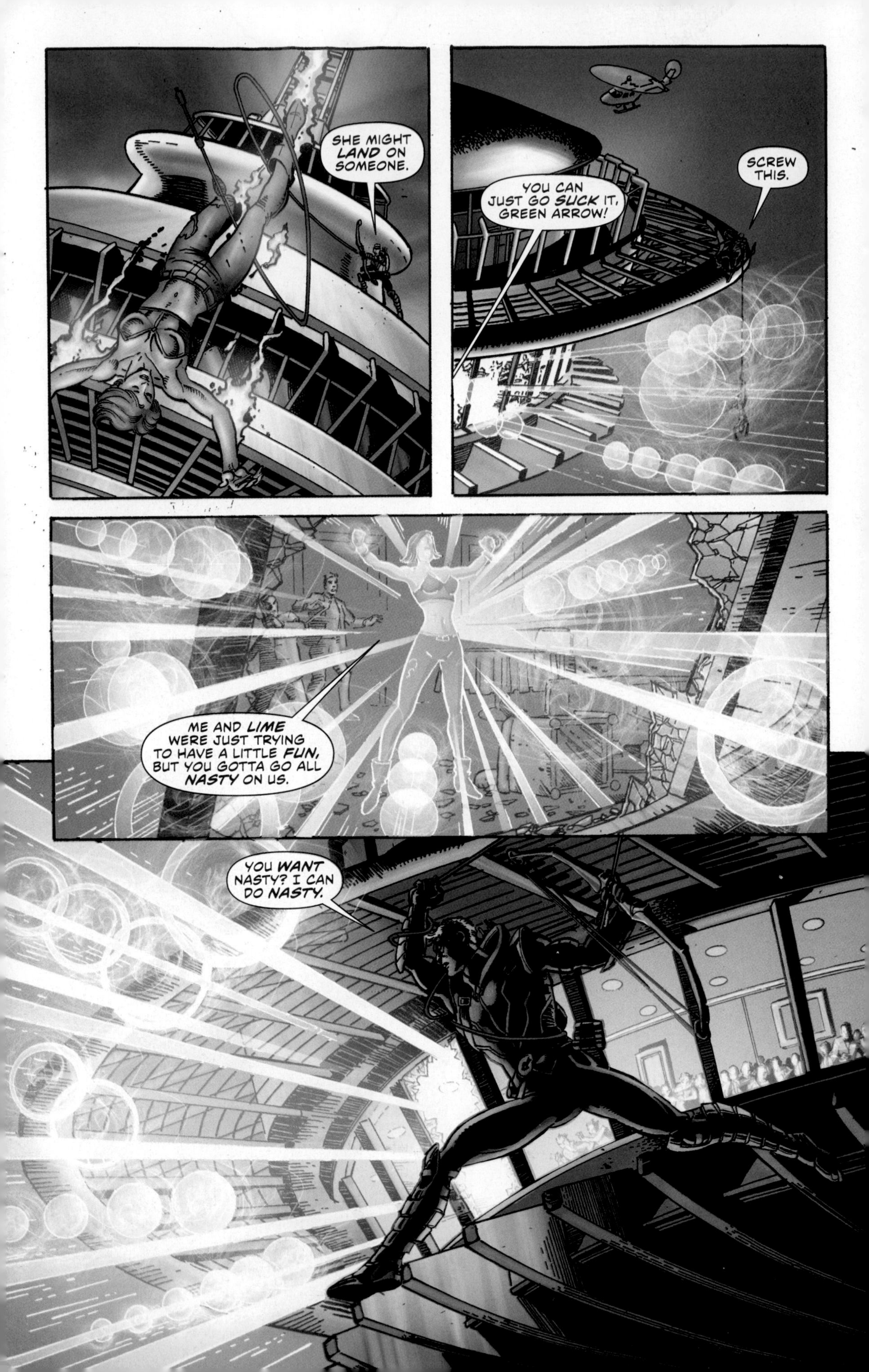
SHE MIGHT LAND ON SOMEONE.
YOU CAN JUST GO SUCK IT, GREEN ARROW!
SCREW THIS.
ME AND LIME WERE JUST TRYING TO HAVE A LITTLE FUN, BUT YOU GOTTA GO ALL NASTY ON US.
YOU WANT NASTY? I CAN DO NASTY.

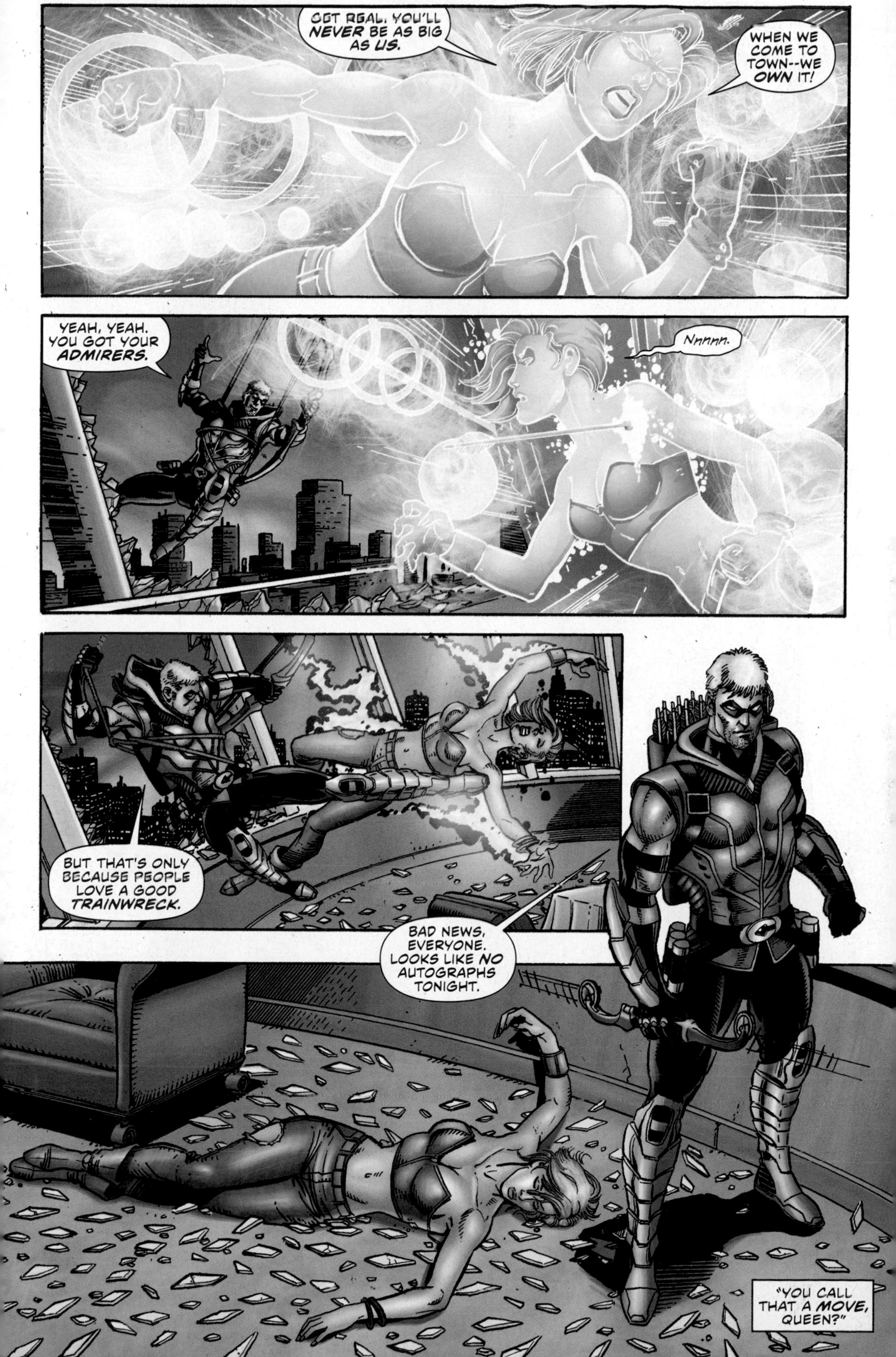
GET REAL. YOU'LL NEVER BE AS BIG AS US.
WHEN WE COME TO TOWN--WE OWN IT!
YEAH, YEAH. YOU GOT YOUR ADMIRERS.
Nnnnn.
BUT THAT'S ONLY BECAUSE PEOPLE LOVE A GOOD TRAINWRECK.
BAD NEWS, EVERYONE. LOOKS LIKE NO AUTOGRAPHS TONIGHT.
"YOU CALL THAT A MOVE, QUEEN?"

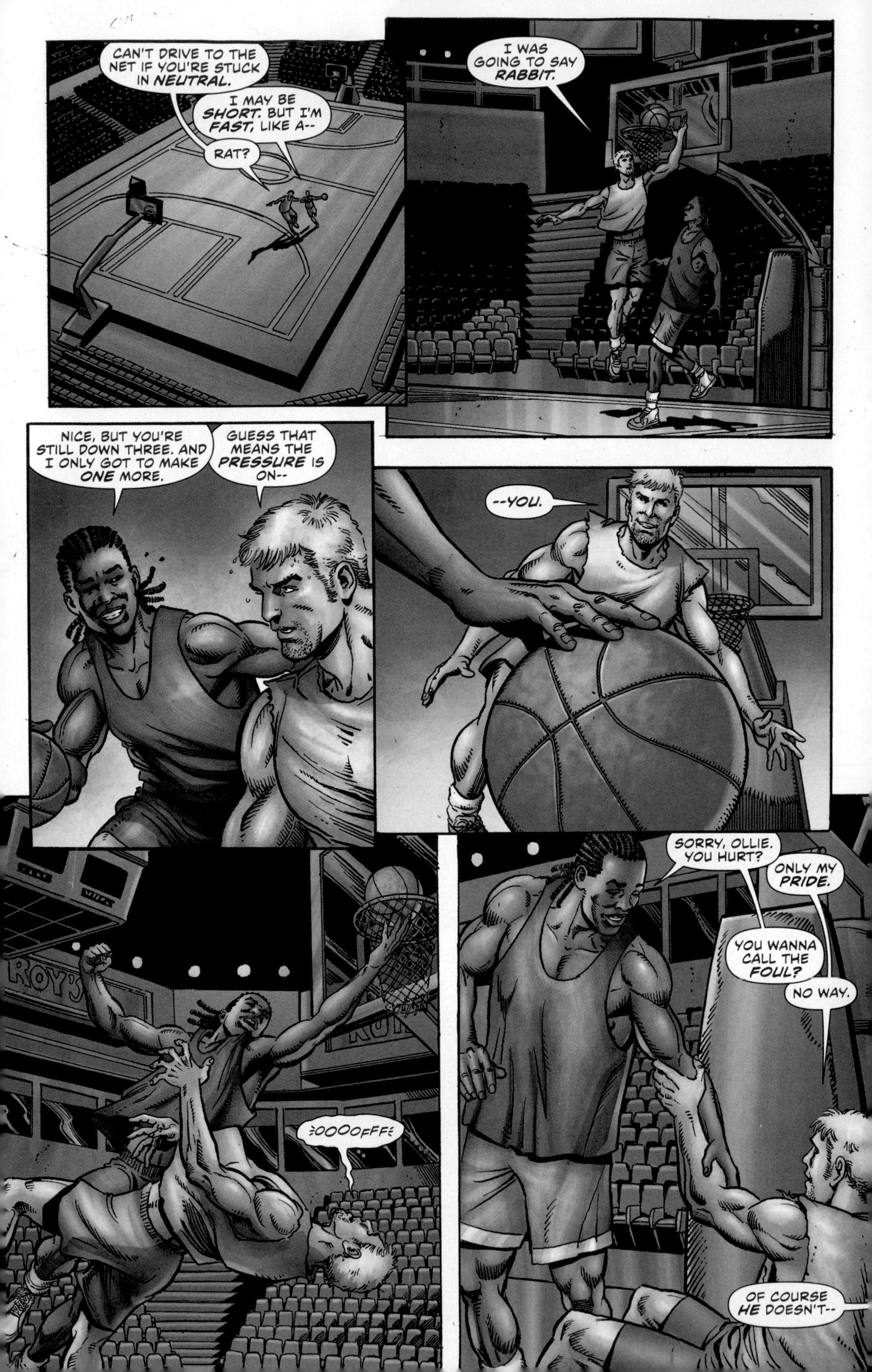
CAN'T DRIVE TO THE NET IF YOU'RE STUCK IN NEUTRAL.
I MAY BE SHORT. BUT I'M FAST, LIKE A--
RAT?
I WAS GOING TO SAY RABBIT.
NICE, BUT YOU'RE STILL DOWN THREE. AND I ONLY GOT TO MAKE ONE MORE.
GUESS THAT MEANS THE PRESSURE IS ON--
--YOU.
ROY'S
OOOOFFF
SORRY, OLLIE. YOU HURT?
ONLY MY PRIDE.
YOU WANNA CALL THE FOUL?
NO WAY.
OF COURSE HE DOESN'T--

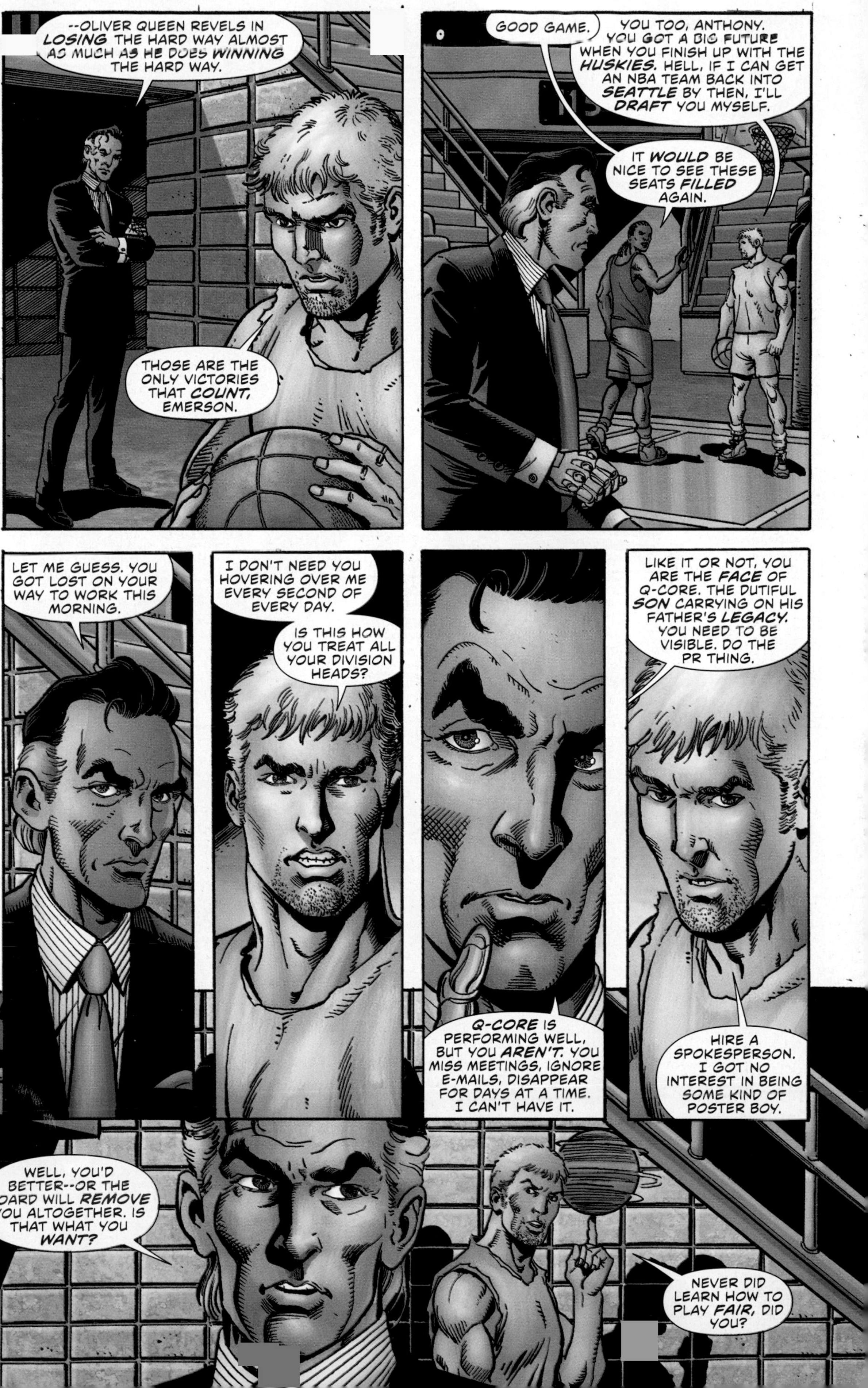
--OLIVER QUEEN REVELS IN LOSING THE HARD WAY ALMOST AS MUCH AS HE DOES WINNING THE HARD WAY.
THOSE ARE THE ONLY VICTORIES THAT COUNT, EMERSON.
GOOD GAME.
YOU TOO, ANTHONY. YOU GOT A BIG FUTURE WHEN YOU FINISH UP WITH THE HUSKIES. HELL, IF I CAN GET AN NBA TEAM BACK INTO SEATTLE BY THEN, I'LL DRAFT YOU MYSELF.
IT WOULD BE NICE TO SEE THESE SEATS FILLED AGAIN.
LET ME GUESS. YOU GOT LOST ON YOUR WAY TO WORK THIS MORNING.
I DON'T NEED YOU HOVERING OVER ME EVERY SECOND OF EVERY DAY.
IS THIS HOW YOU TREAT ALL YOUR DIVISION HEADS?
Q-CORE IS PERFORMING WELL, BUT YOU AREN'T. YOU MISS MEETINGS, IGNORE E-MAILS, DISAPPEAR FOR DAYS AT A TIME. I CAN'T HAVE IT.
LIKE IT OR NOT, YOU ARE THE FACE OF Q-CORE. THE DUTIFUL SON CARRYING ON HIS FATHER'S LEGACY. YOU NEED TO BE VISIBLE. DO THE PR THING.
HIRE A SPOKESPERSON. I GOT NO INTEREST IN BEING SOME KIND OF POSTER BOY.
WELL, YOU'D BETTER--OR THE BOARD WILL REMOVE YOU ALTOGETHER. IS THAT WHAT YOU WANT?
NEVER DID LEARN HOW TO PLAY FAIR, DID YOU?

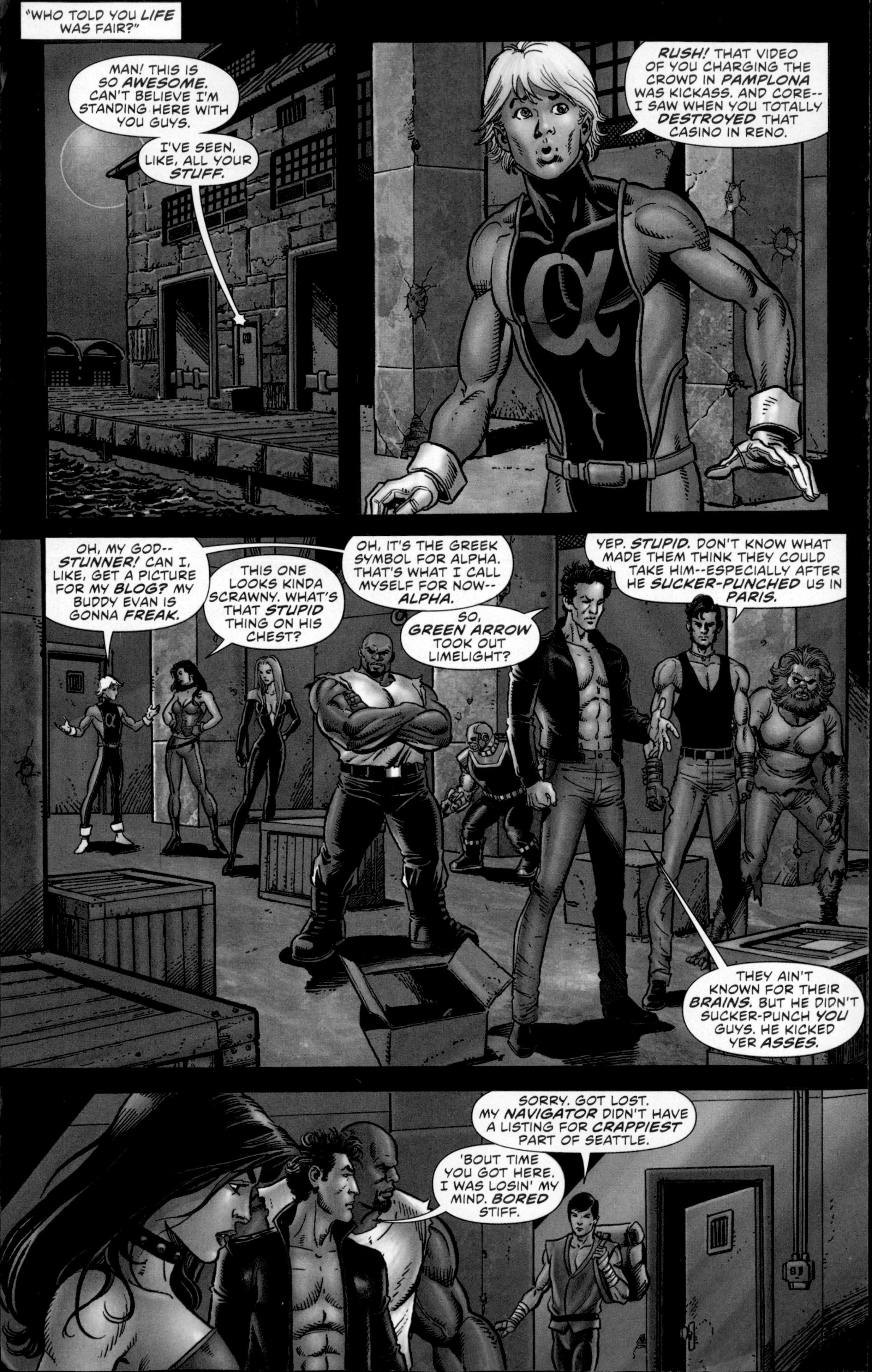
"WHO TOLD YOU LIFE WAS FAIR?"
MAN! THIS IS SO AWESOME. CAN'T BELIEVE I'M STANDING HERE WITH YOU GUYS.
I'VE SEEN, LIKE, ALL YOUR STUFF.
RUSH! THAT VIDEO OF YOU CHARGING THE CROWD IN PAMPLONA WAS KICKASS. AND CORE-- I SAW WHEN YOU TOTALLY DESTROYED THAT CASINO IN RENO.
OH, MY GOD-- STUNNER! CAN I, LIKE, GET A PICTURE FOR MY BLOG? MY BUDDY EVAN IS GONNA FREAK.
THIS ONE LOOKS KINDA SCRAWNY. WHAT'S THAT STUPID THING ON HIS CHEST?
OH, IT'S THE GREEK SYMBOL FOR ALPHA. THAT'S WHAT I CALL MYSELF FOR NOW-- ALPHA.
SO, GREEN ARROW TOOK OUT LIMELIGHT?
YEP. STUPID. DON'T KNOW WHAT MADE THEM THINK THEY COULD TAKE HIM--ESPECIALLY AFTER HE SUCKER-PUNCHED US IN PARIS.
THEY AIN'T KNOWN FOR THEIR BRAINS. BUT HE DIDN'T SUCKER-PUNCH YOU GUYS. HE KICKED YER ASSES.
SORRY. GOT LOST. MY NAVIGATOR DIDN'T HAVE A LISTING FOR CRAPPIEST PART OF SEATTLE.
'BOUT TIME YOU GOT HERE. I WAS LOSIN' MY MIND. BORED STIFF.

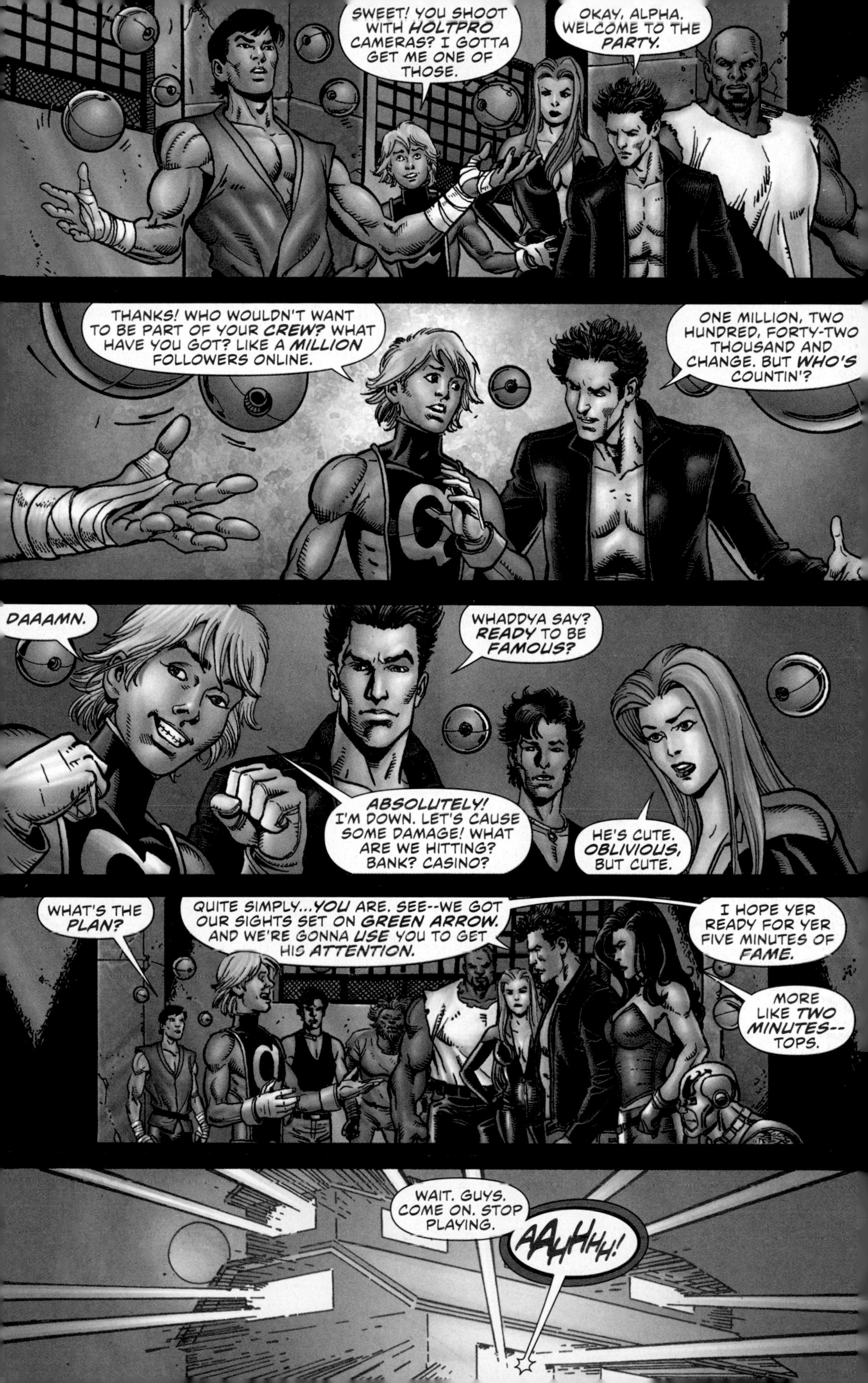
SWEET! YOU SHOOT WITH HOLTPRO CAMERAS? I GOTTA GET ME ONE OF THOSE.
OKAY, ALPHA. WELCOME TO THE PARTY.
THANKS! WHO WOULDN'T WANT TO BE PART OF YOUR CREW? WHAT HAVE YOU GOT? LIKE A MILLION FOLLOWERS ONLINE.
ONE MILLION, TWO HUNDRED, FORTY-TWO THOUSAND AND CHANGE. BUT WHO'S COUNTIN'?
DAAAMN.
WHADDYA SAY? READY TO BE FAMOUS?
ABSOLUTELY! I'M DOWN. LET'S CAUSE SOME DAMAGE! WHAT ARE WE HITTING? BANK? CASINO?
HE'S CUTE. OBLIVIOUS, BUT CUTE.
WHAT'S THE PLAN?
QUITE SIMPLY...YOU ARE. SEE--WE GOT OUR SIGHTS SET ON GREEN ARROW. AND WE'RE GONNA USE YOU TO GET HIS ATTENTION.
I HOPE YER READY FOR YER FIVE MINUTES OF FAME.
MORE LIKE TWO MINUTES-- TOPS.
WAIT. GUYS. COME ON. STOP PLAYING.
AAHHHH!

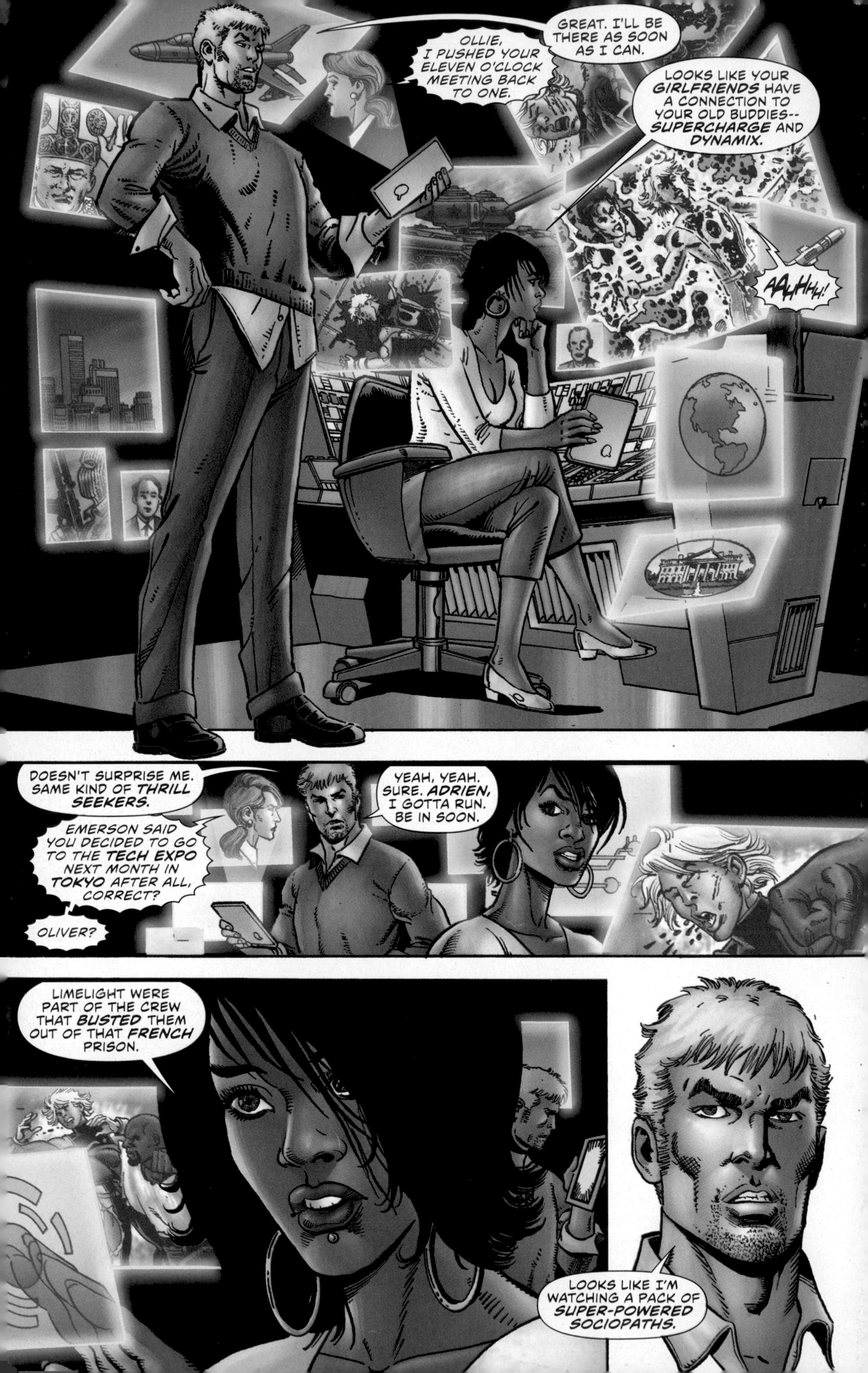
OLLIE, I PUSHED YOUR ELEVEN O'CLOCK MEETING BACK TO ONE.
GREAT. I'LL BE THERE AS SOON AS I CAN.
LOOKS LIKE YOUR GIRLFRIENDS HAVE A CONNECTION TO YOUR OLD BUDDIES-- SUPERCHARGE AND DYNAMIX.
AAHHHH!
DOESN'T SURPRISE ME. SAME KIND OF THRILL SEEKERS.
EMERSON SAID YOU DECIDED TO GO TO THE TECH EXPO NEXT MONTH IN TOKYO AFTER ALL, CORRECT?
OLIVER?
YEAH, YEAH. SURE. ADRIEN, I GOTTA RUN. BE IN SOON.
LIMELIGHT WERE PART OF THE CREW THAT BUSTED THEM OUT OF THAT FRENCH PRISON.
LOOKS LIKE I'M WATCHING A PACK OF SUPER-POWERED SOCIOPATHS.

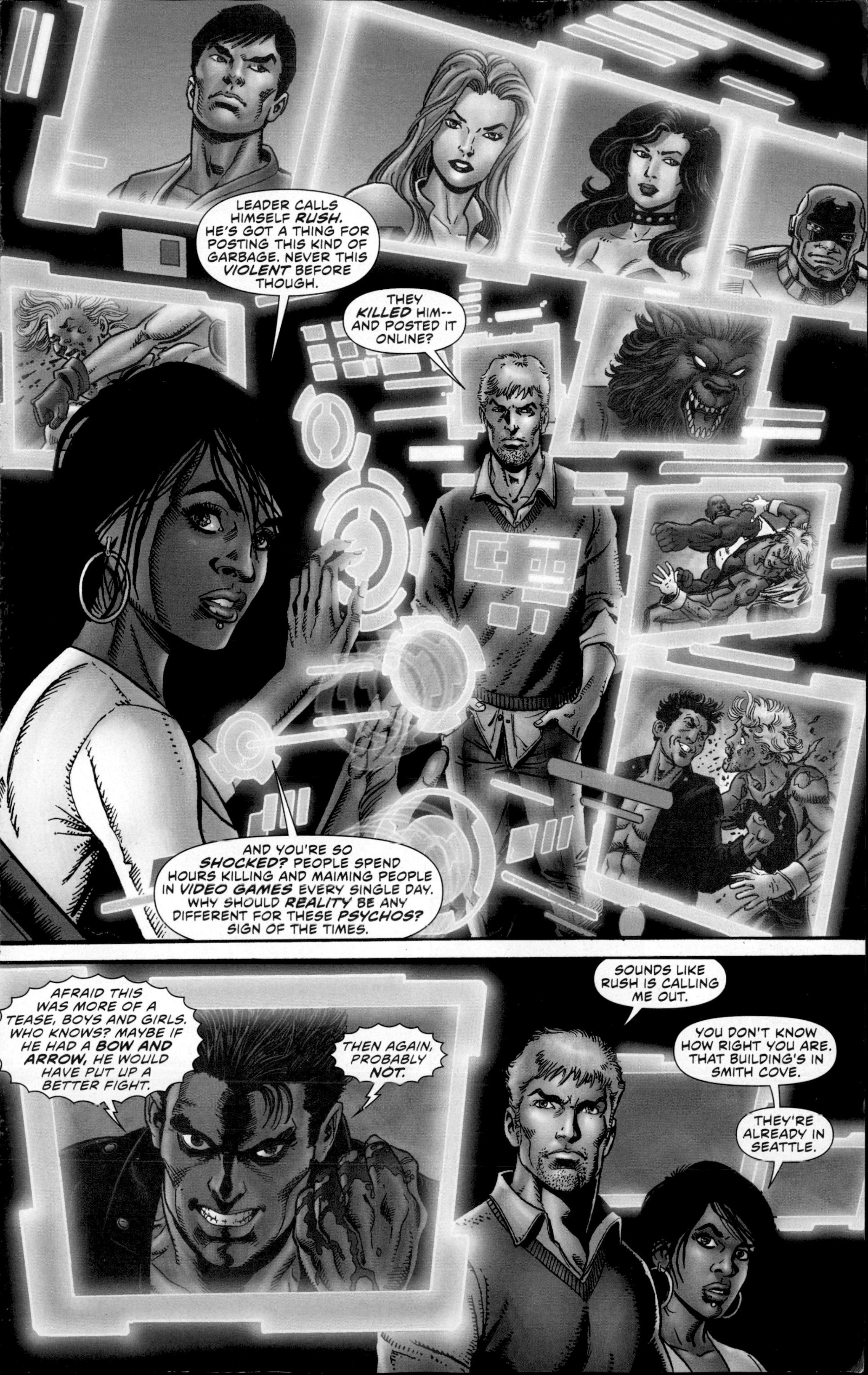

LEADER CALLS HIMSELF RUSH. HE'S GOT A THING FOR POSTING THIS KIND OF GARBAGE. NEVER THIS VIOLENT BEFORE THOUGH.
THEY KILLED HIM-- AND POSTED IT ONLINE?
AND YOU'RE SO SHOCKED? PEOPLE SPEND HOURS KILLING AND MAIMING PEOPLE IN VIDEO GAMES EVERY SINGLE DAY. WHY SHOULD REALITY BE ANY DIFFERENT FOR THESE PSYCHOS? SIGN OF THE TIMES.
AFRAID THIS WAS MORE OF A TEASE, BOYS AND GIRLS. WHO KNOWS? MAYBE IF HE HAD A BOW AND ARROW, HE WOULD HAVE PUT UP A BETTER FIGHT.
THEN AGAIN, PROBABLY NOT.
SOUNDS LIKE RUSH IS CALLING ME OUT.
YOU DON'T KNOW HOW RIGHT YOU ARE. THAT BUILDING'S IN SMITH COVE.
THEY'RE ALREADY IN SEATTLE.

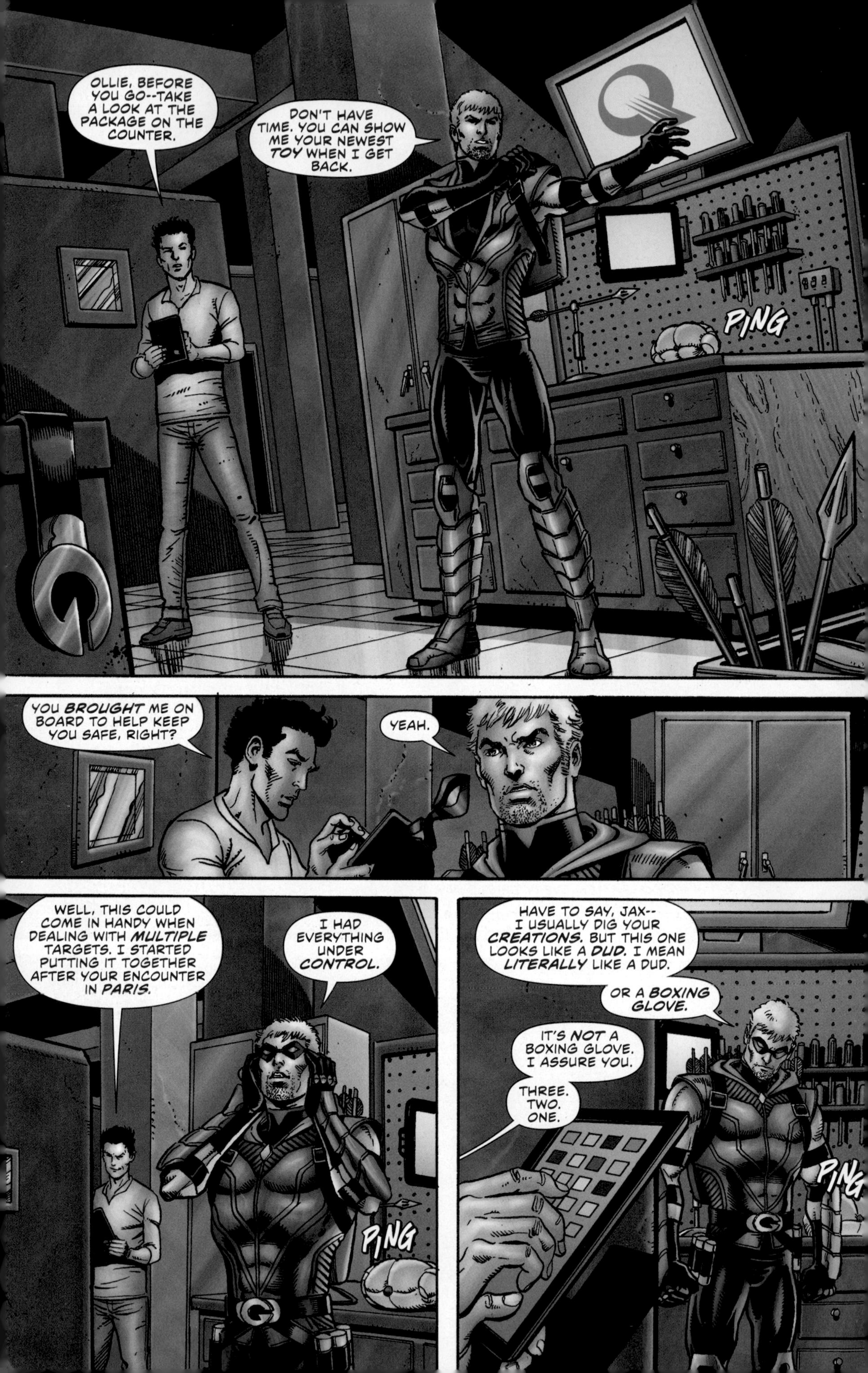

OLLIE, BEFORE YOU GO--TAKE A LOOK AT THE PACKAGE ON THE COUNTER.
DON'T HAVE TIME. YOU CAN SHOW ME YOUR NEWEST TOY WHEN I GET BACK.
PING
YOU BROUGHT ME ON BOARD TO HELP KEEP YOU SAFE, RIGHT?
YEAH.
WELL, THIS COULD COME IN HANDY WHEN DEALING WITH MULTIPLE TARGETS. I STARTED PUTTING IT TOGETHER AFTER YOUR ENCOUNTER IN PARIS.
I HAD EVERYTHING UNDER CONTROL.
PING
HAVE TO SAY, JAX-- I USUALLY DIG YOUR CREATIONS. BUT THIS ONE LOOKS LIKE A DUD. I MEAN LITERALLY LIKE A DUD.
OR A BOXING GLOVE.
IT'S NOT A BOXING GLOVE. I ASSURE YOU.
THREE. TWO. ONE.
PING

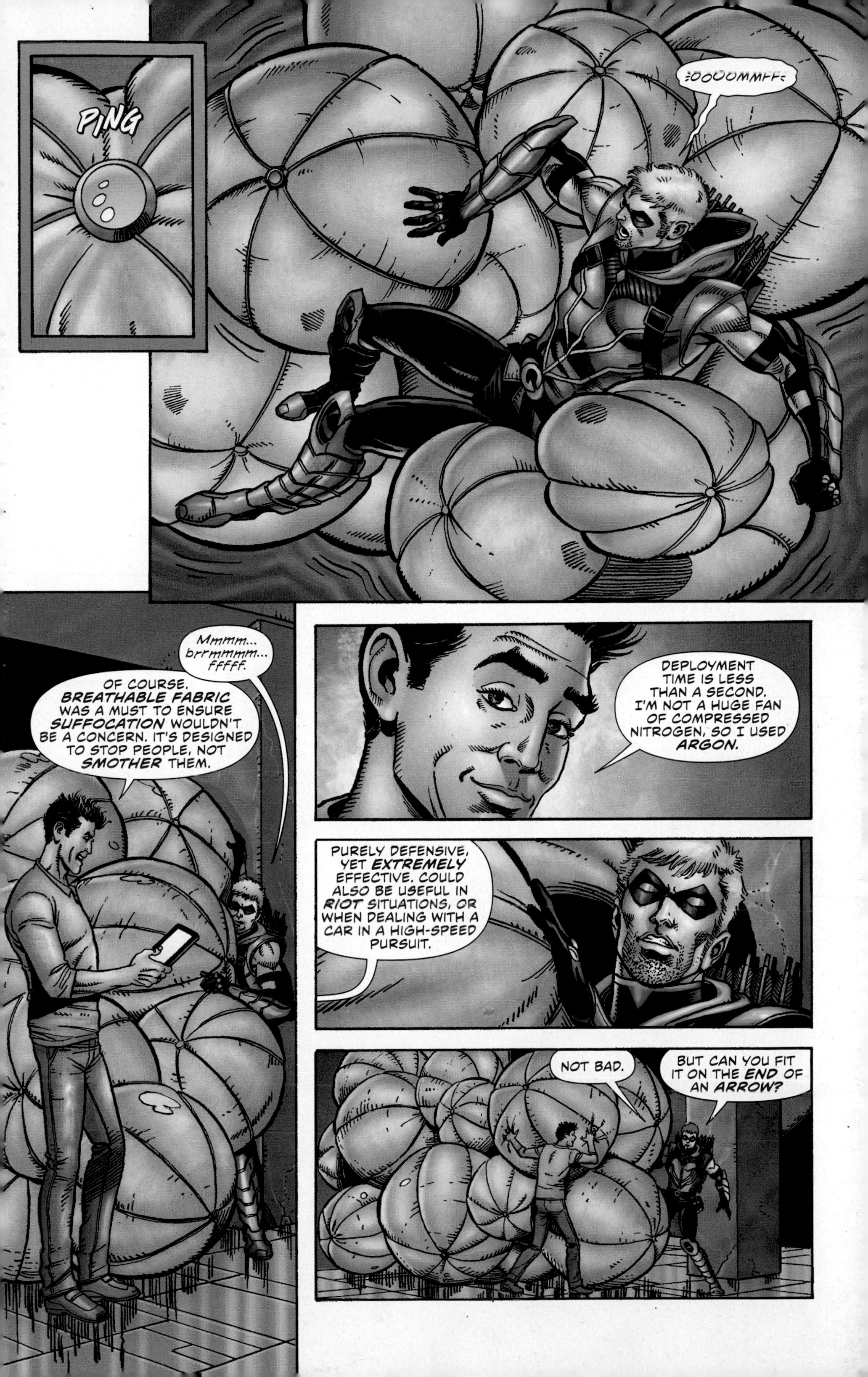
PING
:OOOOMMFF:
Mmmm... brrmmmmm... fffff.
OF COURSE. BREATHABLE FABRIC WAS A MUST TO ENSURE SUFFOCATION WOULDN'T BE A CONCERN. IT'S DESIGNED TO STOP PEOPLE, NOT SMOTHER THEM.
DEPLOYMENT TIME IS LESS THAN A SECOND. I'M NOT A HUGE FAN OF COMPRESSED NITROGEN, SO I USED ARGON.
PURELY DEFENSIVE, YET EXTREMELY EFFECTIVE. COULD ALSO BE USEFUL IN RIOT SITUATIONS, OR WHEN DEALING WITH A CAR IN A HIGH-SPEED PURSUIT.
NOT BAD.
BUT CAN YOU FIT IT ON THE END OF AN ARROW?

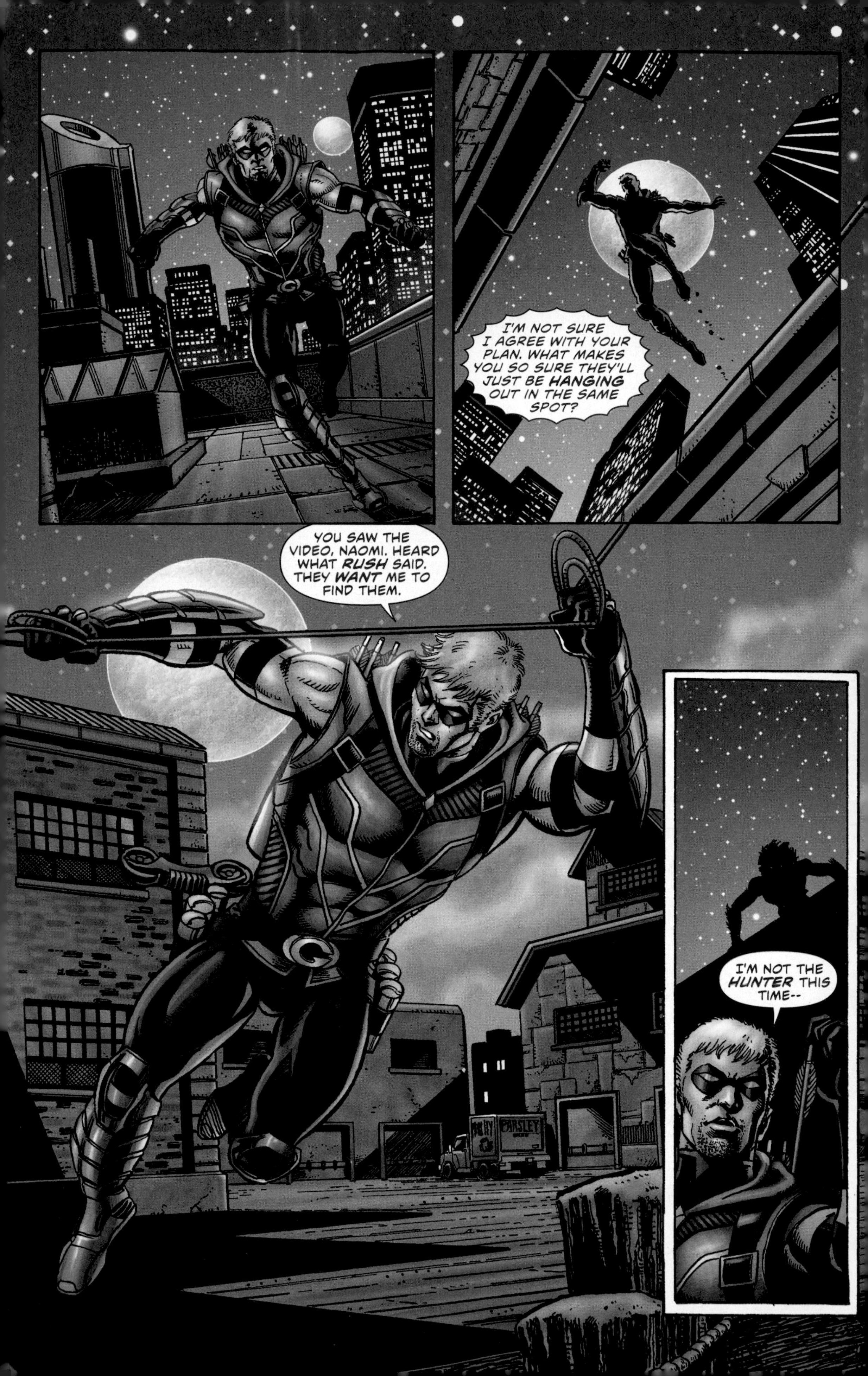

I'M NOT SURE I AGREE WITH YOUR PLAN. WHAT MAKES YOU SO SURE THEY'LL JUST BE HANGING OUT IN THE SAME SPOT?
YOU SAW THE VIDEO, NAOMI. HEARD WHAT RUSH SAID. THEY WANT ME TO FIND THEM.
I'M NOT THE HUNTER THIS TIME--

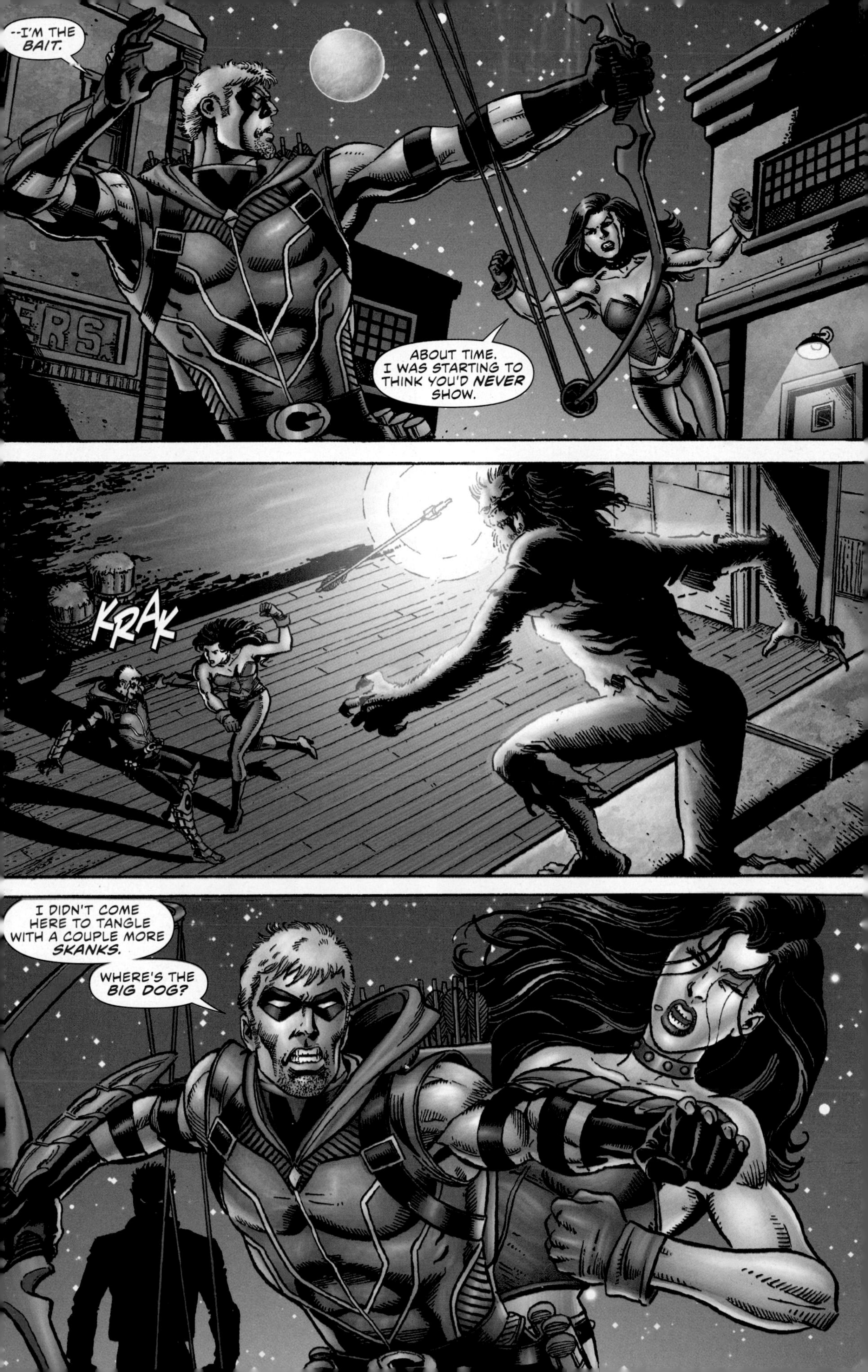
--I'M THE BAIT.
ABOUT TIME. I WAS STARTING TO THINK YOU'D NEVER SHOW.
KRAK
I DIDN'T COME HERE TO TANGLE WITH A COUPLE MORE SKANKS.
WHERE'S THE BIG DOG?

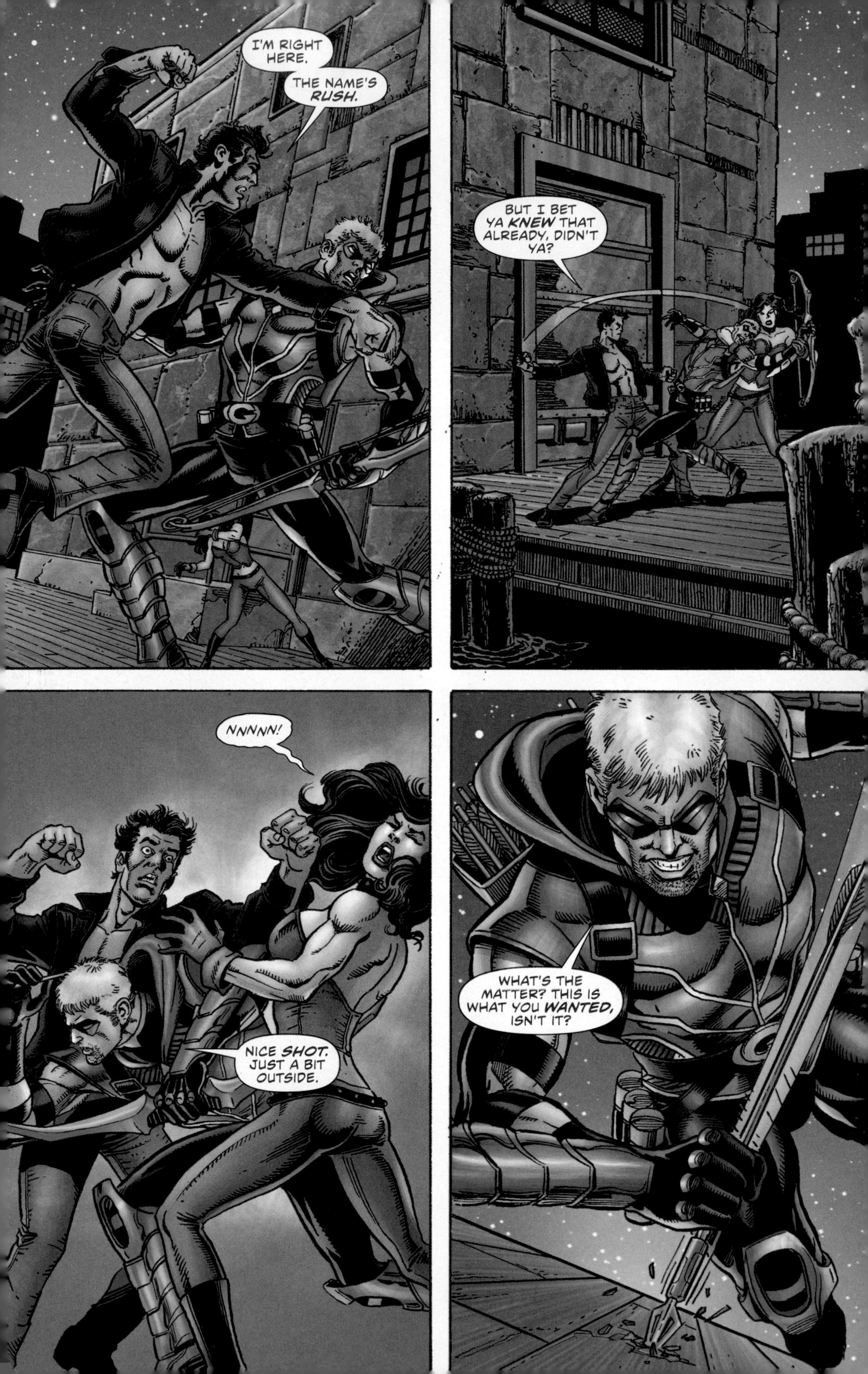
I'M RIGHT HERE.
THE NAME'S *RUSH.*
BUT I BET YA *KNEW* THAT ALREADY, DIDN'T YA?
NNNNN!
NICE *SHOT.* JUST A BIT OUTSIDE.
WHAT'S THE MATTER? THIS IS WHAT YOU *WANTED,* ISN'T IT?

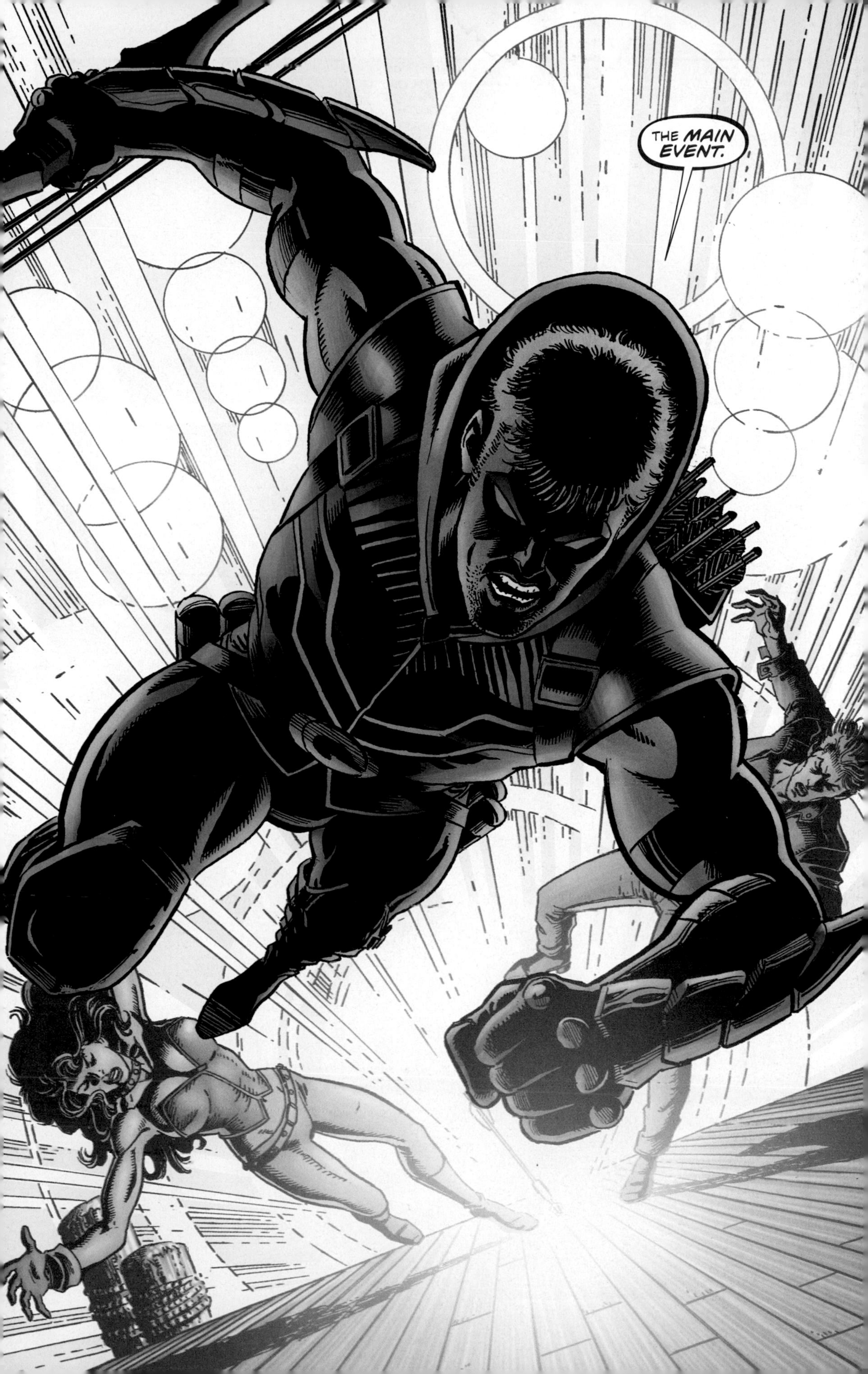
THE MAIN EVENT.

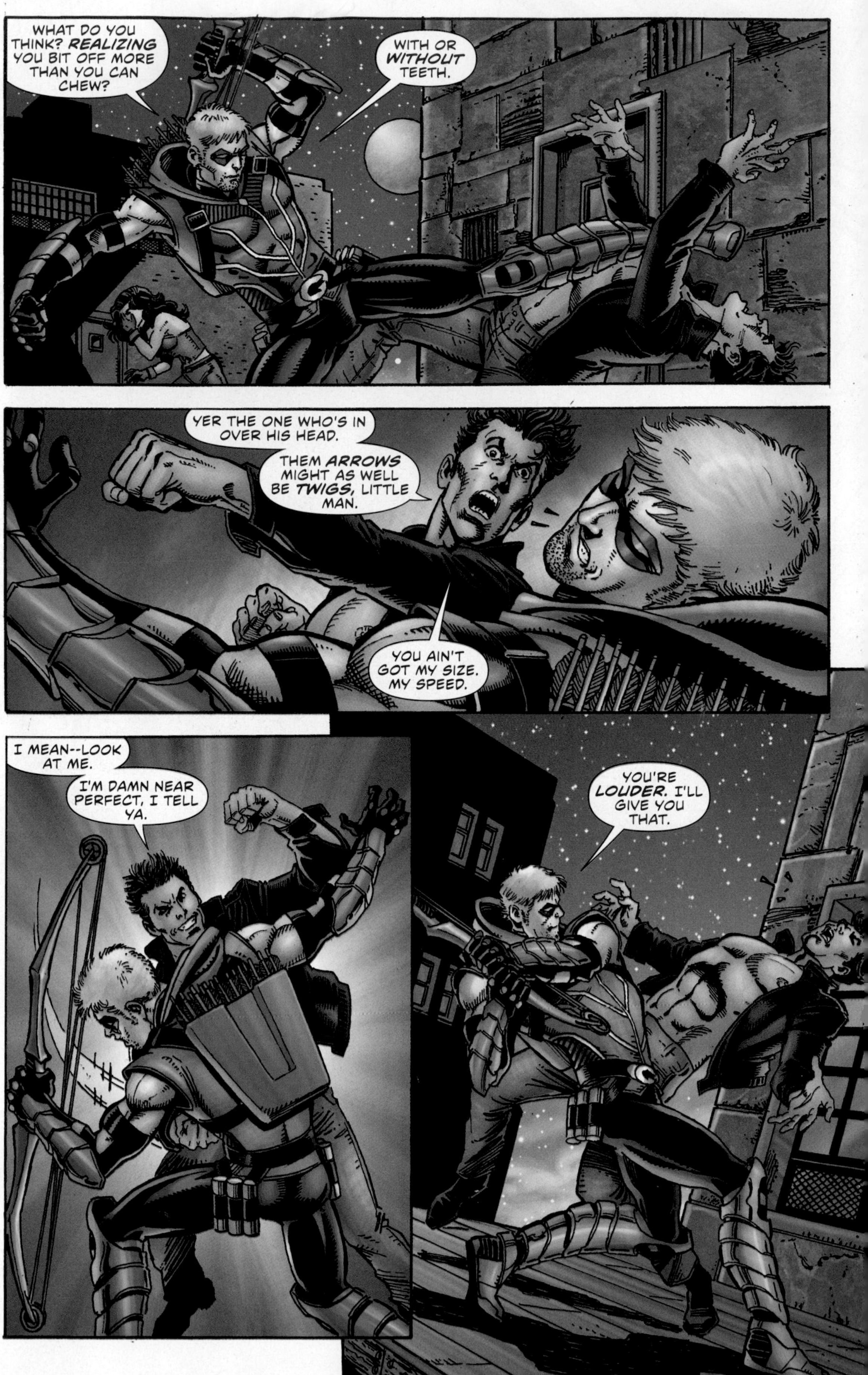
WHAT DO YOU THINK? REALIZING YOU BIT OFF MORE THAN YOU CAN CHEW?
WITH OR WITHOUT TEETH.
YER THE ONE WHO'S IN OVER HIS HEAD.
THEM ARROWS MIGHT AS WELL BE TWIGS, LITTLE MAN.
YOU AIN'T GOT MY SIZE. MY SPEED.
I MEAN--LOOK AT ME.
I'M DAMN NEAR PERFECT, I TELL YA.
YOU'RE LOUDER. I'LL GIVE YOU THAT.

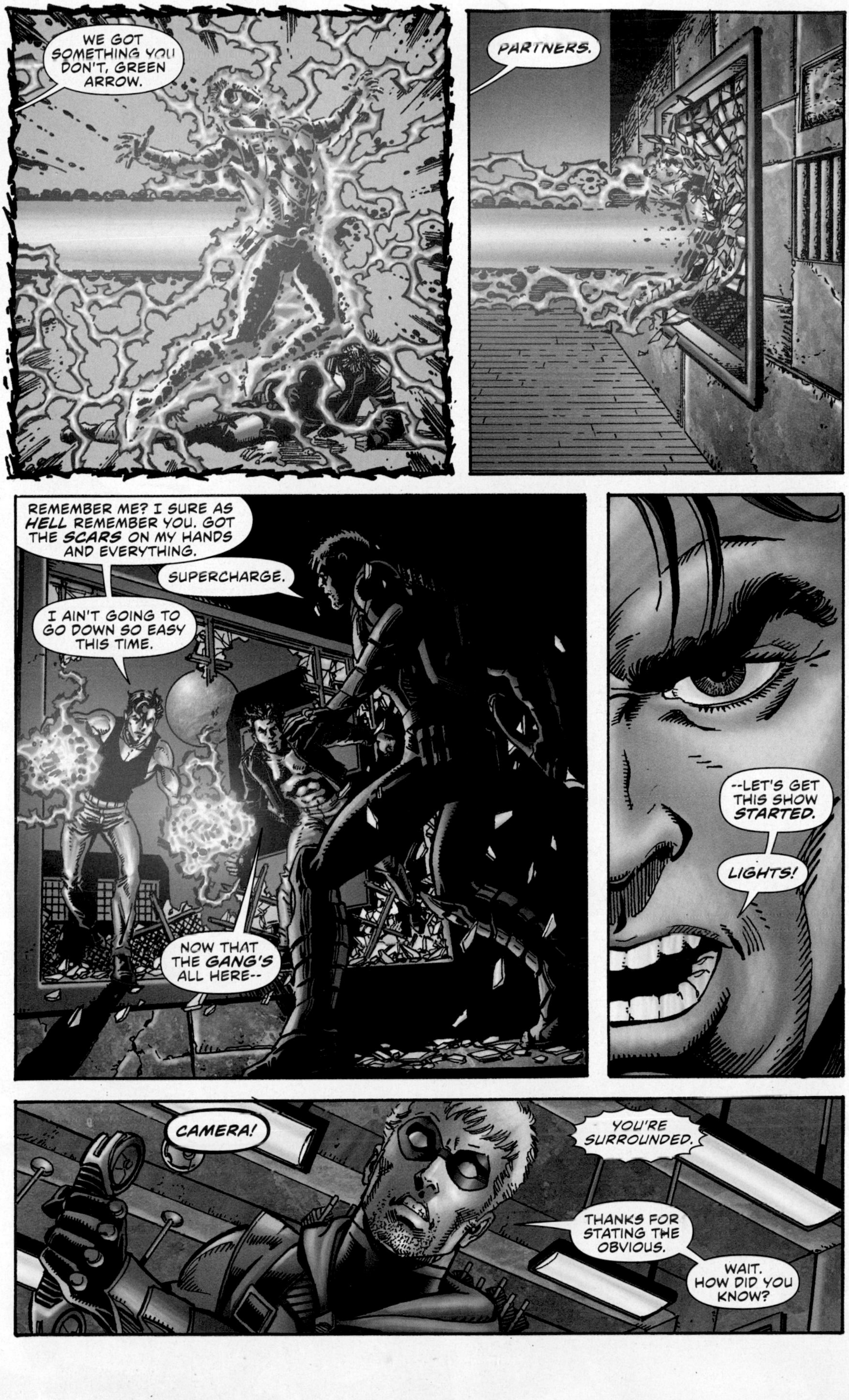
WE GOT SOMETHING YOU DON'T, GREEN ARROW.
PARTNERS.
REMEMBER ME? I SURE AS HELL REMEMBER YOU. GOT THE SCARS ON MY HANDS AND EVERYTHING.
SUPERCHARGE.
I AIN'T GOING TO GO DOWN SO EASY THIS TIME.
NOW THAT THE GANG'S ALL HERE--
--LET'S GET THIS SHOW STARTED.
LIGHTS!
CAMERA!
YOU'RE SURROUNDED.
THANKS FOR STATING THE OBVIOUS.
WAIT. HOW DID YOU KNOW?

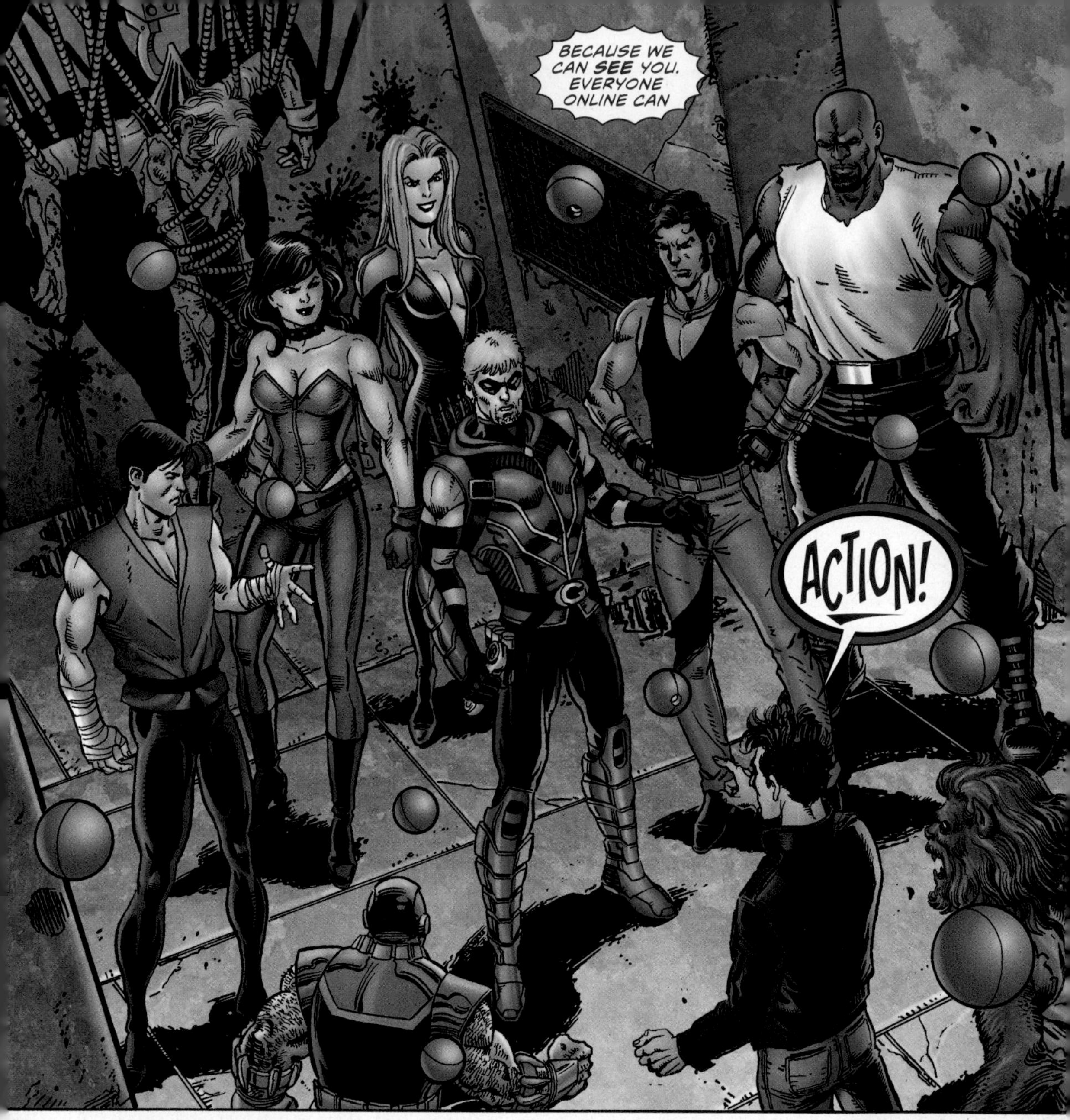
BECAUSE WE CAN SEE YOU. EVERYONE ONLINE CAN
ACTION!
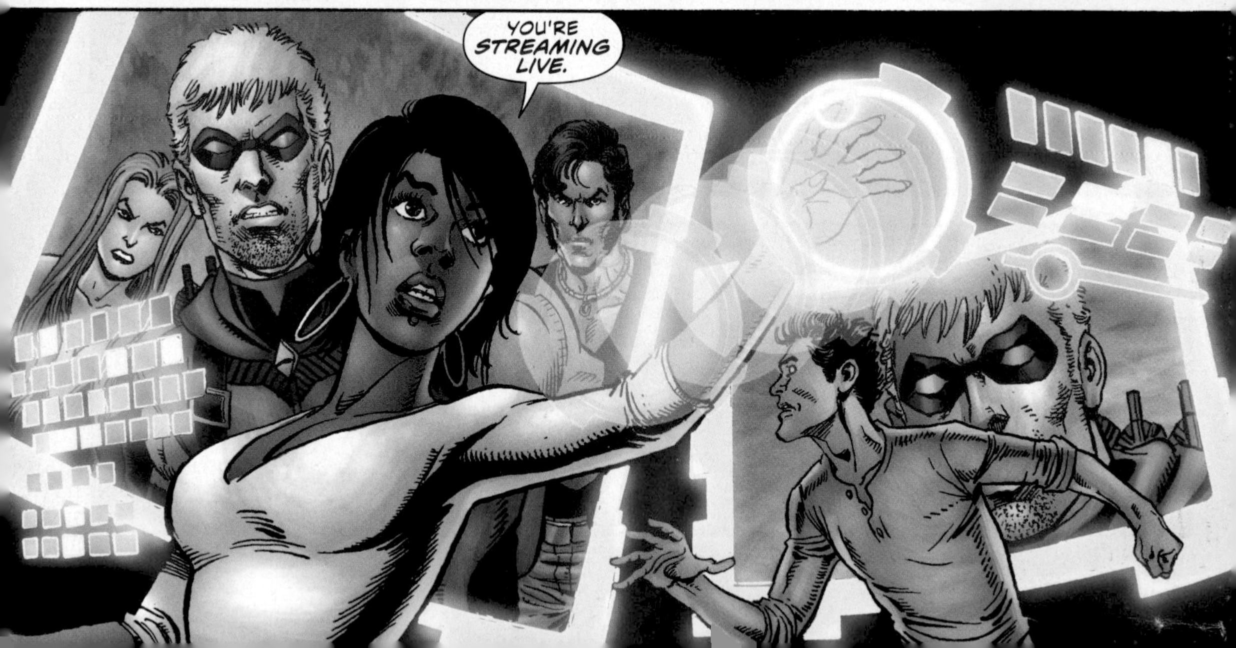
YOU'RE STREAMING LIVE.

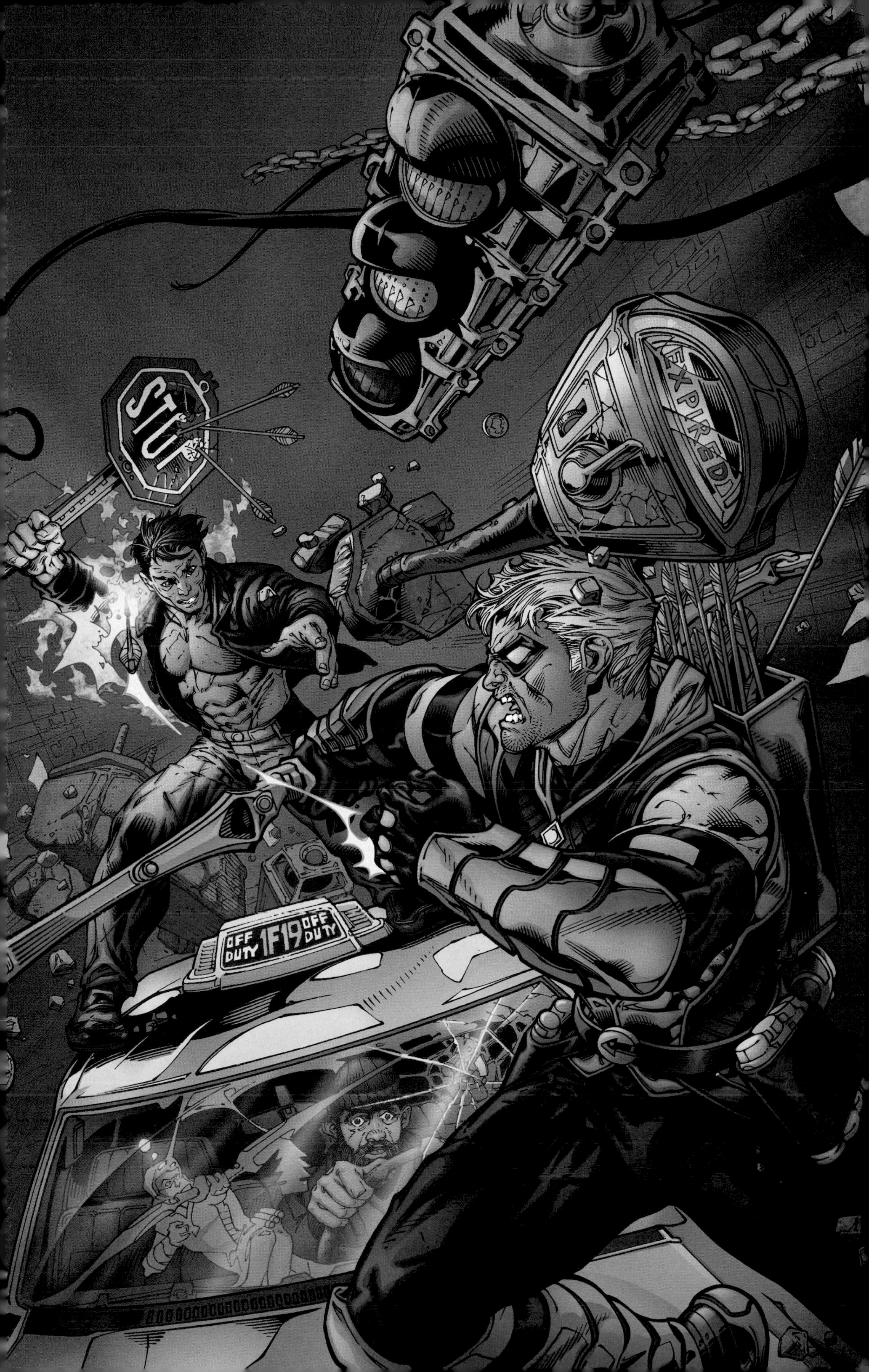
EXPIRED
OFF DUTY
1F19
OFF DUTY

GREEN ARROW'S LAST STAND

J.T. KRUL
writer / co-plotter

DAN JURGENS
layouts / co-plotter

GEORGE PÉREZ
RAY McCARTHY
finishes

cover by HOWARD PORTER, RAY McCARTHY & ALLEN PASSALAQUA

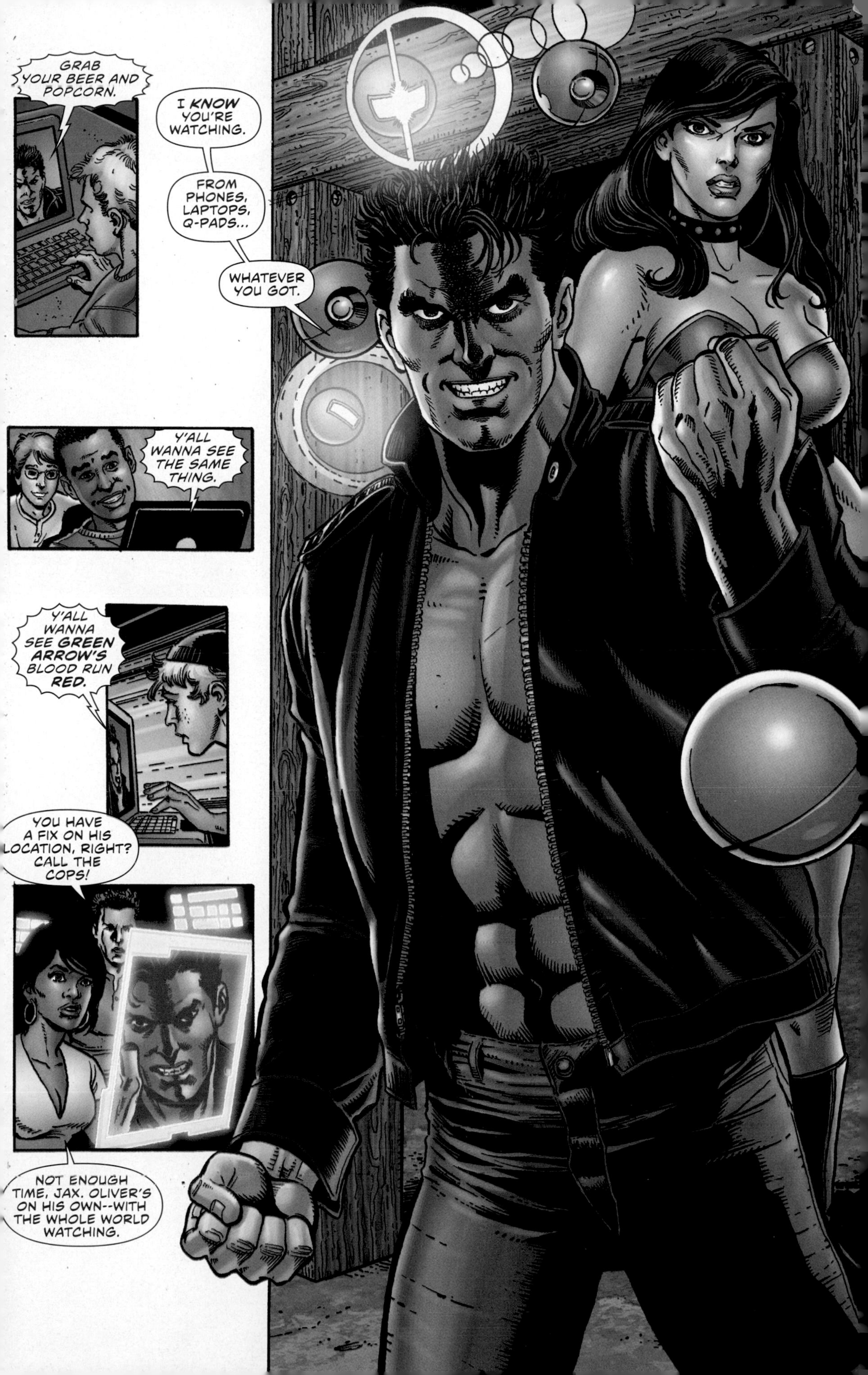
GRAB YOUR BEER AND POPCORN.
I KNOW YOU'RE WATCHING.
FROM PHONES, LAPTOPS, Q-PADS...
WHATEVER YOU GOT.
Y'ALL WANNA SEE THE SAME THING.
Y'ALL WANNA SEE GREEN ARROW'S BLOOD RUN RED.
YOU HAVE A FIX ON HIS LOCATION, RIGHT? CALL THE COPS!
NOT ENOUGH TIME, JAX. OLIVER'S ON HIS OWN--WITH THE WHOLE WORLD WATCHING.

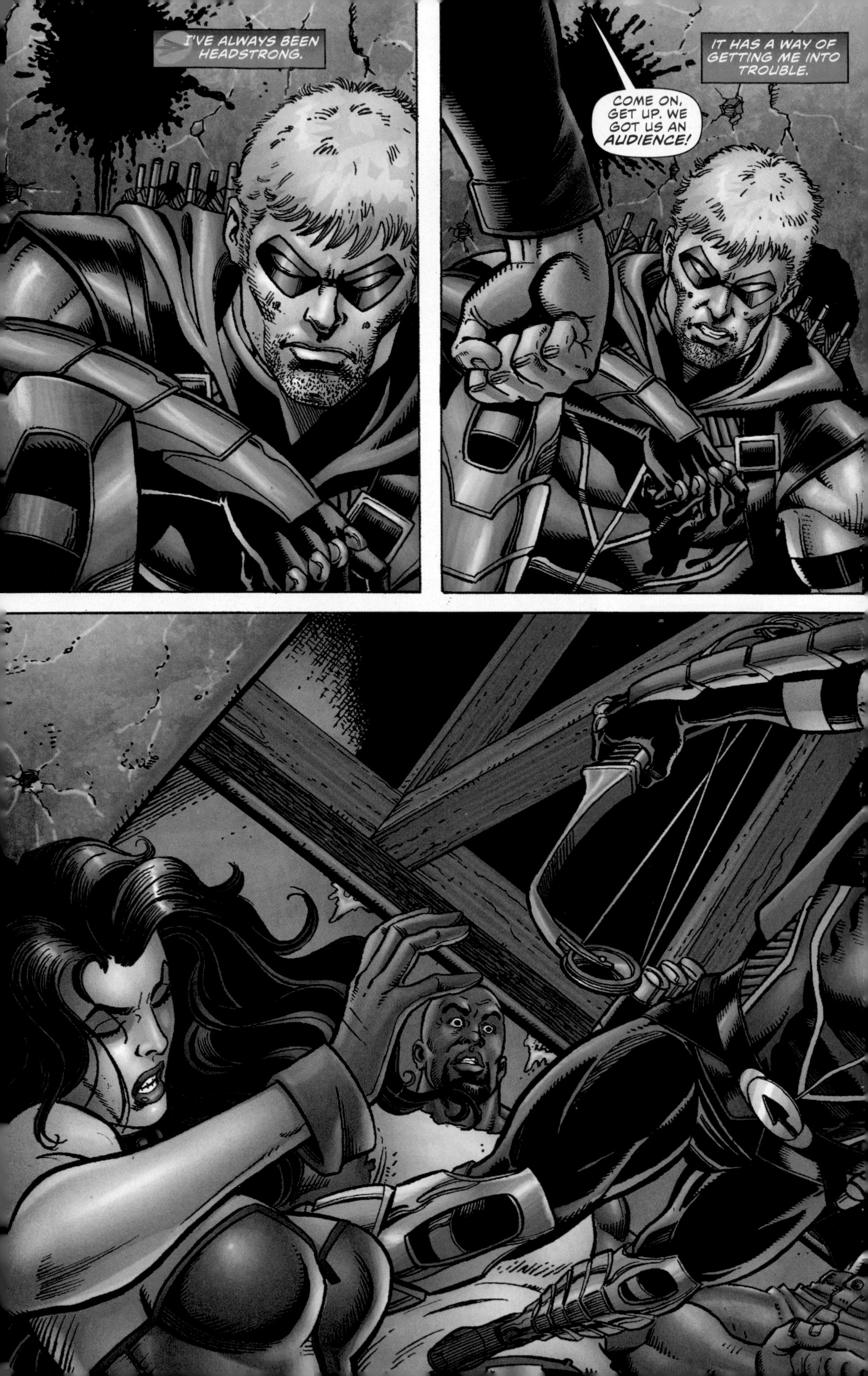
I'VE ALWAYS BEEN HEADSTRONG.
IT HAS A WAY OF GETTING ME INTO TROUBLE.
COME ON, GET UP. WE GOT US AN AUDIENCE!

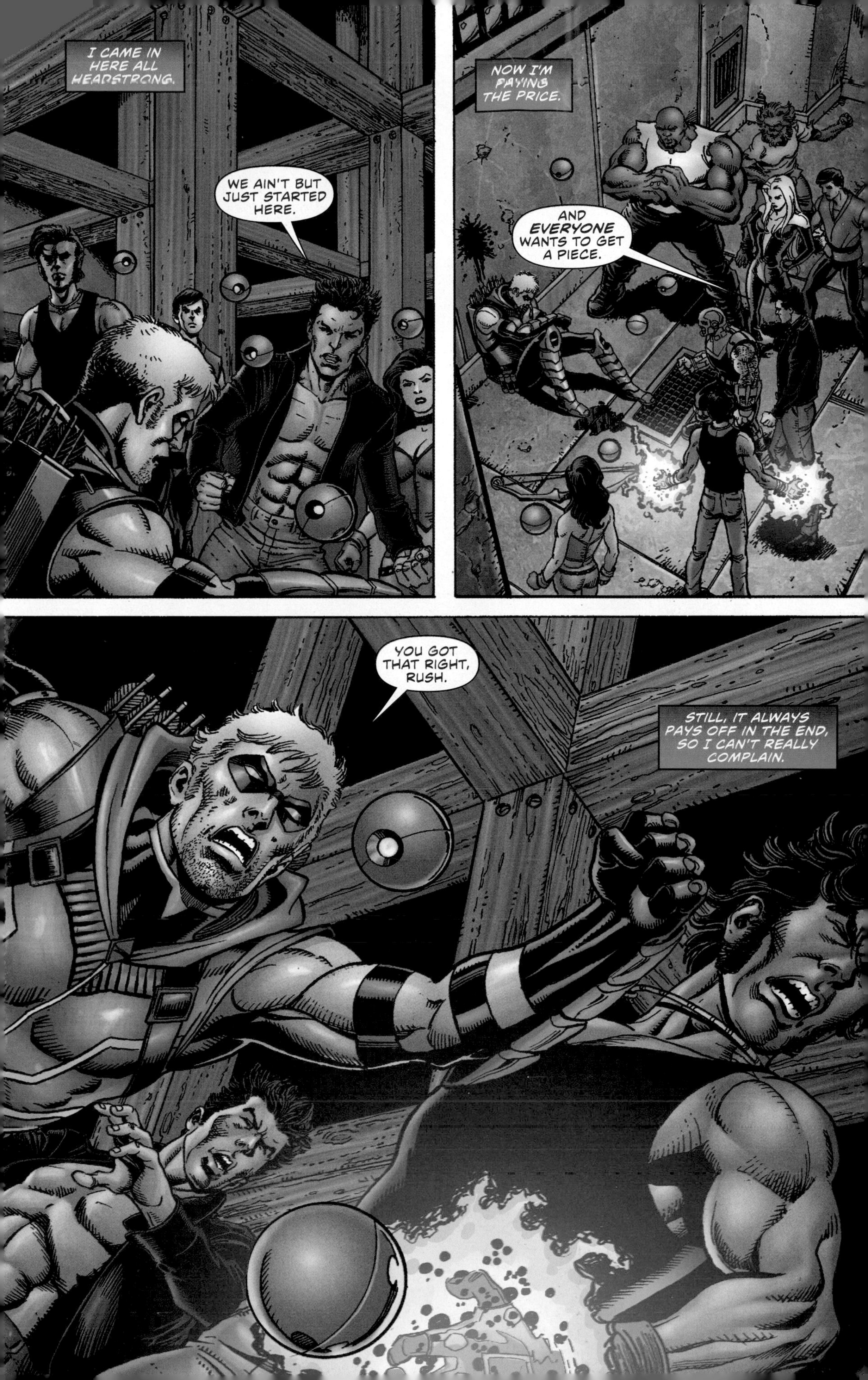
I CAME IN HERE ALL HEADSTRONG.
WE AIN'T BUT JUST STARTED HERE.
NOW I'M PAYING THE PRICE.
AND EVERYONE WANTS TO GET A PIECE.
YOU GOT THAT RIGHT, RUSH.
STILL, IT ALWAYS PAYS OFF IN THE END, SO I CAN'T REALLY COMPLAIN.

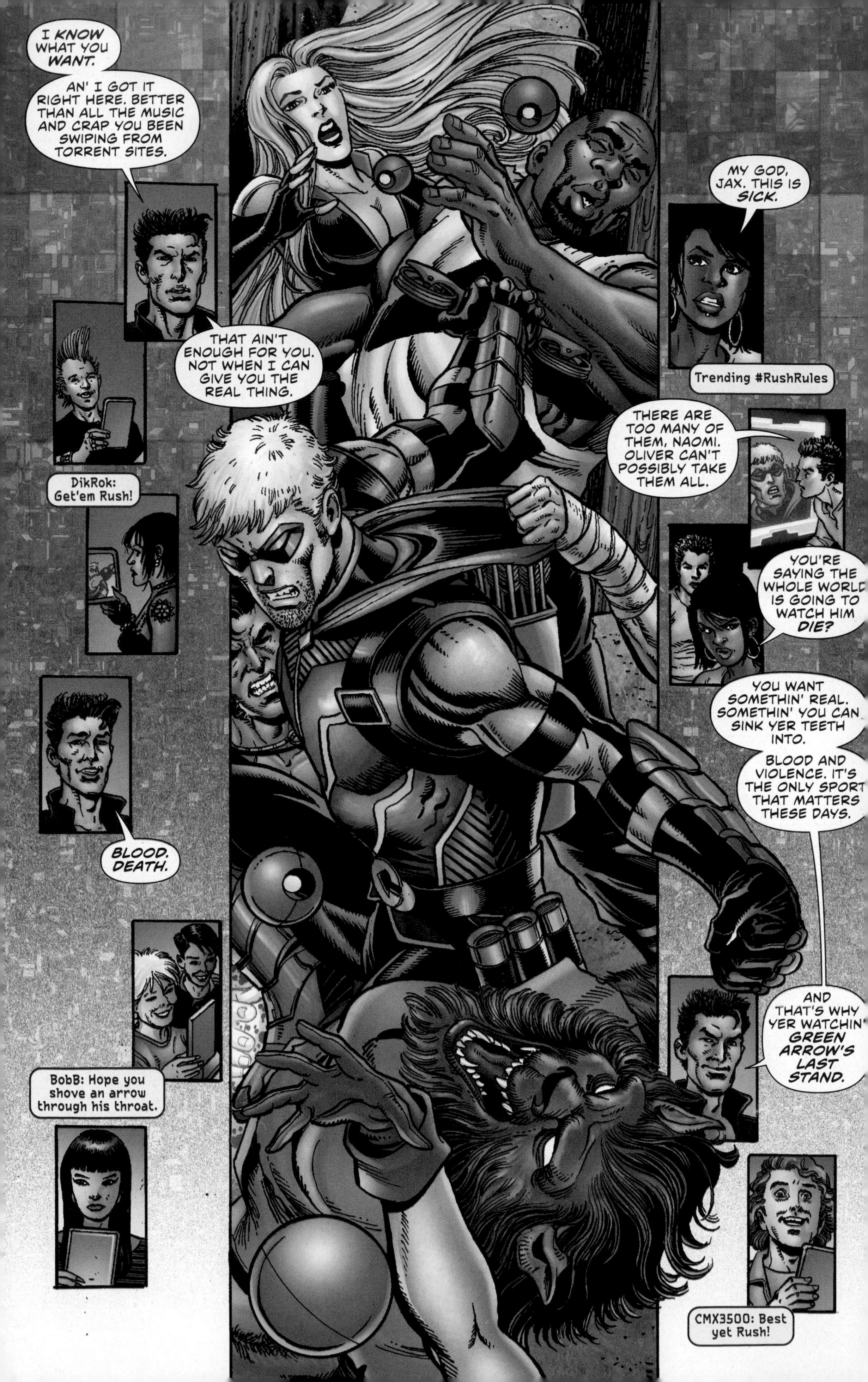
I KNOW WHAT YOU WANT.
AN' I GOT IT RIGHT HERE. BETTER THAN ALL THE MUSIC AND CRAP YOU BEEN SWIPING FROM TORRENT SITES.
THAT AIN'T ENOUGH FOR YOU. NOT WHEN I CAN GIVE YOU THE REAL THING.
DikRok: Get'em Rush!
BLOOD. DEATH.
BobB: Hope you shove an arrow through his throat.
MY GOD, JAX. THIS IS SICK.
Trending #RushRules
THERE ARE TOO MANY OF THEM, NAOMI. OLIVER CAN'T POSSIBLY TAKE THEM ALL.
YOU'RE SAYING THE WHOLE WORLD IS GOING TO WATCH HIM DIE?
YOU WANT SOMETHIN' REAL. SOMETHIN' YOU CAN SINK YER TEETH INTO.
BLOOD AND VIOLENCE. IT'S THE ONLY SPORT THAT MATTERS THESE DAYS.
AND THAT'S WHY YER WATCHIN' GREEN ARROW'S LAST STAND.
CMX3500: Best yet Rush!

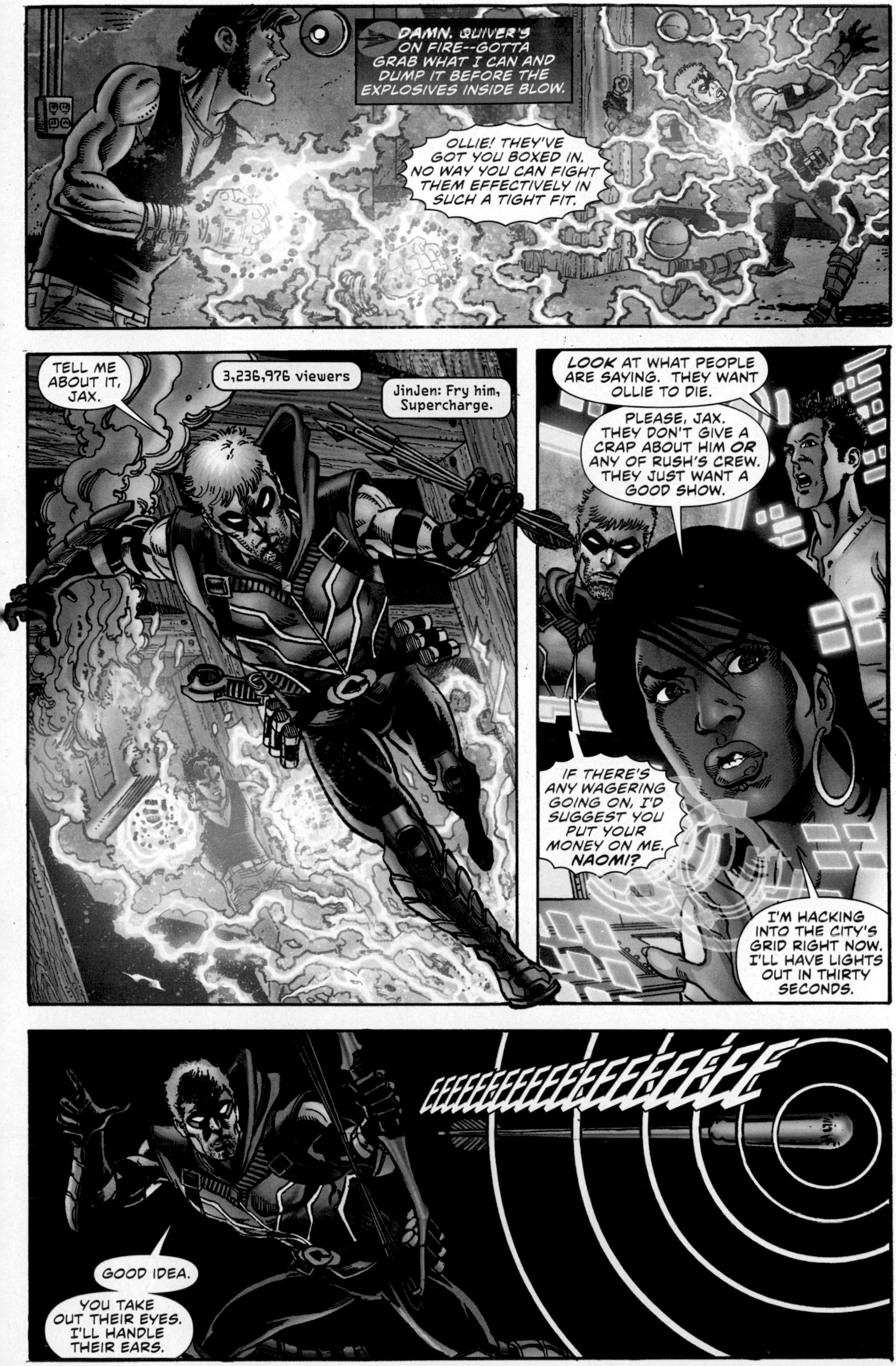
DAMN. QUIVER'S ON FIRE--GOTTA GRAB WHAT I CAN AND DUMP IT BEFORE THE EXPLOSIVES INSIDE BLOW.
OLLIE! THEY'VE GOT YOU BOXED IN. NO WAY YOU CAN FIGHT THEM EFFECTIVELY IN SUCH A TIGHT FIT.
TELL ME ABOUT IT, JAX.
3,236,976 viewers
JinJen: Fry him, Supercharge.
LOOK AT WHAT PEOPLE ARE SAYING. THEY WANT OLLIE TO DIE.
PLEASE, JAX. THEY DON'T GIVE A CRAP ABOUT HIM OR ANY OF RUSH'S CREW. THEY JUST WANT A GOOD SHOW.
IF THERE'S ANY WAGERING GOING ON, I'D SUGGEST YOU PUT YOUR MONEY ON ME. NAOMI?
I'M HACKING INTO THE CITY'S GRID RIGHT NOW. I'LL HAVE LIGHTS OUT IN THIRTY SECONDS.
EEEEEEEEEEEEEEEEEEEEEE
GOOD IDEA.
YOU TAKE OUT THEIR EYES. I'LL HANDLE THEIR EARS.

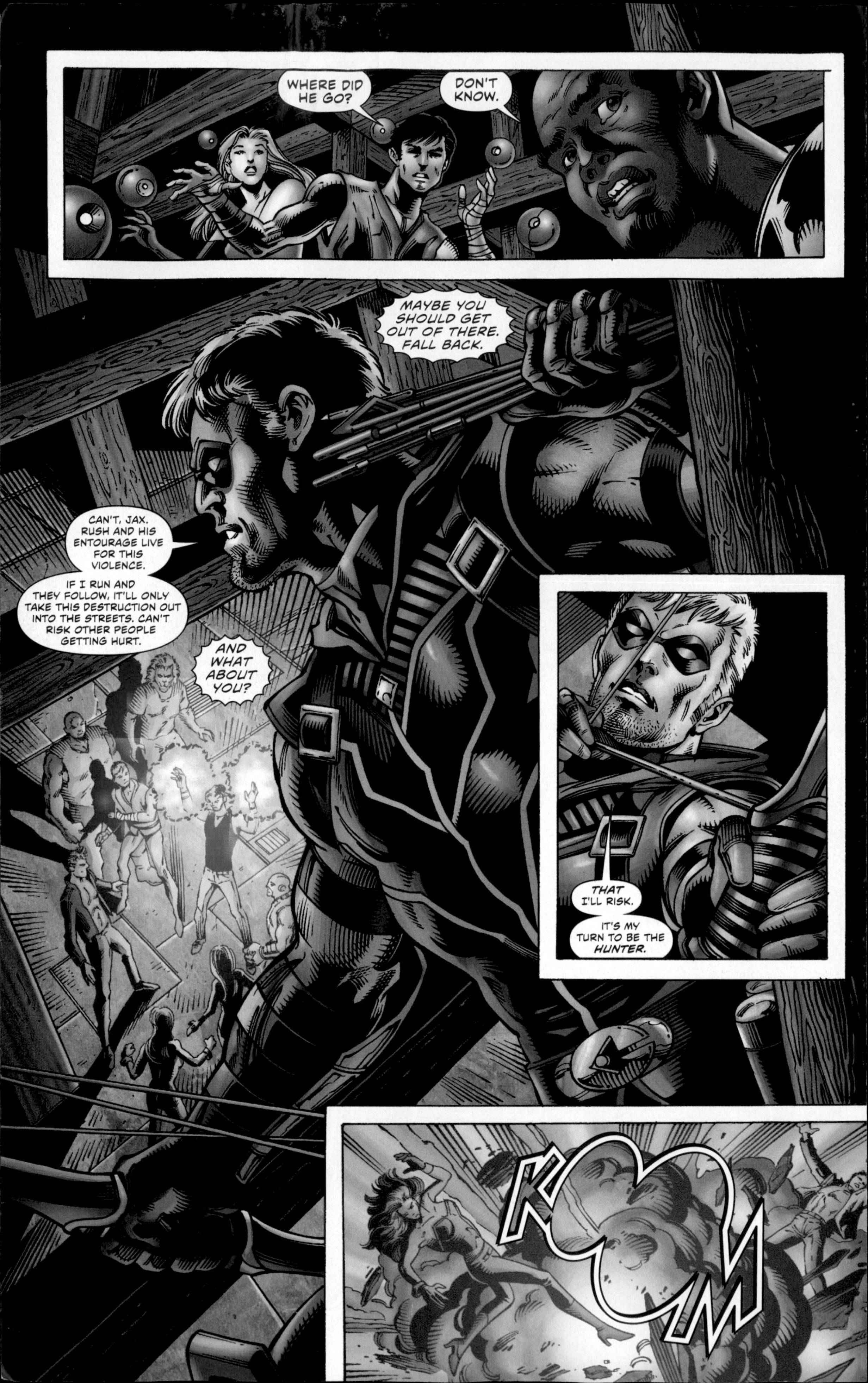

WHERE DID HE GO?
DON'T KNOW.
MAYBE YOU SHOULD GET OUT OF THERE. FALL BACK.
CAN'T, JAX. RUSH AND HIS ENTOURAGE LIVE FOR THIS VIOLENCE.
IF I RUN AND THEY FOLLOW, IT'LL ONLY TAKE THIS DESTRUCTION OUT INTO THE STREETS. CAN'T RISK OTHER PEOPLE GETTING HURT.
AND WHAT ABOUT YOU?
THAT I'LL RISK.
IT'S MY TURN TO BE THE HUNTER.
KOOM

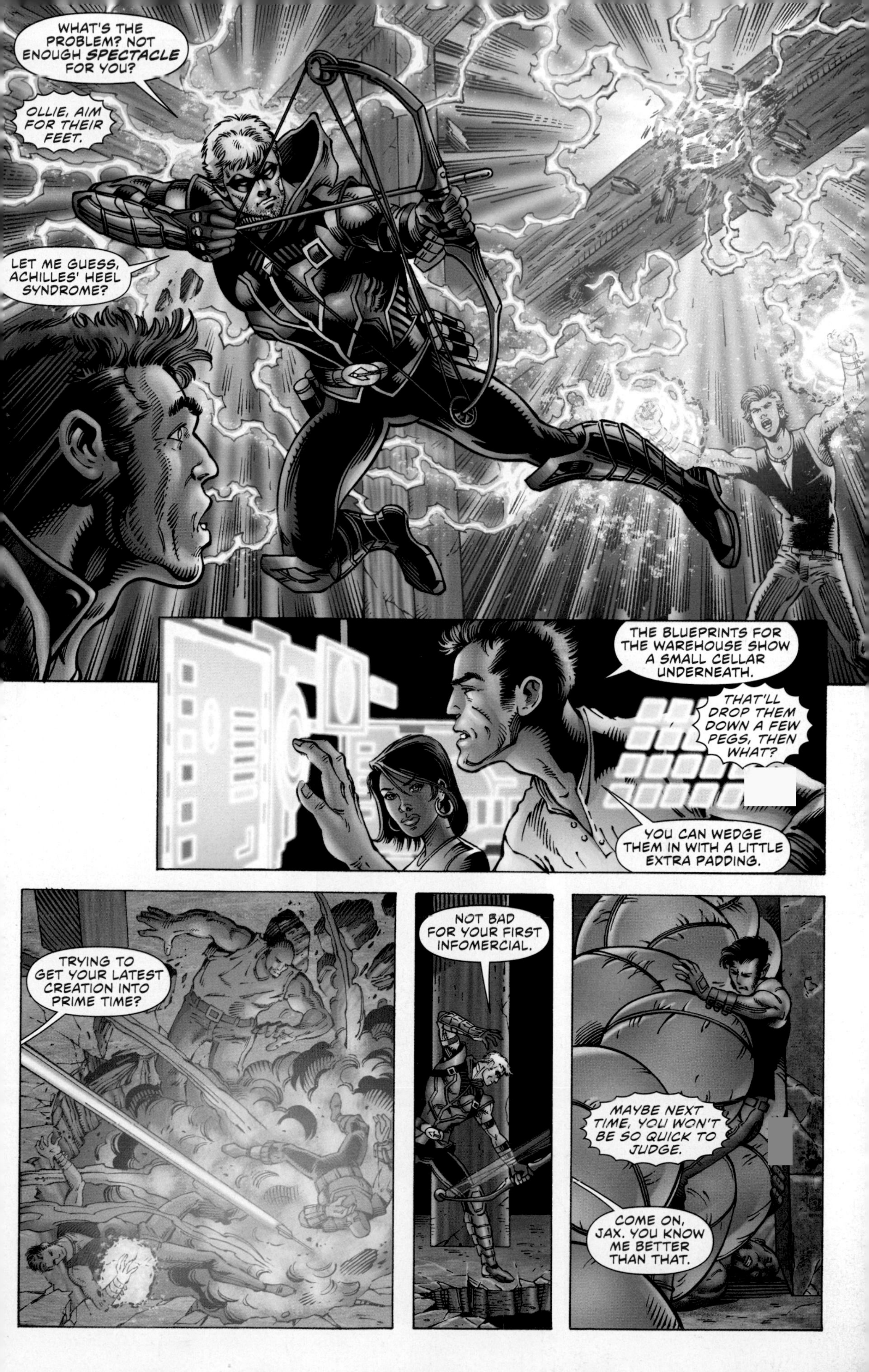
WHAT'S THE PROBLEM? NOT ENOUGH SPECTACLE FOR YOU?
OLLIE, AIM FOR THEIR FEET.
LET ME GUESS, ACHILLES' HEEL SYNDROME?
THE BLUEPRINTS FOR THE WAREHOUSE SHOW A SMALL CELLAR UNDERNEATH.
THAT'LL DROP THEM DOWN A FEW PEGS, THEN WHAT?
YOU CAN WEDGE THEM IN WITH A LITTLE EXTRA PADDING.
TRYING TO GET YOUR LATEST CREATION INTO PRIME TIME?
NOT BAD FOR YOUR FIRST INFOMERCIAL.
MAYBE NEXT TIME, YOU WON'T BE SO QUICK TO JUDGE.
COME ON, JAX. YOU KNOW ME BETTER THAN THAT.

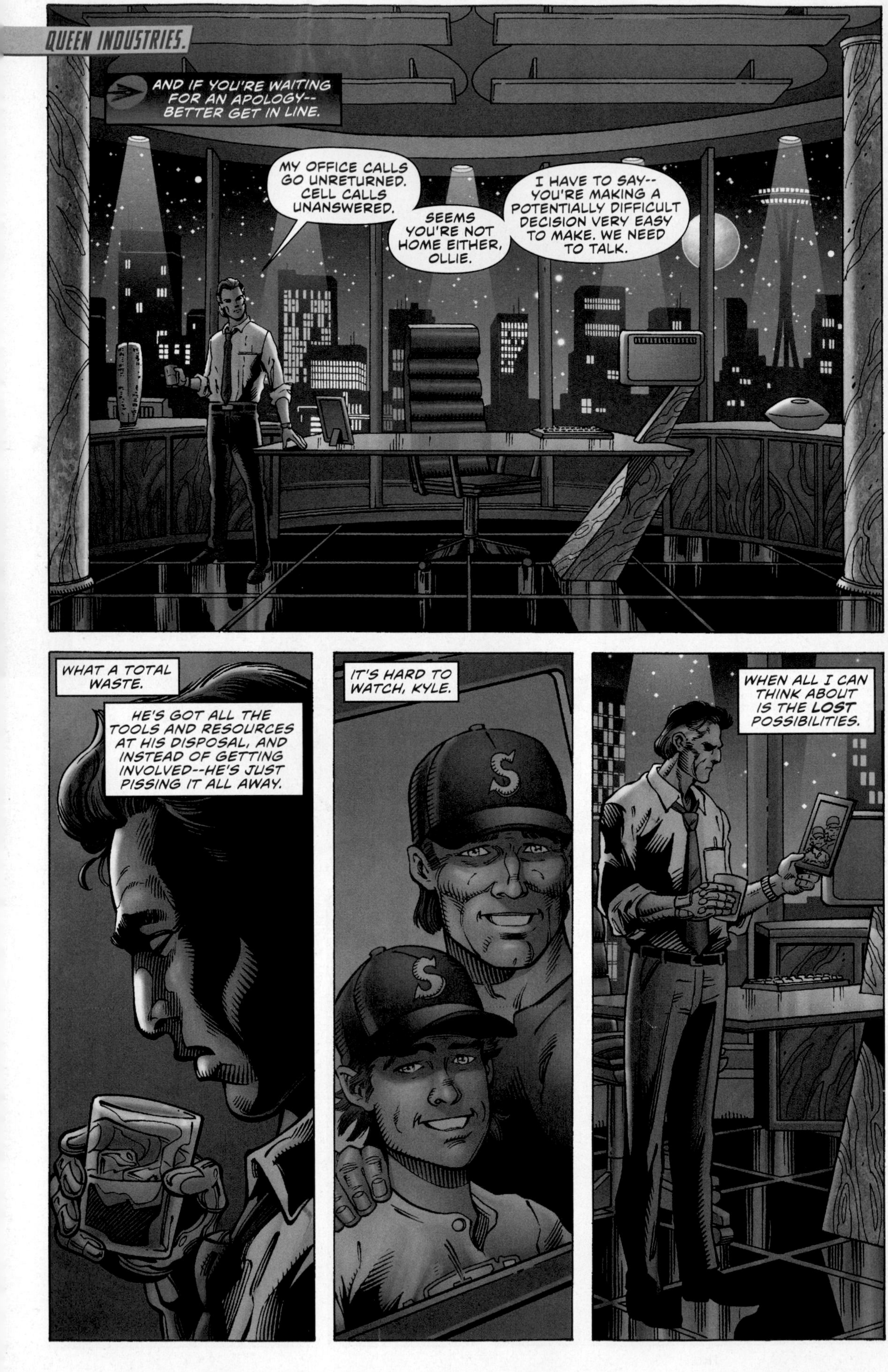
QUEEN INDUSTRIES.
AND IF YOU'RE WAITING FOR AN APOLOGY-- BETTER GET IN LINE.
MY OFFICE CALLS GO UNRETURNED. CELL CALLS UNANSWERED.
SEEMS YOU'RE NOT HOME EITHER, OLLIE.
I HAVE TO SAY-- YOU'RE MAKING A POTENTIALLY DIFFICULT DECISION VERY EASY TO MAKE. WE NEED TO TALK.
WHAT A TOTAL WASTE.
HE'S GOT ALL THE TOOLS AND RESOURCES AT HIS DISPOSAL, AND INSTEAD OF GETTING INVOLVED--HE'S JUST PISSING IT ALL AWAY.
IT'S HARD TO WATCH, KYLE.
WHEN ALL I CAN THINK ABOUT IS THE LOST POSSIBILITIES.

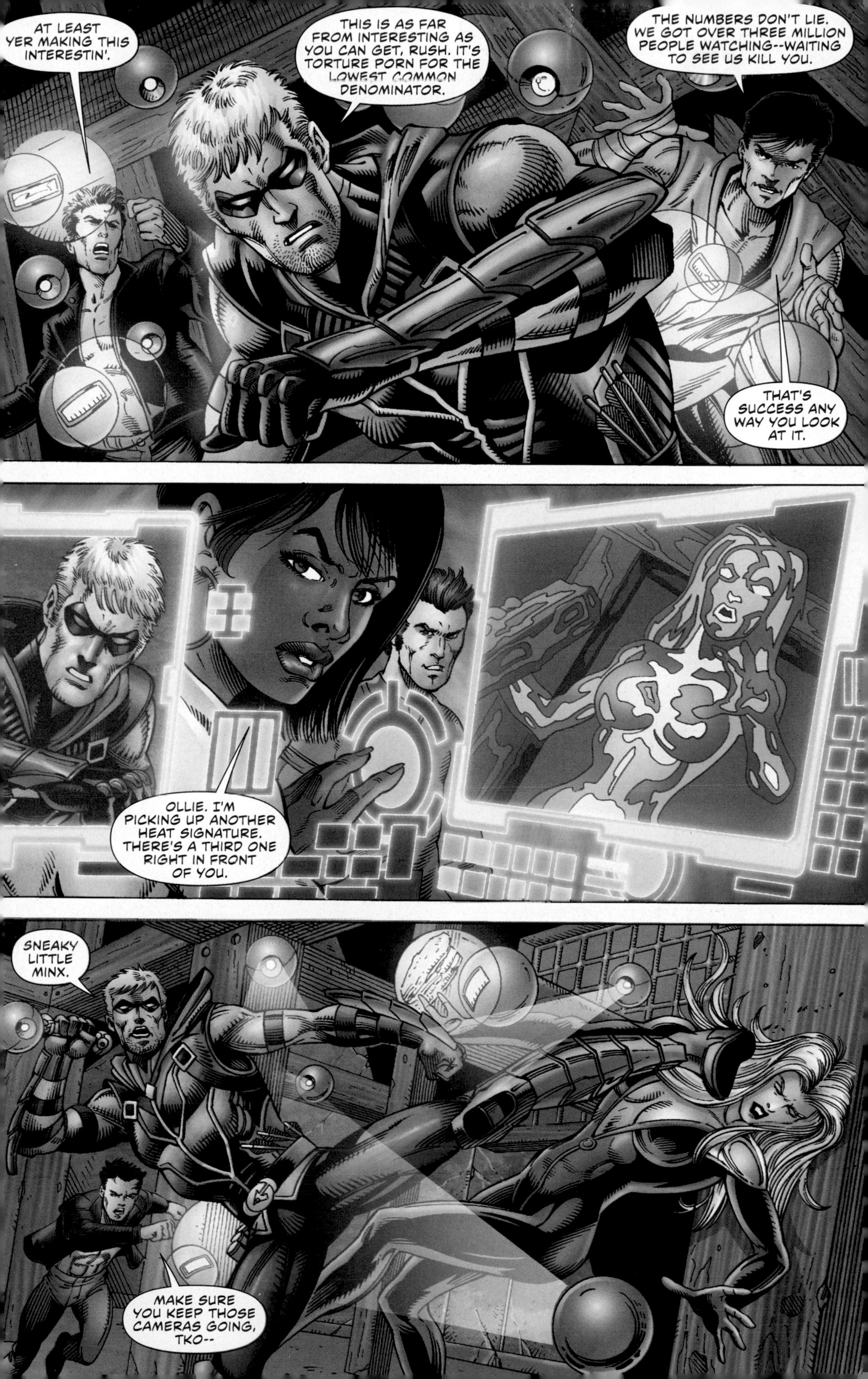
AT LEAST YER MAKING THIS INTERESTIN'.
THIS IS AS FAR FROM INTERESTING AS YOU CAN GET, RUSH. IT'S TORTURE PORN FOR THE LOWEST COMMON DENOMINATOR.
THE NUMBERS DON'T LIE. WE GOT OVER THREE MILLION PEOPLE WATCHING--WAITING TO SEE US KILL YOU.
THAT'S SUCCESS ANY WAY YOU LOOK AT IT.
OLLIE. I'M PICKING UP ANOTHER HEAT SIGNATURE. THERE'S A THIRD ONE RIGHT IN FRONT OF YOU.
SNEAKY LITTLE MINX.
MAKE SURE YOU KEEP THOSE CAMERAS GOING, TKO--

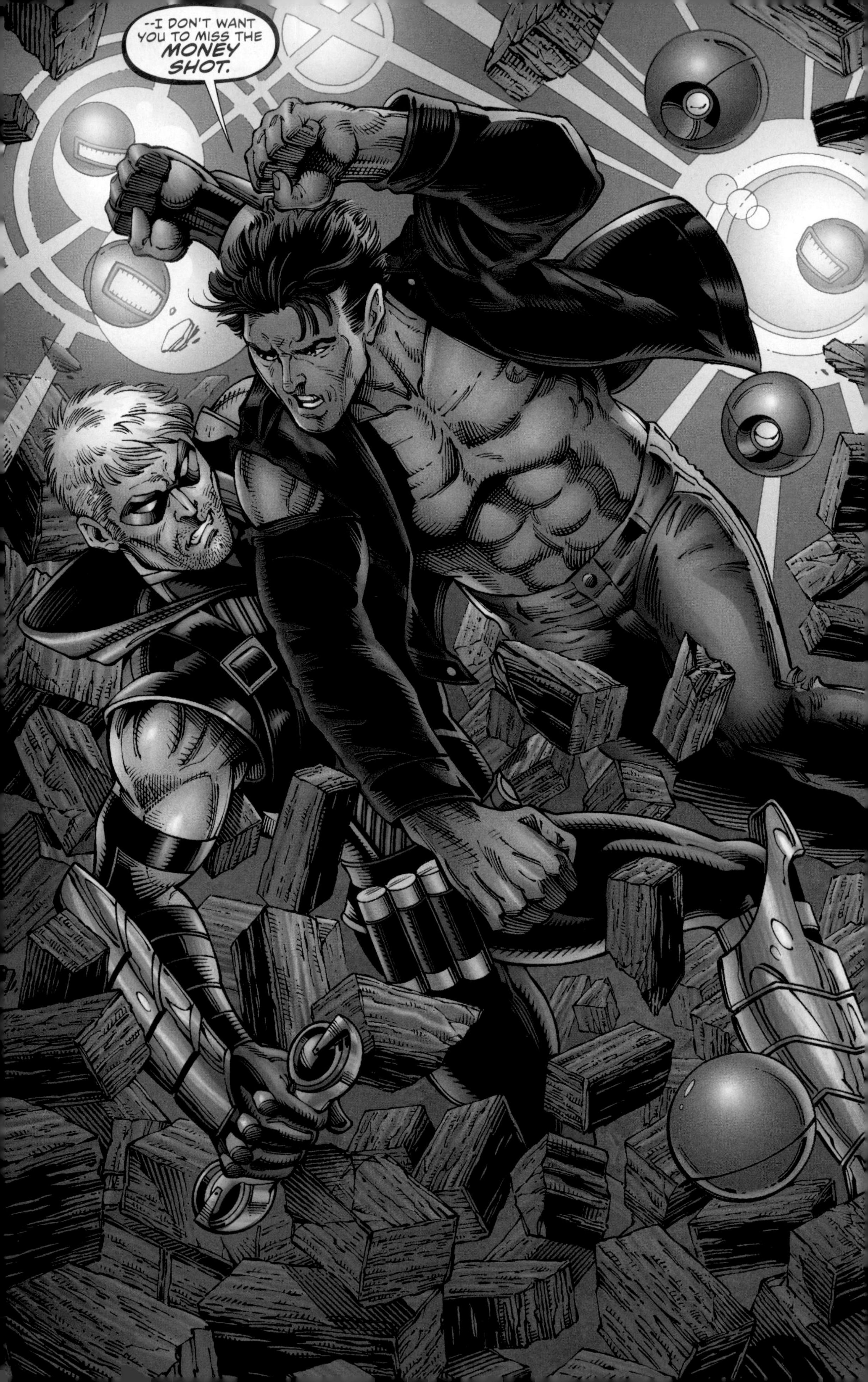
--I DON'T WANT YOU TO MISS THE MONEY SHOT.

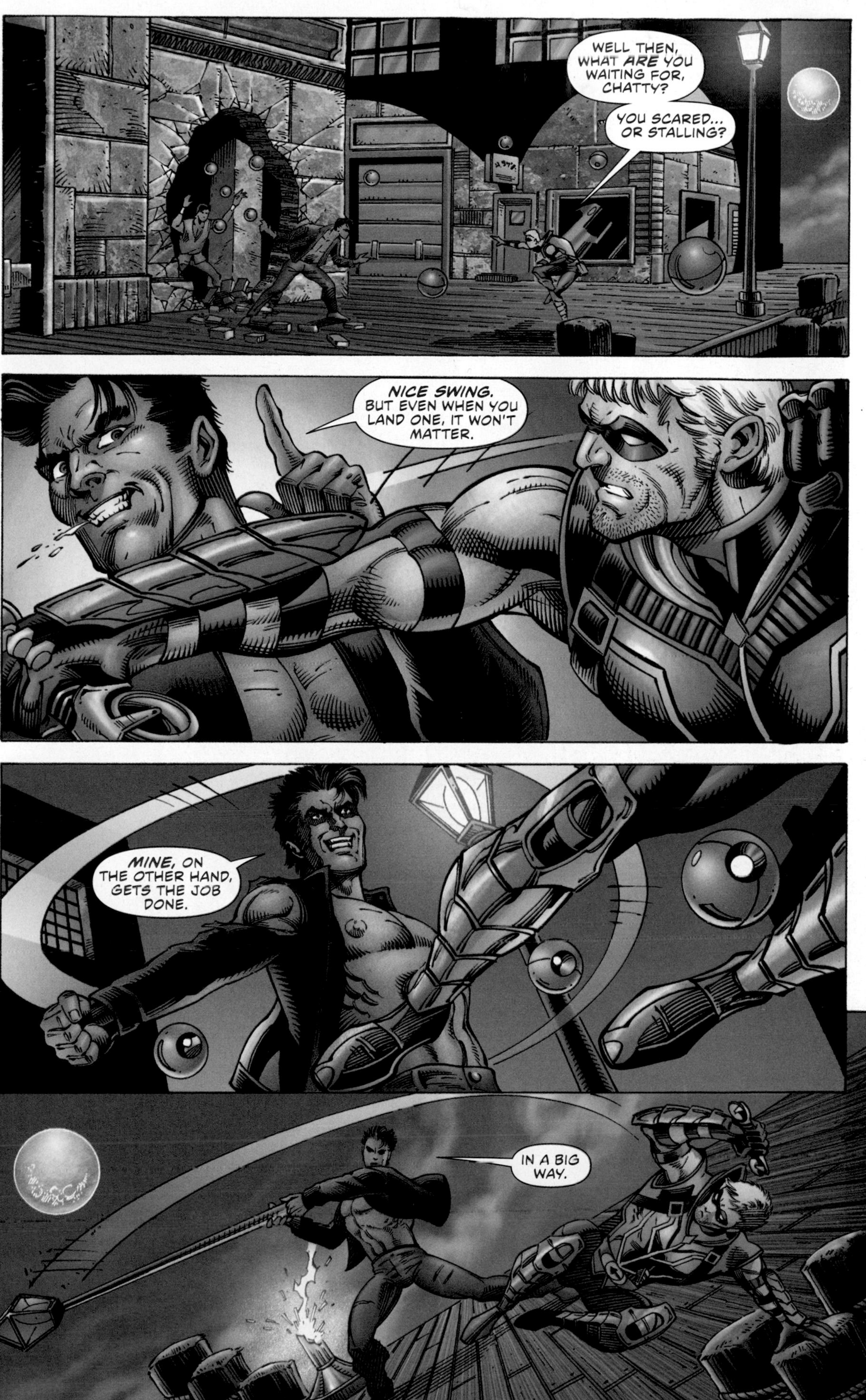
WELL THEN, WHAT ARE YOU WAITING FOR, CHATTY?
YOU SCARED... OR STALLING?
NICE SWING. BUT EVEN WHEN YOU LAND ONE, IT WON'T MATTER.
MINE, ON THE OTHER HAND, GETS THE JOB DONE.
IN A BIG WAY.

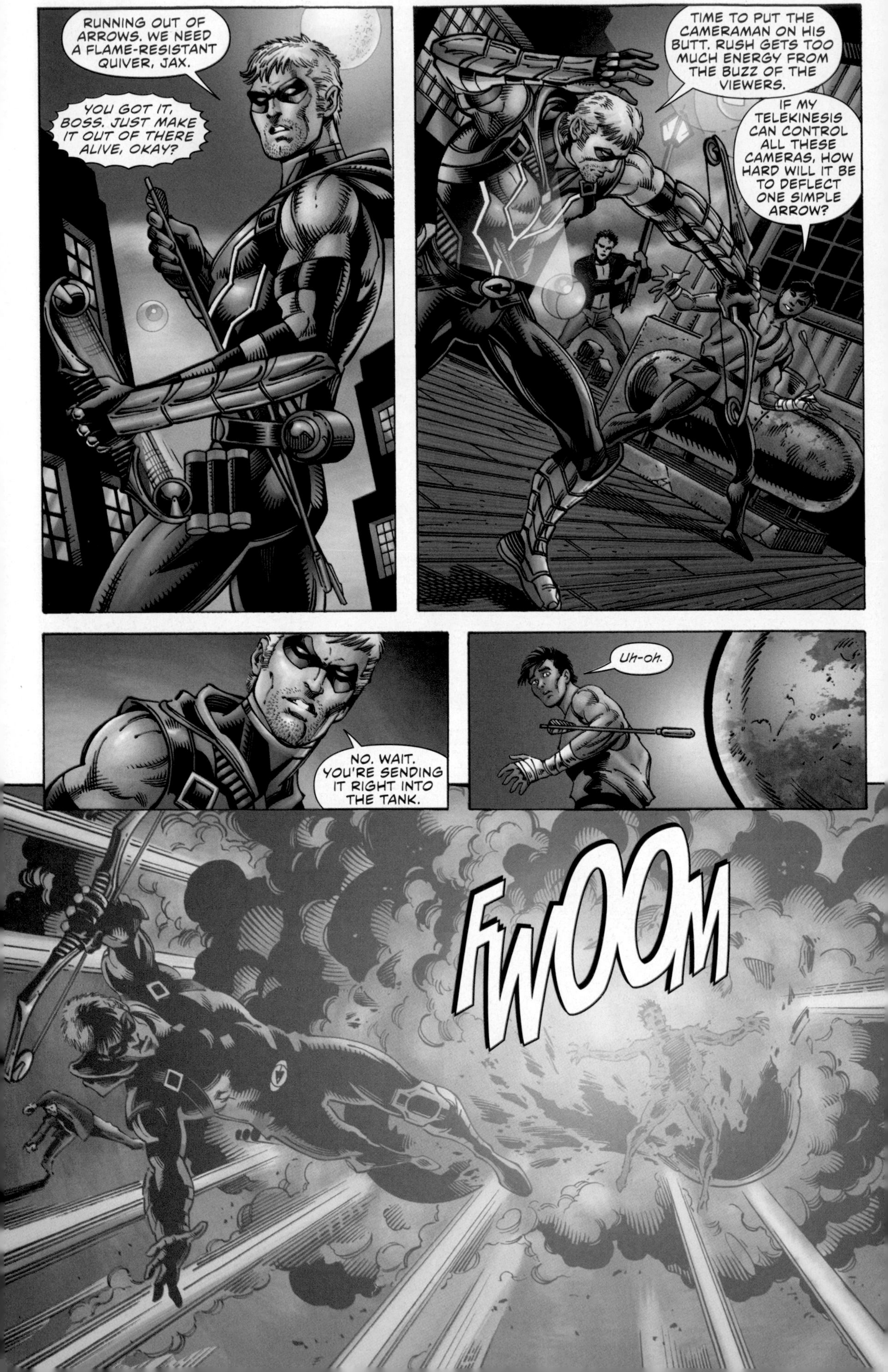
RUNNING OUT OF ARROWS. WE NEED A FLAME-RESISTANT QUIVER, JAX.
YOU GOT IT, BOSS. JUST MAKE IT OUT OF THERE ALIVE, OKAY?
TIME TO PUT THE CAMERAMAN ON HIS BUTT. RUSH GETS TOO MUCH ENERGY FROM THE BUZZ OF THE VIEWERS.
IF MY TELEKINESIS CAN CONTROL ALL THESE CAMERAS, HOW HARD WILL IT BE TO DEFLECT ONE SIMPLE ARROW?
NO. WAIT. YOU'RE SENDING IT RIGHT INTO THE TANK.
Uh-oh.
FWOOM

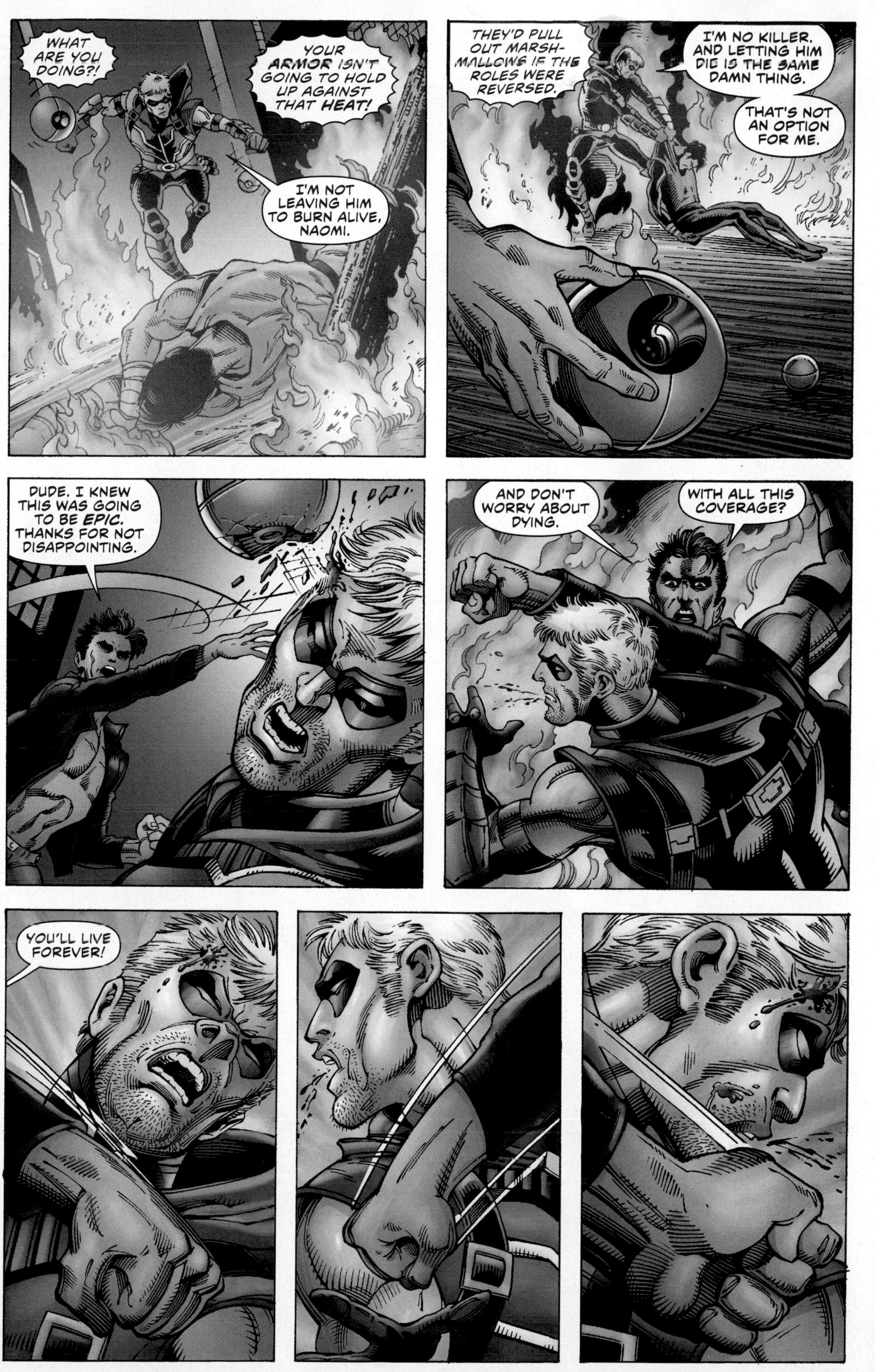
WHAT ARE YOU DOING?!
YOUR ARMOR ISN'T GOING TO HOLD UP AGAINST THAT HEAT!
I'M NOT LEAVING HIM TO BURN ALIVE, NAOMI.
THEY'D PULL OUT MARSH-MALLOWS IF THE ROLES WERE REVERSED.
I'M NO KILLER. AND LETTING HIM DIE IS THE SAME DAMN THING.
THAT'S NOT AN OPTION FOR ME.
DUDE. I KNEW THIS WAS GOING TO BE EPIC. THANKS FOR NOT DISAPPOINTING.
AND DON'T WORRY ABOUT DYING.
WITH ALL THIS COVERAGE?
YOU'LL LIVE FOREVER!

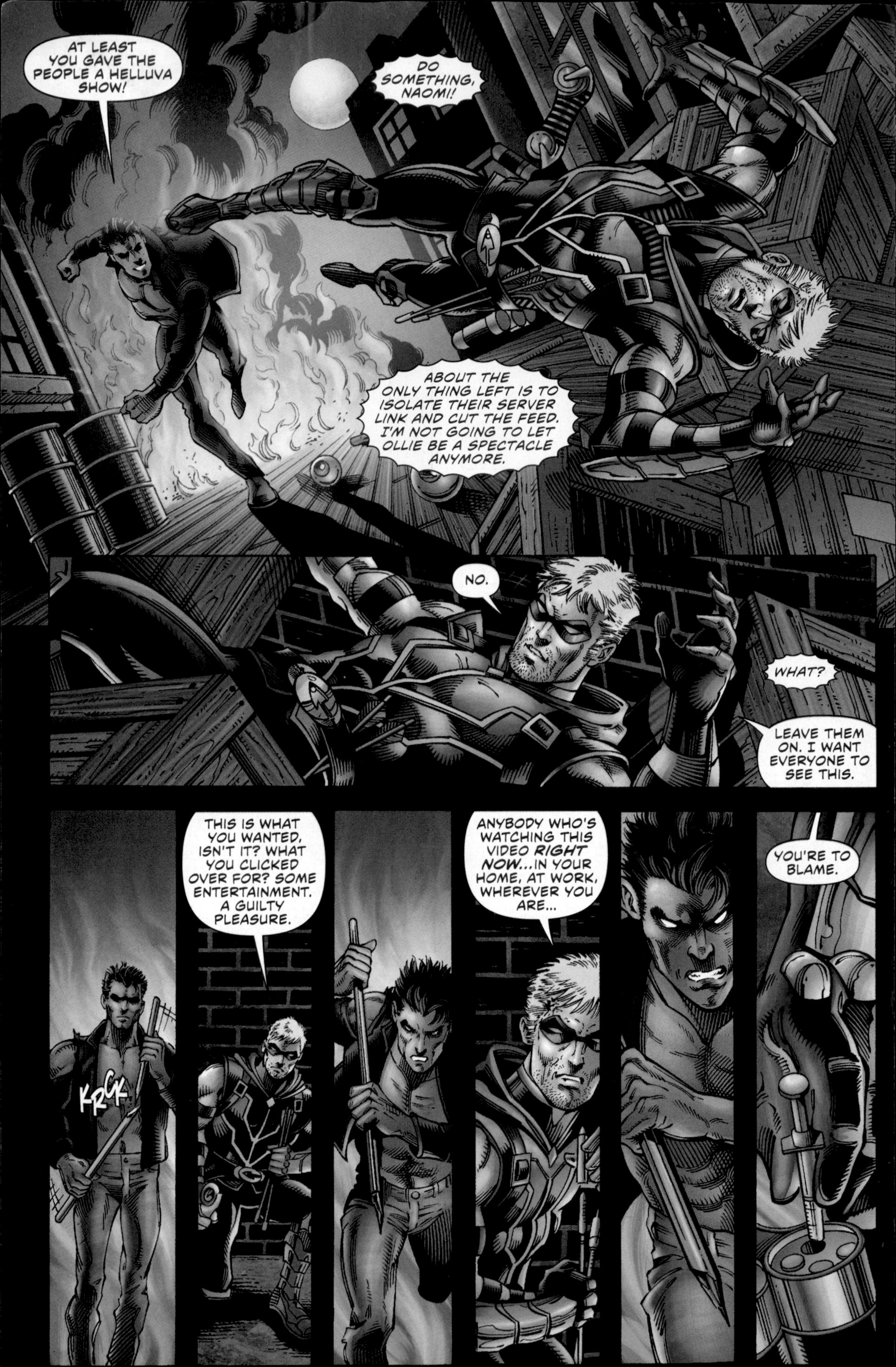
AT LEAST YOU GAVE THE PEOPLE A HELLUVA SHOW!
DO SOMETHING, NAOMI!
ABOUT THE ONLY THING LEFT IS TO ISOLATE THEIR SERVER LINK AND CUT THE FEED. I'M NOT GOING TO LET OLLIE BE A SPECTACLE ANYMORE.
NO.
WHAT?
LEAVE THEM ON. I WANT EVERYONE TO SEE THIS.
KRCK
THIS IS WHAT YOU WANTED, ISN'T IT? WHAT YOU CLICKED OVER FOR? SOME ENTERTAINMENT. A GUILTY PLEASURE.
ANYBODY WHO'S WATCHING THIS VIDEO RIGHT NOW...IN YOUR HOME, AT WORK, WHEREVER YOU ARE...
YOU'RE TO BLAME.

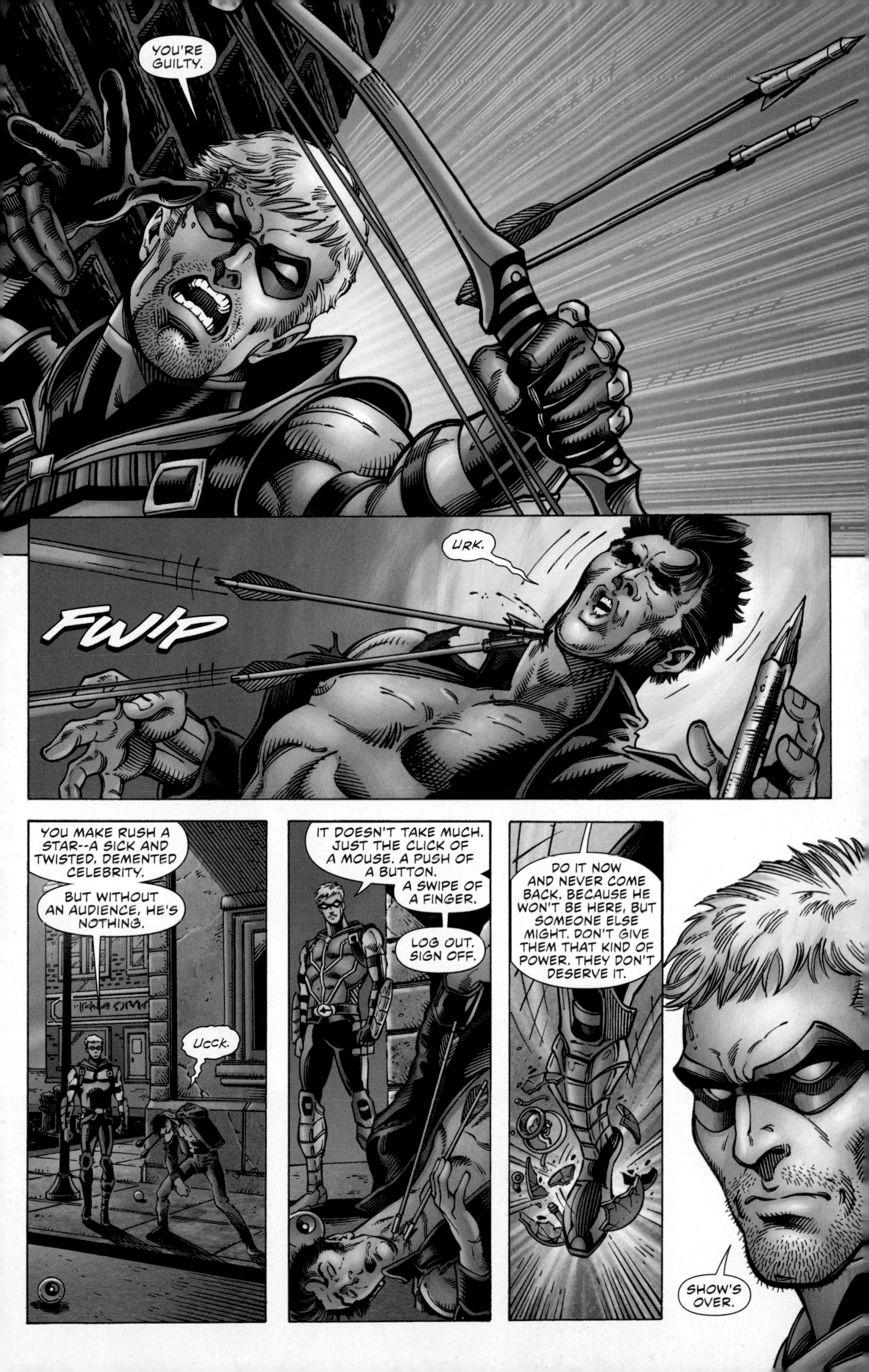
YOU'RE GUILTY.
URK.
FWIP
YOU MAKE RUSH A STAR--A SICK AND TWISTED, DEMENTED CELEBRITY.
BUT WITHOUT AN AUDIENCE, HE'S NOTHING.
UCCK.
IT DOESN'T TAKE MUCH. JUST THE CLICK OF A MOUSE. A PUSH OF A BUTTON.
A SWIPE OF A FINGER.
LOG OUT. SIGN OFF.
DO IT NOW AND NEVER COME BACK. BECAUSE HE WON'T BE HERE, BUT SOMEONE ELSE MIGHT. DON'T GIVE THEM THAT KIND OF POWER. THEY DON'T DESERVE IT.
SHOW'S OVER.

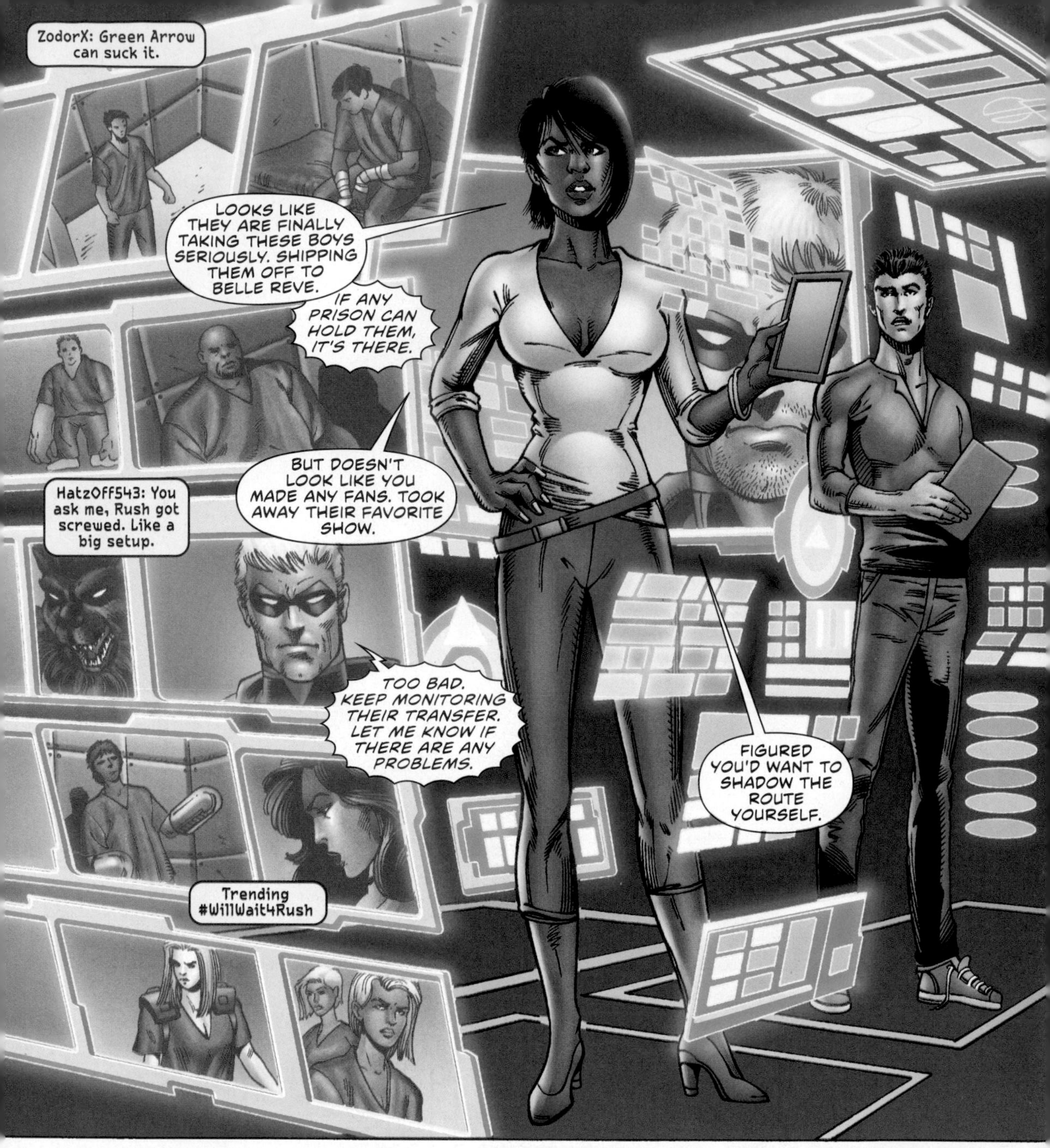
ZodorX: Green Arrow can suck it.
LOOKS LIKE THEY ARE FINALLY TAKING THESE BOYS SERIOUSLY. SHIPPING THEM OFF TO BELLE REVE.
IF ANY PRISON CAN HOLD THEM, IT'S THERE.
BUT DOESN'T LOOK LIKE YOU MADE ANY FANS. TOOK AWAY THEIR FAVORITE SHOW.
HatzOff543: You ask me, Rush got screwed. Like a big setup.
TOO BAD. KEEP MONITORING THEIR TRANSFER. LET ME KNOW IF THERE ARE ANY PROBLEMS.
FIGURED YOU'D WANT TO SHADOW THE ROUTE YOURSELF.
Trending #WillWait4Rush

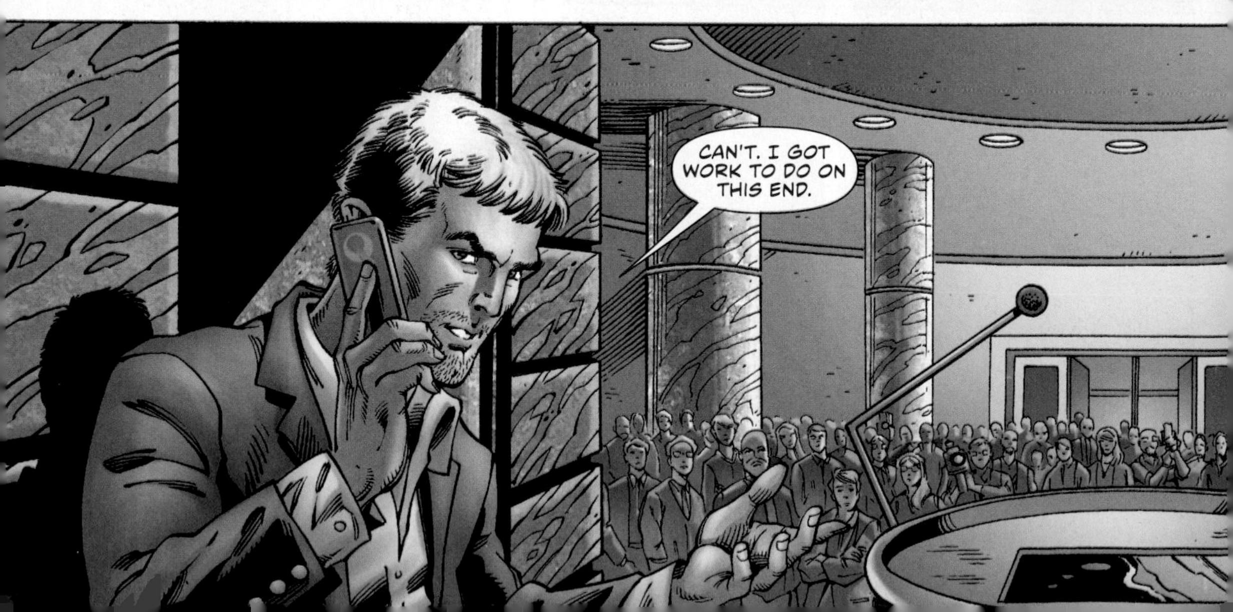
CAN'T. I GOT WORK TO DO ON THIS END.

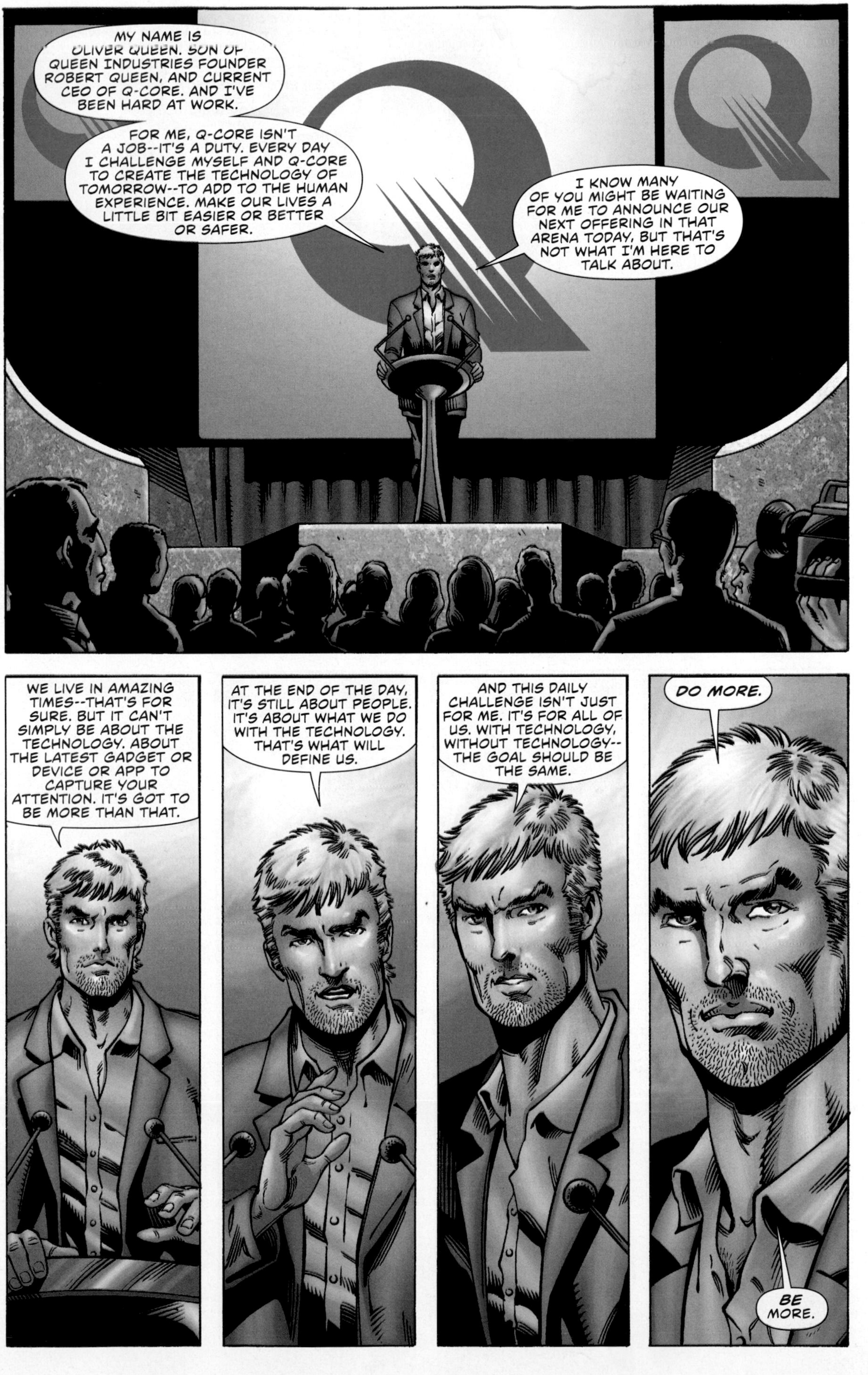
MY NAME IS OLIVER QUEEN. SON OF QUEEN INDUSTRIES FOUNDER ROBERT QUEEN, AND CURRENT CEO OF Q-CORE. AND I'VE BEEN HARD AT WORK.
FOR ME, Q-CORE ISN'T A JOB--IT'S A DUTY. EVERY DAY I CHALLENGE MYSELF AND Q-CORE TO CREATE THE TECHNOLOGY OF TOMORROW--TO ADD TO THE HUMAN EXPERIENCE. MAKE OUR LIVES A LITTLE BIT EASIER OR BETTER OR SAFER.
I KNOW MANY OF YOU MIGHT BE WAITING FOR ME TO ANNOUNCE OUR NEXT OFFERING IN THAT ARENA TODAY, BUT THAT'S NOT WHAT I'M HERE TO TALK ABOUT.
WE LIVE IN AMAZING TIMES--THAT'S FOR SURE. BUT IT CAN'T SIMPLY BE ABOUT THE TECHNOLOGY. ABOUT THE LATEST GADGET OR DEVICE OR APP TO CAPTURE YOUR ATTENTION. IT'S GOT TO BE MORE THAN THAT.
AT THE END OF THE DAY, IT'S STILL ABOUT PEOPLE. IT'S ABOUT WHAT WE DO WITH THE TECHNOLOGY. THAT'S WHAT WILL DEFINE US.
AND THIS DAILY CHALLENGE ISN'T JUST FOR ME. IT'S FOR ALL OF US. WITH TECHNOLOGY, WITHOUT TECHNOLOGY--THE GOAL SHOULD BE THE SAME.
DO MORE.
BE MORE.

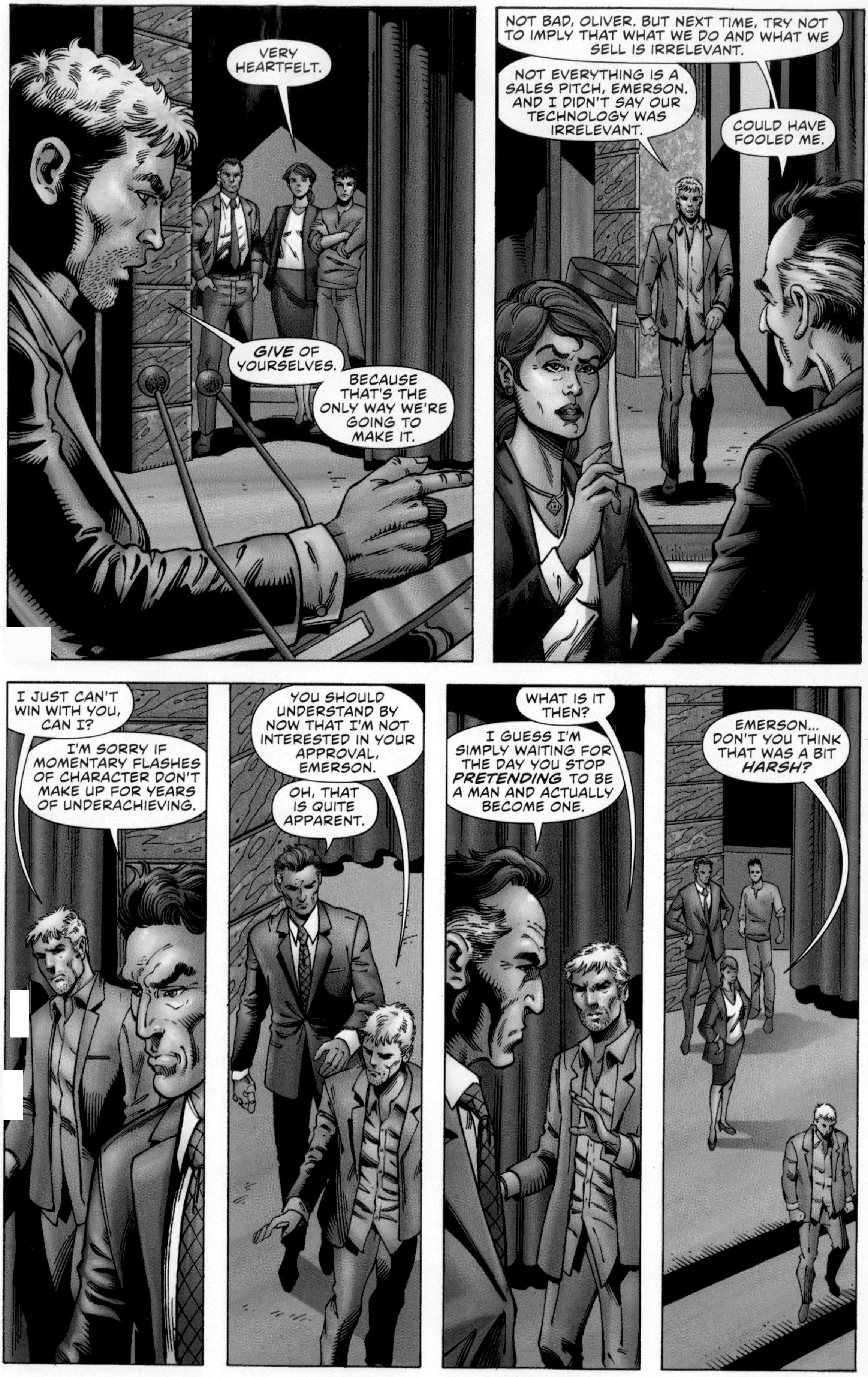
VERY HEARTFELT.
GIVE OF YOURSELVES.
BECAUSE THAT'S THE ONLY WAY WE'RE GOING TO MAKE IT.
NOT BAD, OLIVER. BUT NEXT TIME, TRY NOT TO IMPLY THAT WHAT WE DO AND WHAT WE SELL IS IRRELEVANT.
NOT EVERYTHING IS A SALES PITCH, EMERSON. AND I DIDN'T SAY OUR TECHNOLOGY WAS IRRELEVANT.
COULD HAVE FOOLED ME.
I JUST CAN'T WIN WITH YOU, CAN I?
I'M SORRY IF MOMENTARY FLASHES OF CHARACTER DON'T MAKE UP FOR YEARS OF UNDERACHIEVING.
YOU SHOULD UNDERSTAND BY NOW THAT I'M NOT INTERESTED IN YOUR APPROVAL, EMERSON.
OH, THAT IS QUITE APPARENT.
WHAT IS IT THEN?
I GUESS I'M SIMPLY WAITING FOR THE DAY YOU STOP PRETENDING TO BE A MAN AND ACTUALLY BECOME ONE.
EMERSON... DON'T YOU THINK THAT WAS A BIT HARSH?

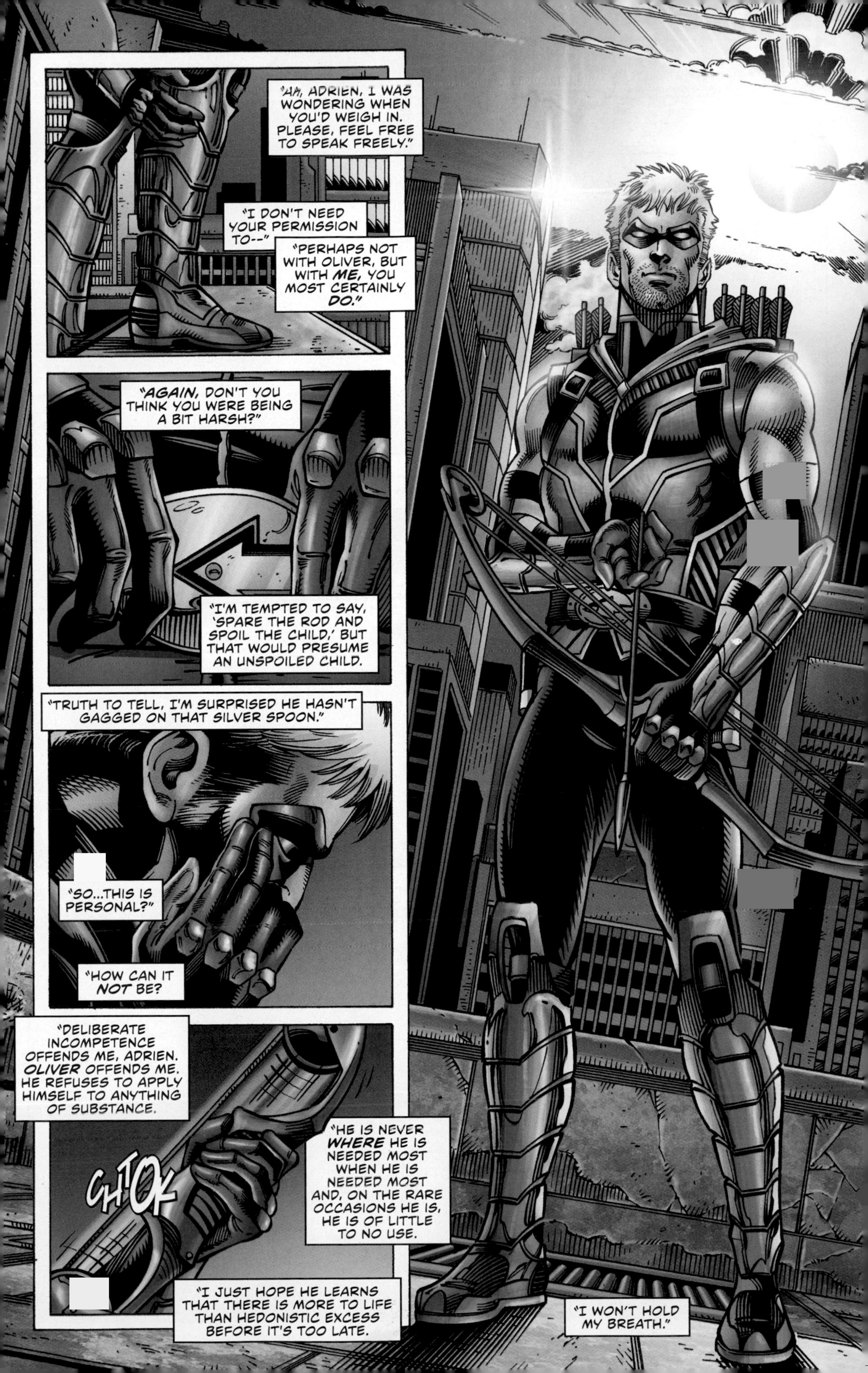

"AH, ADRIEN, I WAS WONDERING WHEN YOU'D WEIGH IN. PLEASE, FEEL FREE TO SPEAK FREELY."
"I DON'T NEED YOUR PERMISSION TO--"
"PERHAPS NOT WITH OLIVER, BUT WITH ME, YOU MOST CERTAINLY DO."
"AGAIN, DON'T YOU THINK YOU WERE BEING A BIT HARSH?"
"I'M TEMPTED TO SAY, 'SPARE THE ROD AND SPOIL THE CHILD,' BUT THAT WOULD PRESUME AN UNSPOILED CHILD.
"TRUTH TO TELL, I'M SURPRISED HE HASN'T GAGGED ON THAT SILVER SPOON."
"SO...THIS IS PERSONAL?"
"HOW CAN IT NOT BE?
"DELIBERATE INCOMPETENCE OFFENDS ME, ADRIEN. OLIVER OFFENDS ME. HE REFUSES TO APPLY HIMSELF TO ANYTHING OF SUBSTANCE.
CHTOK
"HE IS NEVER WHERE HE IS NEEDED MOST WHEN HE IS NEEDED MOST AND, ON THE RARE OCCASIONS HE IS, HE IS OF LITTLE TO NO USE.
"I JUST HOPE HE LEARNS THAT THERE IS MORE TO LIFE THAN HEDONISTIC EXCESS BEFORE IT'S TOO LATE.
"I WON'T HOLD MY BREATH."

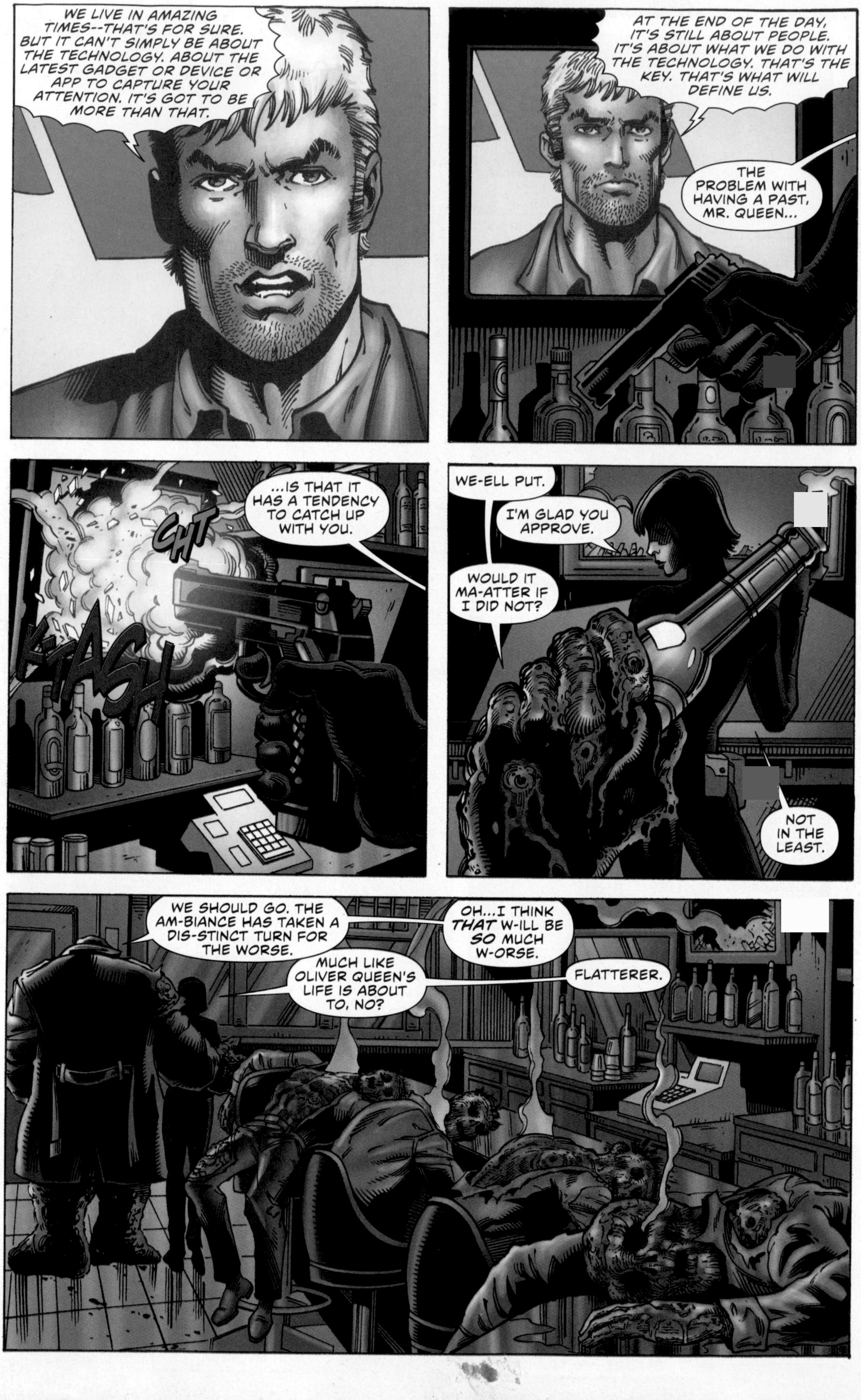

WE LIVE IN AMAZING TIMES--THAT'S FOR SURE. BUT IT CAN'T SIMPLY BE ABOUT THE TECHNOLOGY. ABOUT THE LATEST GADGET OR DEVICE OR APP TO CAPTURE YOUR ATTENTION. IT'S GOT TO BE MORE THAN THAT.
AT THE END OF THE DAY, IT'S STILL ABOUT PEOPLE. IT'S ABOUT WHAT WE DO WITH THE TECHNOLOGY. THAT'S THE KEY. THAT'S WHAT WILL DEFINE US.
THE PROBLEM WITH HAVING A PAST, MR. QUEEN...
...IS THAT IT HAS A TENDENCY TO CATCH UP WITH YOU.
CHT
KASH
WE-ELL PUT.
I'M GLAD YOU APPROVE.
WOULD IT MA-ATTER IF I DID NOT?
NOT IN THE LEAST.
WE SHOULD GO. THE AM-BIANCE HAS TAKEN A DIS-STINCT TURN FOR THE WORSE.
OH...I THINK THAT W-ILL BE SO MUCH W-ORSE.
MUCH LIKE OLIVER QUEEN'S LIFE IS ABOUT TO, NO?
FLATTERER.

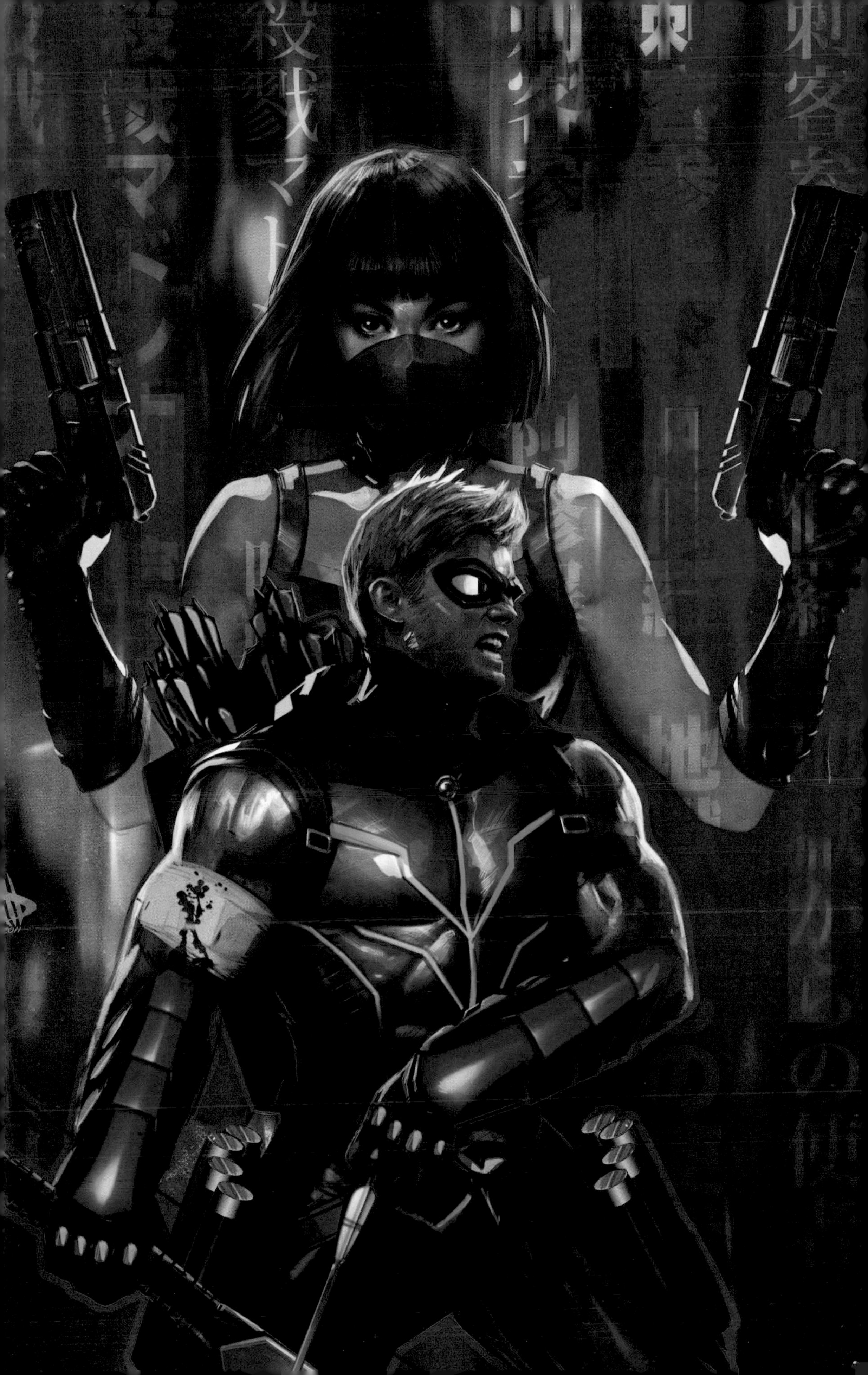

THE THINGS WE DO FOR LOVE HATE!

KEITH GIFFEN
writer / co-plotter

DAN JURGENS
layouts / co-plotter

GEORGE PÉREZ
finishes

cover by DAVE WILKINS

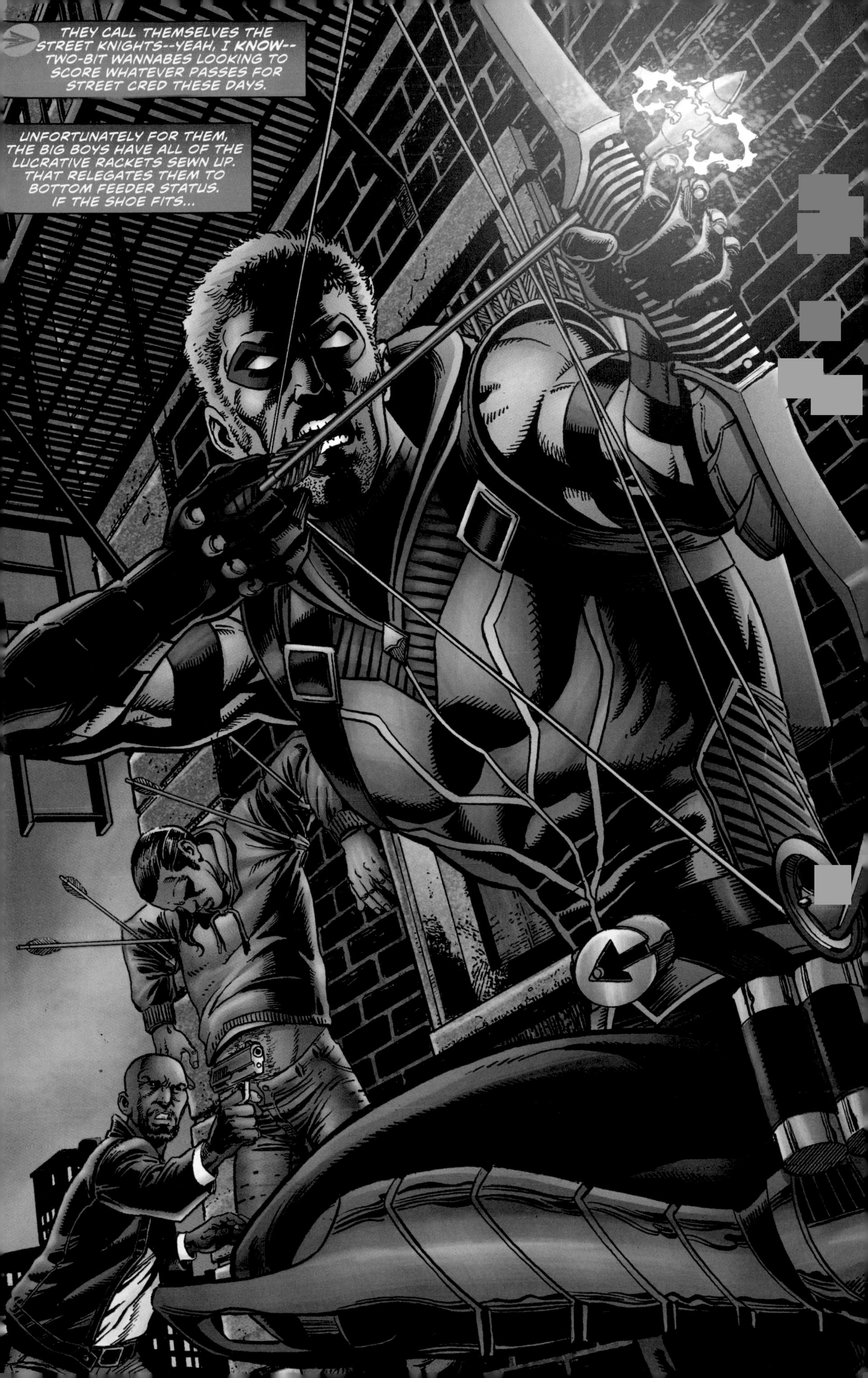
THEY CALL THEMSELVES THE STREET KNIGHTS--YEAH, I KNOW-- TWO-BIT WANNABES LOOKING TO SCORE WHATEVER PASSES FOR STREET CRED THESE DAYS.
UNFORTUNATELY FOR THEM, THE BIG BOYS HAVE ALL OF THE LUCRATIVE RACKETS SEWN UP. THAT RELEGATES THEM TO BOTTOM FEEDER STATUS. IF THE SHOE FITS...

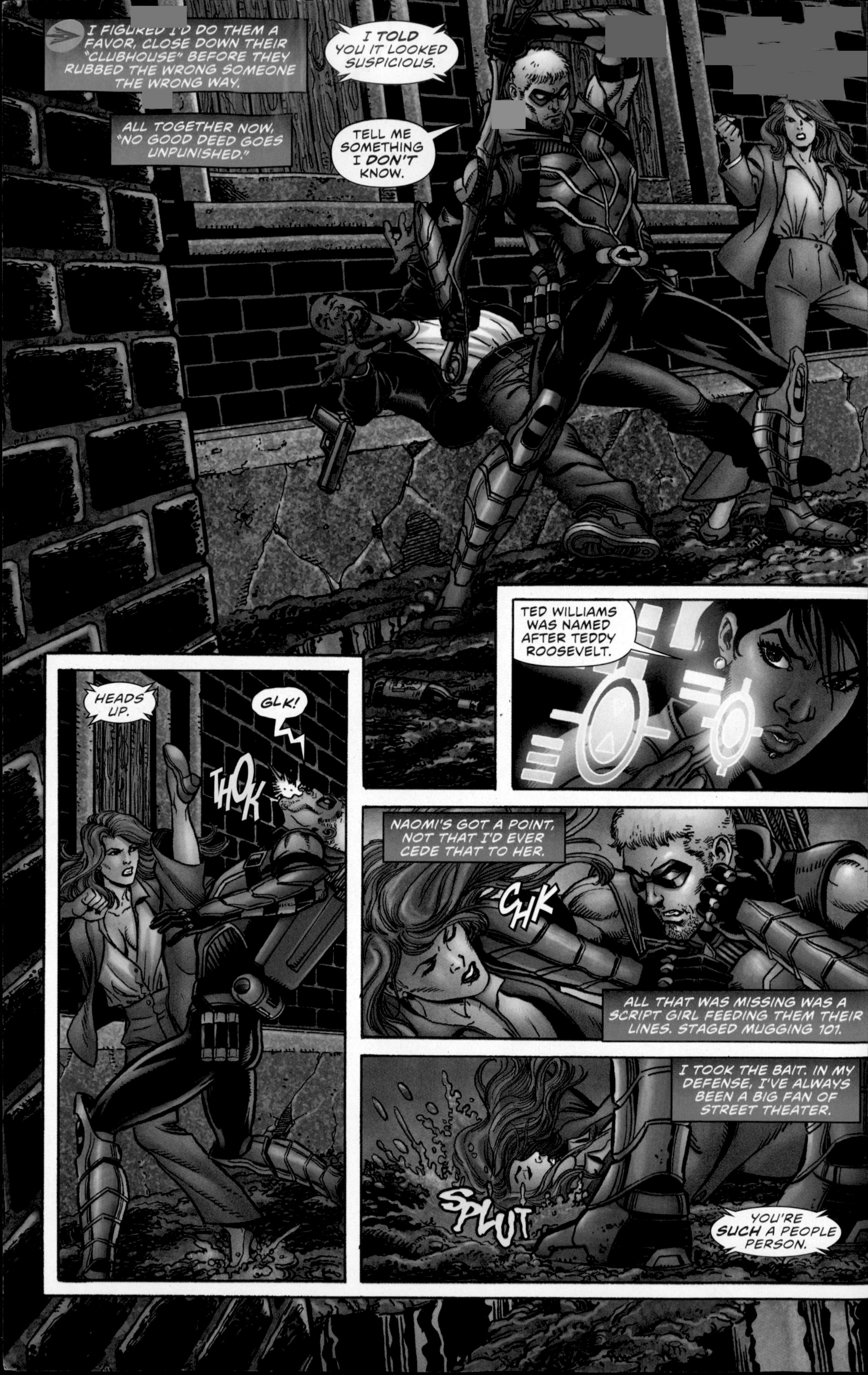

I FIGURED I'D DO THEM A FAVOR, CLOSE DOWN THEIR "CLUBHOUSE" BEFORE THEY RUBBED THE WRONG SOMEONE THE WRONG WAY.
ALL TOGETHER NOW, "NO GOOD DEED GOES UNPUNISHED."
I TOLD YOU IT LOOKED SUSPICIOUS.
TELL ME SOMETHING I DON'T KNOW.
TED WILLIAMS WAS NAMED AFTER TEDDY ROOSEVELT.
HEADS UP.
GLK!
THOK
NAOMI'S GOT A POINT, NOT THAT I'D EVER CEDE THAT TO HER.
CHK
ALL THAT WAS MISSING WAS A SCRIPT GIRL FEEDING THEM THEIR LINES. STAGED MUGGING 101.
I TOOK THE BAIT. IN MY DEFENSE, I'VE ALWAYS BEEN A BIG FAN OF STREET THEATER.
SPLUT
YOU'RE SUCH A PEOPLE PERSON.

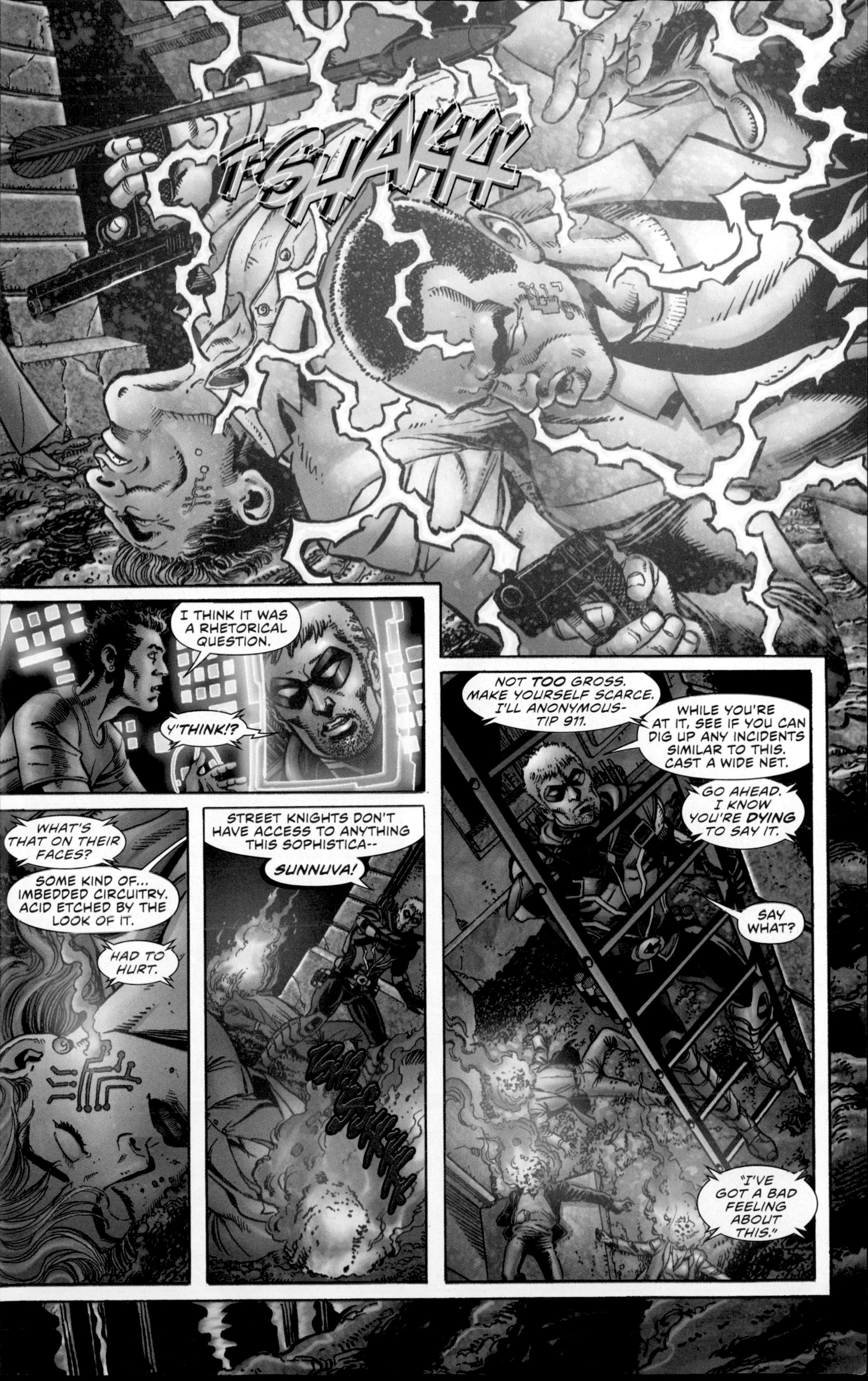
T-SHAKK!
I THINK IT WAS A RHETORICAL QUESTION.
Y'THINK!?
NOT TOO GROSS. MAKE YOURSELF SCARCE. I'LL ANONYMOUS-TIP 911.
WHILE YOU'RE AT IT, SEE IF YOU CAN DIG UP ANY INCIDENTS SIMILAR TO THIS. CAST A WIDE NET.
GO AHEAD. I KNOW YOU'RE DYING TO SAY IT.
SAY WHAT?
"I'VE GOT A BAD FEELING ABOUT THIS."
WHAT'S THAT ON THEIR FACES?
SOME KIND OF... IMBEDDED CIRCUITRY. ACID ETCHED BY THE LOOK OF IT.
HAD TO HURT.
STREET KNIGHTS DON'T HAVE ACCESS TO ANYTHING THIS SOPHISTICA--
SUNNUVA!

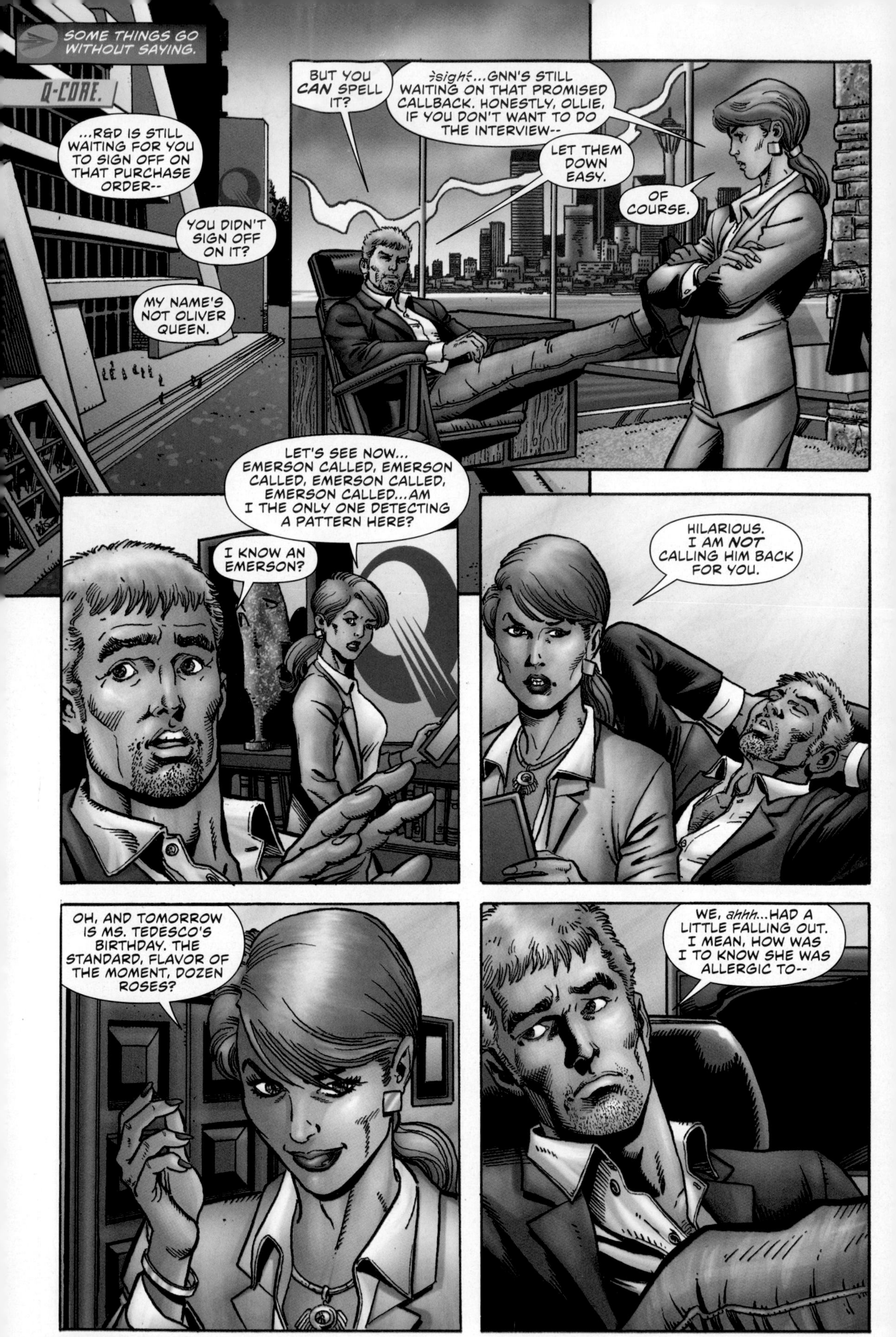
SOME THINGS GO WITHOUT SAYING.
Q-CORE.
...R&D IS STILL WAITING FOR YOU TO SIGN OFF ON THAT PURCHASE ORDER--
YOU DIDN'T SIGN OFF ON IT?
MY NAME'S NOT OLIVER QUEEN.
BUT YOU CAN SPELL IT?
sigh...GNN'S STILL WAITING ON THAT PROMISED CALLBACK. HONESTLY, OLLIE, IF YOU DON'T WANT TO DO THE INTERVIEW--
LET THEM DOWN EASY.
OF COURSE.
LET'S SEE NOW... EMERSON CALLED, EMERSON CALLED, EMERSON CALLED, EMERSON CALLED...AM I THE ONLY ONE DETECTING A PATTERN HERE?
I KNOW AN EMERSON?
HILARIOUS. I AM NOT CALLING HIM BACK FOR YOU.
OH, AND TOMORROW IS MS. TEDESCO'S BIRTHDAY. THE STANDARD, FLAVOR OF THE MOMENT, DOZEN ROSES?
WE, ahhh...HAD A LITTLE FALLING OUT. I MEAN, HOW WAS I TO KNOW SHE WAS ALLERGIC TO--

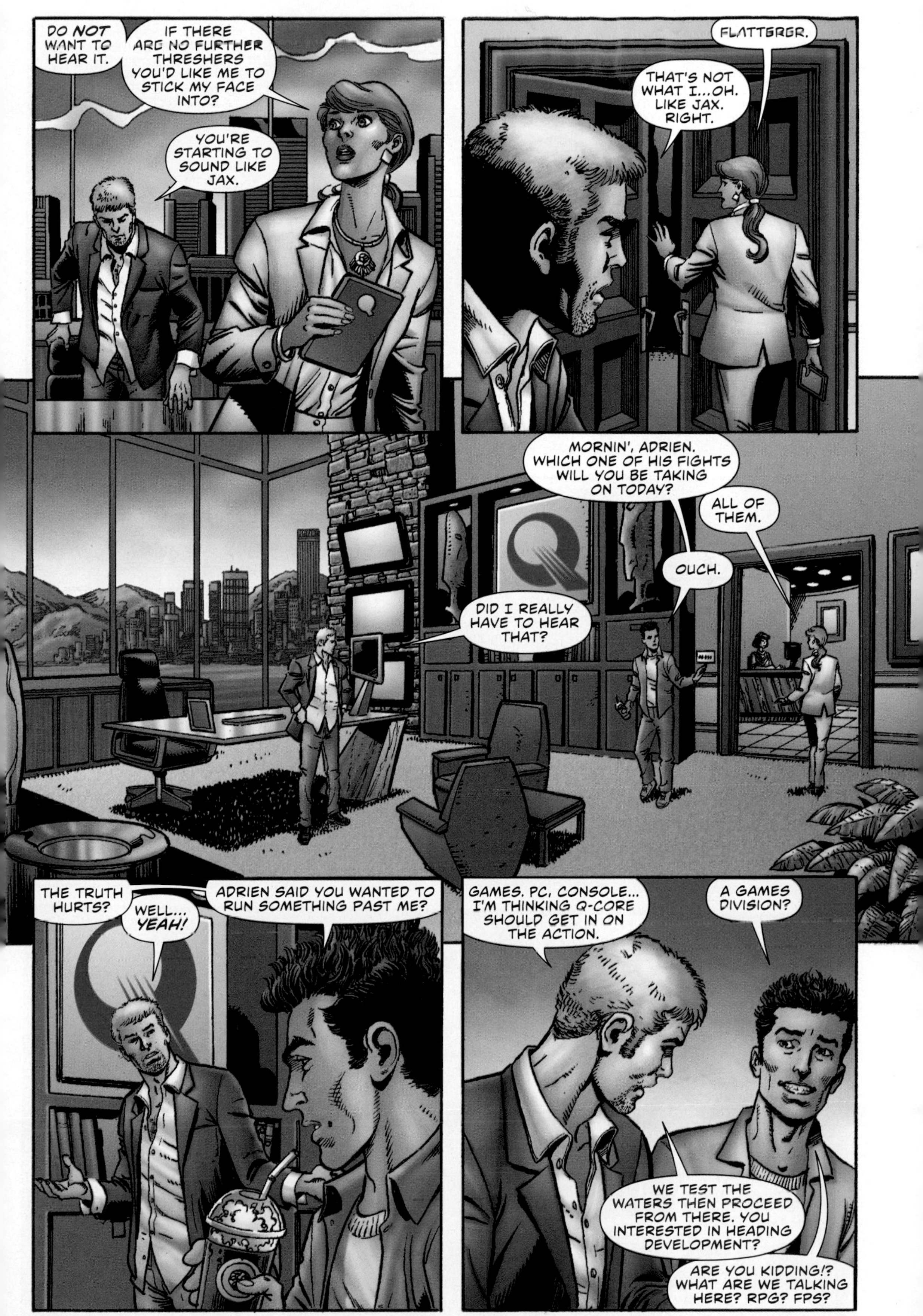

DO **NOT** WANT TO HEAR IT.
IF THERE ARE NO FURTHER THRESHERS YOU'D LIKE ME TO STICK MY FACE INTO?
YOU'RE STARTING TO SOUND LIKE JAX.
THAT'S NOT WHAT I...OH. LIKE JAX. RIGHT.
FLATTERER.
MORNIN', ADRIEN. WHICH ONE OF HIS FIGHTS WILL YOU BE TAKING ON TODAY?
ALL OF THEM.
OUCH.
DID I REALLY HAVE TO HEAR THAT?
THE TRUTH HURTS?
WELL... *YEAH!*
ADRIEN SAID YOU WANTED TO RUN SOMETHING PAST ME?
GAMES. PC, CONSOLE... I'M THINKING Q-CORE SHOULD GET IN ON THE ACTION.
A GAMES DIVISION?
WE TEST THE WATERS THEN PROCEED FROM THERE. YOU INTERESTED IN HEADING DEVELOPMENT?
ARE YOU KIDDING!? WHAT ARE WE TALKING HERE? RPG? FPS?

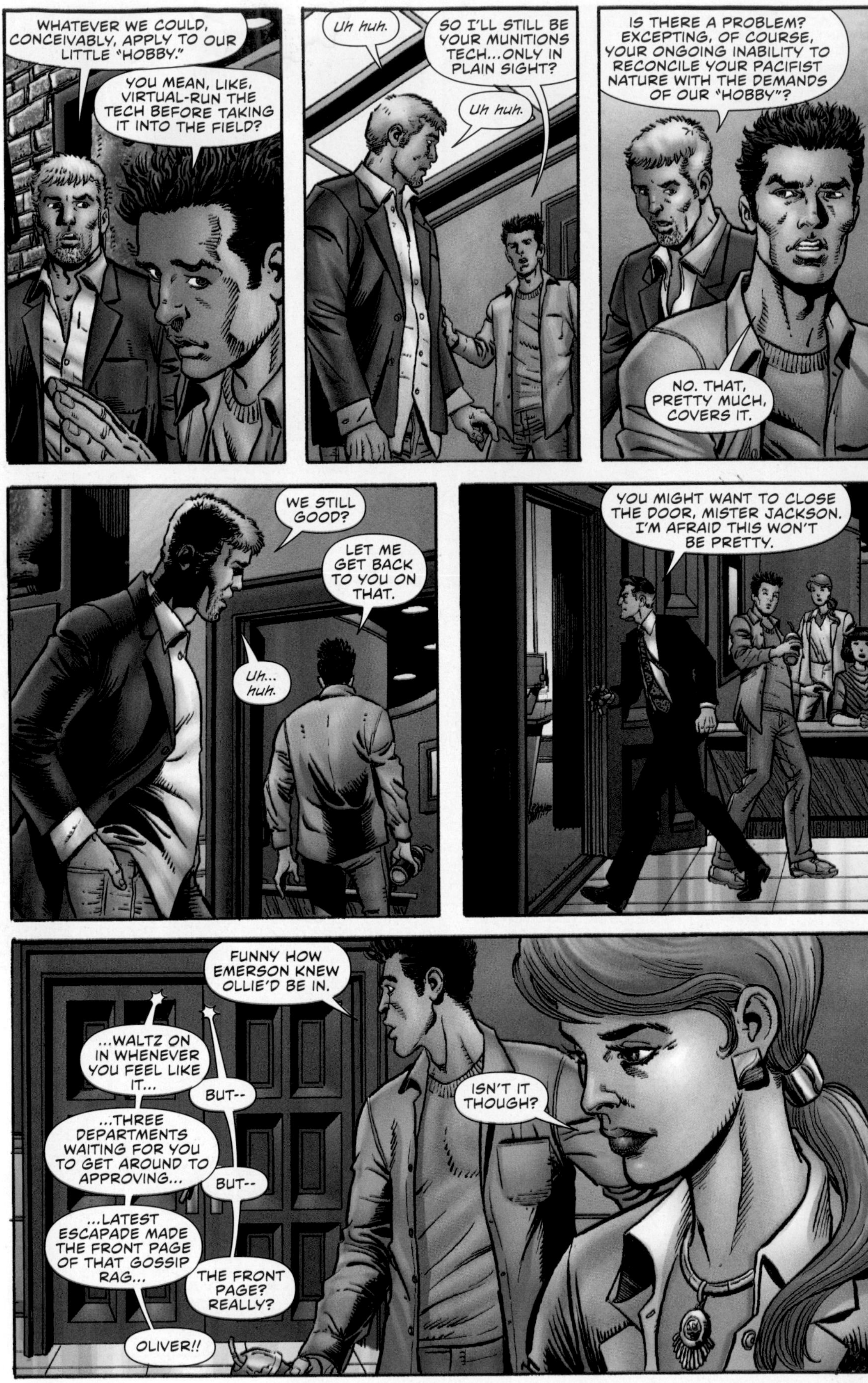

WHATEVER WE COULD, CONCEIVABLY, APPLY TO OUR LITTLE "HOBBY."
YOU MEAN, LIKE, VIRTUAL-RUN THE TECH BEFORE TAKING IT INTO THE FIELD?
Uh huh.
SO I'LL STILL BE YOUR MUNITIONS TECH...ONLY IN PLAIN SIGHT?
Uh huh.
IS THERE A PROBLEM? EXCEPTING, OF COURSE, YOUR ONGOING INABILITY TO RECONCILE YOUR PACIFIST NATURE WITH THE DEMANDS OF OUR "HOBBY"?
NO. THAT, PRETTY MUCH, COVERS IT.
WE STILL GOOD?
LET ME GET BACK TO YOU ON THAT.
Uh... huh.
YOU MIGHT WANT TO CLOSE THE DOOR, MISTER JACKSON. I'M AFRAID THIS WON'T BE PRETTY.
FUNNY HOW EMERSON KNEW OLLIE'D BE IN.
...WALTZ ON IN WHENEVER YOU FEEL LIKE IT...
BUT--
...THREE DEPARTMENTS WAITING FOR YOU TO GET AROUND TO APPROVING...
BUT--
...LATEST ESCAPADE MADE THE FRONT PAGE OF THAT GOSSIP RAG...
THE FRONT PAGE? REALLY?
OLIVER!!
ISN'T IT THOUGH?

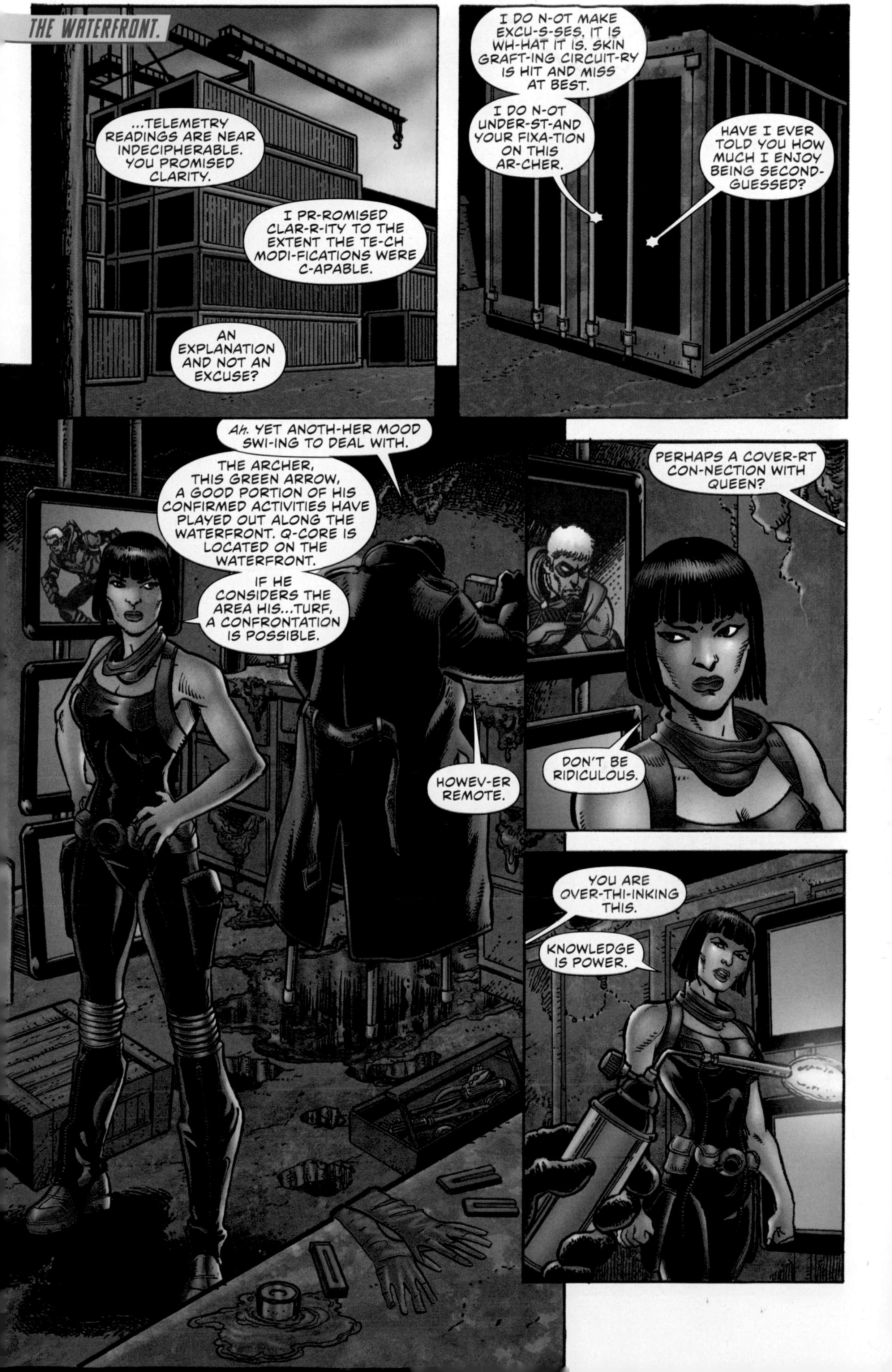
THE WATERFRONT.
...TELEMETRY READINGS ARE NEAR INDECIPHERABLE. YOU PROMISED CLARITY.
I PR-ROMISED CLAR-R-ITY TO THE EXTENT THE TE-CH MODI-FICATIONS WERE C-APABLE.
AN EXPLANATION AND NOT AN EXCUSE?
I DO N-OT MAKE EXCU-S-SES. IT IS WH-HAT IT IS. SKIN GRAFT-ING CIRCUIT-RY IS HIT AND MISS AT BEST.
I DO N-OT UNDER-ST-AND YOUR FIXA-TION ON THIS AR-CHER.
HAVE I EVER TOLD YOU HOW MUCH I ENJOY BEING SECOND-GUESSED?
AH. YET ANOTH-HER MOOD SWI-ING TO DEAL WITH.
THE ARCHER, THIS GREEN ARROW, A GOOD PORTION OF HIS CONFIRMED ACTIVITIES HAVE PLAYED OUT ALONG THE WATERFRONT. Q-CORE IS LOCATED ON THE WATERFRONT.
IF HE CONSIDERS THE AREA HIS...TURF, A CONFRONTATION IS POSSIBLE.
HOWEV-ER REMOTE.
PERHAPS A COVER-RT CON-NECTION WITH QUEEN?
DON'T BE RIDICULOUS.
YOU ARE OVER-THI-INKING THIS.
KNOWLEDGE IS POWER.

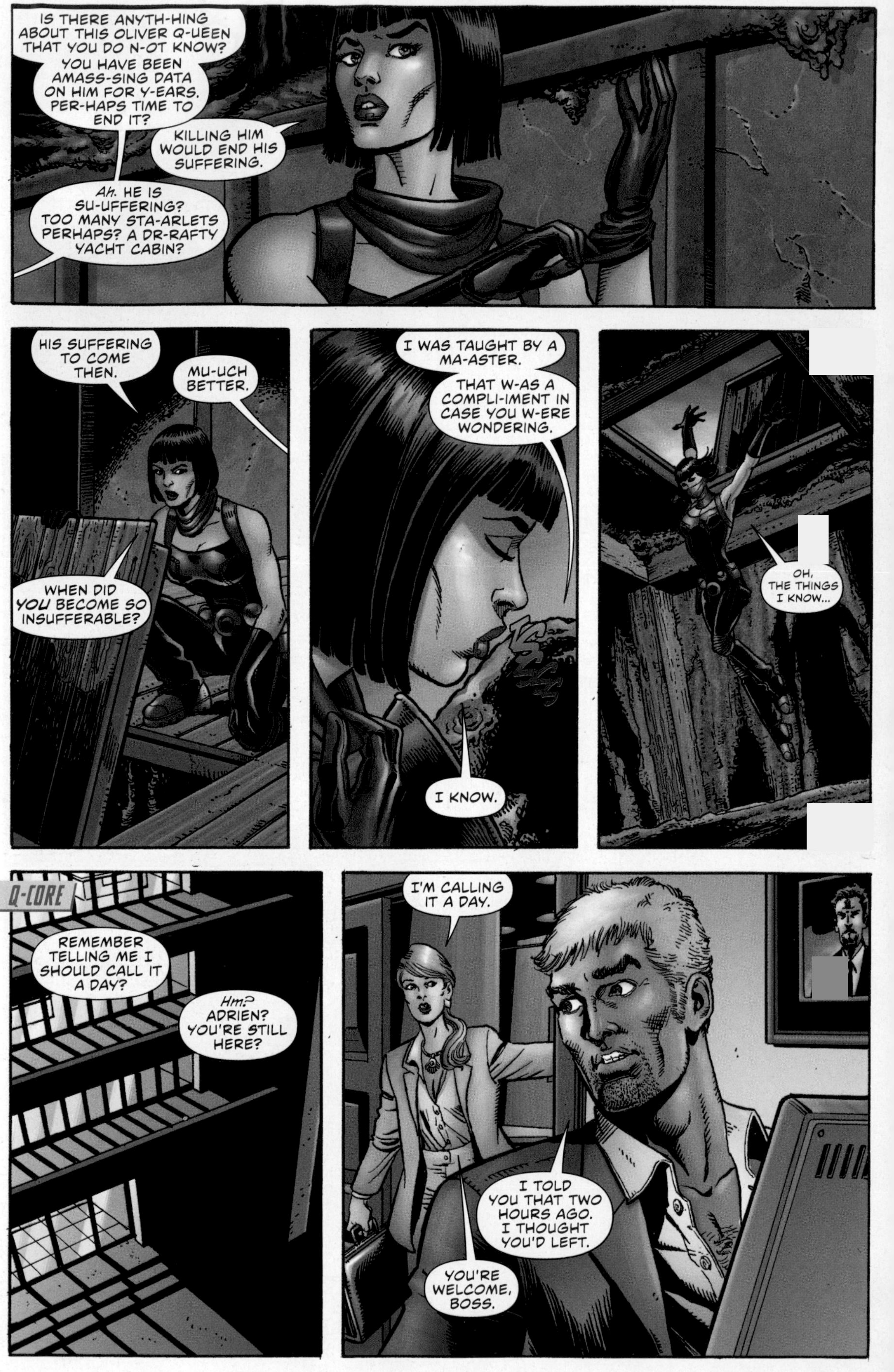
IS THERE ANYTH-HING ABOUT THIS OLIVER Q-UEEN THAT YOU DO N-OT KNOW? YOU HAVE BEEN AMASS-SING DATA ON HIM FOR Y-EARS. PER-HAPS TIME TO END IT?
KILLING HIM WOULD END HIS SUFFERING.
Ah. HE IS SU-UFFERING? TOO MANY STA-ARLETS PERHAPS? A DR-RAFTY YACHT CABIN?
HIS SUFFERING TO COME THEN.
MU-UCH BETTER.
WHEN DID *YOU* BECOME SO INSUFFERABLE?
I WAS TAUGHT BY A MA-ASTER.
THAT W-AS A COMPLI-IMENT IN CASE YOU W-ERE WONDERING.
I KNOW.
OH, THE THINGS I KNOW...
Q-CORE
REMEMBER TELLING ME I SHOULD CALL IT A DAY?
Hm? ADRIEN? YOU'RE STILL HERE?
I'M CALLING IT A DAY.
I TOLD YOU THAT TWO HOURS AGO. I THOUGHT YOU'D LEFT.
YOU'RE WELCOME, BOSS.

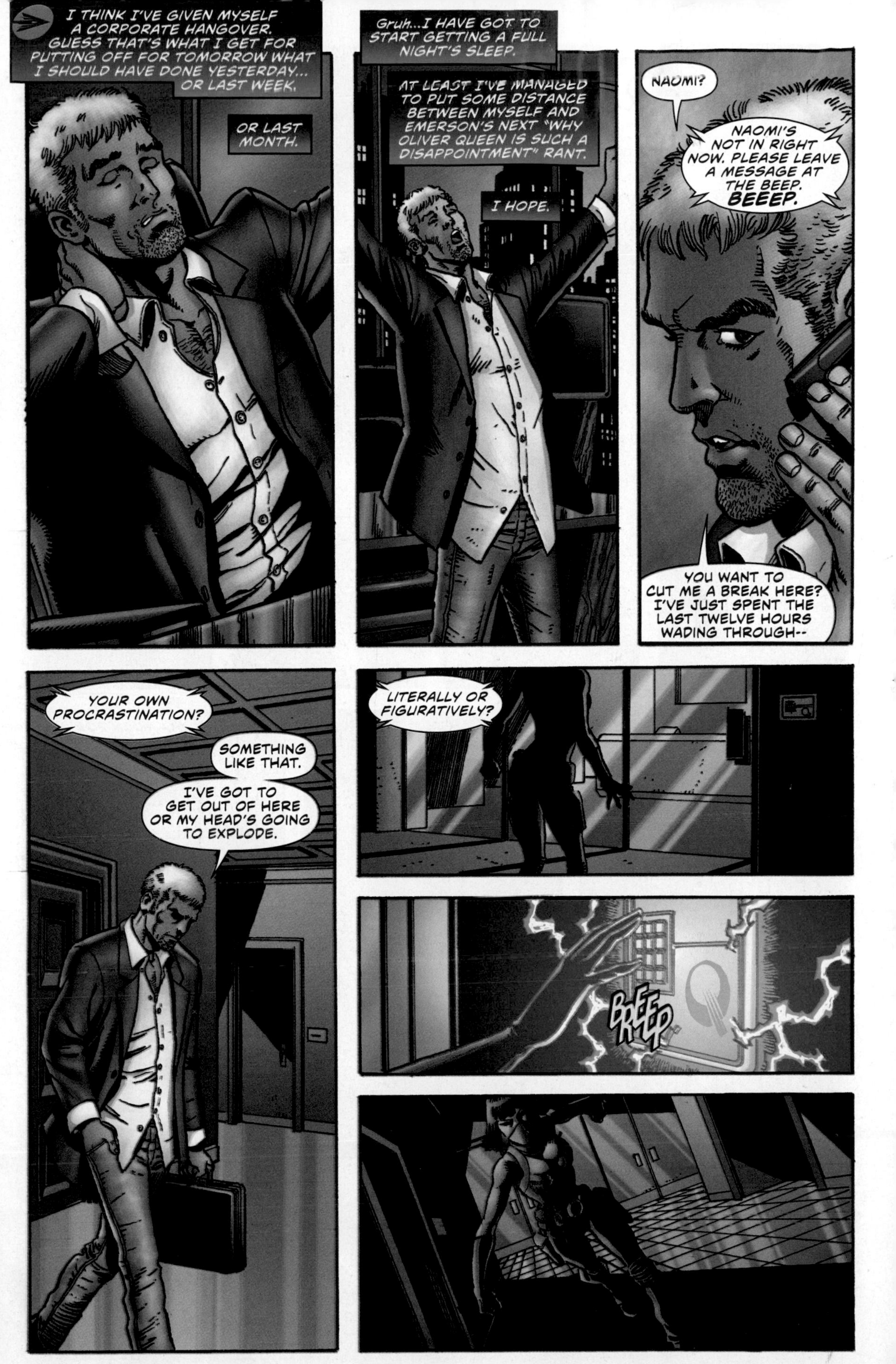
I THINK I'VE GIVEN MYSELF A CORPORATE HANGOVER. GUESS THAT'S WHAT I GET FOR PUTTING OFF FOR TOMORROW WHAT I SHOULD HAVE DONE YESTERDAY...
...OR LAST WEEK.
OR LAST MONTH.
Gruh...I HAVE GOT TO START GETTING A FULL NIGHT'S SLEEP.
AT LEAST I'VE MANAGED TO PUT SOME DISTANCE BETWEEN MYSELF AND EMERSON'S NEXT "WHY OLIVER QUEEN IS SUCH A DISAPPOINTMENT" RANT.
I HOPE.
NAOMI?
NAOMI'S NOT IN RIGHT NOW. PLEASE LEAVE A MESSAGE AT THE BEEP. BEEEP.
YOU WANT TO CUT ME A BREAK HERE? I'VE JUST SPENT THE LAST TWELVE HOURS WADING THROUGH--
YOUR OWN PROCRASTINATION?
SOMETHING LIKE THAT.
I'VE GOT TO GET OUT OF HERE OR MY HEAD'S GOING TO EXPLODE.
LITERALLY OR FIGURATIVELY?
BREEEP

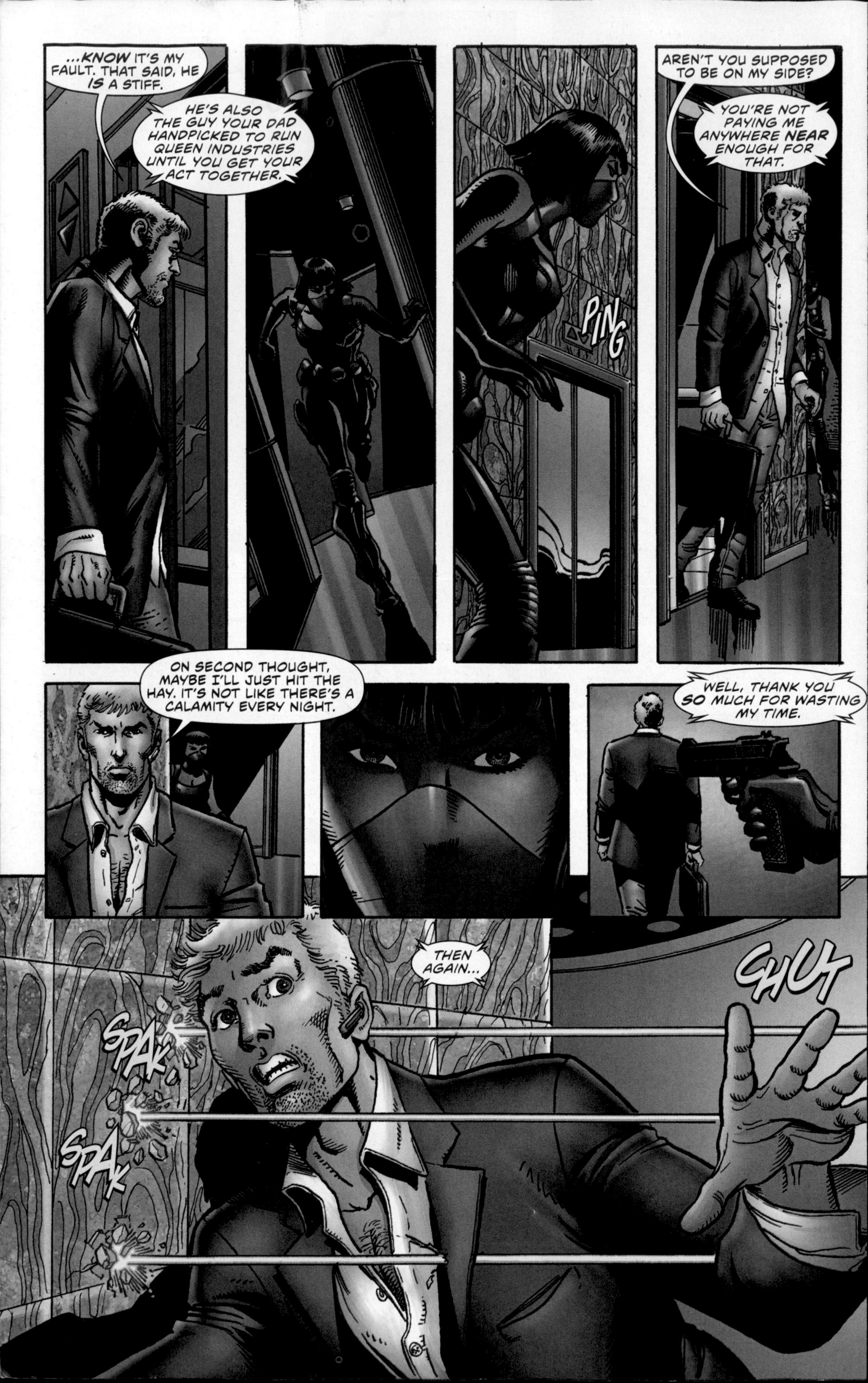
...KNOW IT'S MY FAULT. THAT SAID, HE IS A STIFF.
HE'S ALSO THE GUY YOUR DAD HANDPICKED TO RUN QUEEN INDUSTRIES UNTIL YOU GET YOUR ACT TOGETHER.
PING
AREN'T YOU SUPPOSED TO BE ON MY SIDE?
YOU'RE NOT PAYING ME ANYWHERE NEAR ENOUGH FOR THAT.
ON SECOND THOUGHT, MAYBE I'LL JUST HIT THE HAY. IT'S NOT LIKE THERE'S A CALAMITY EVERY NIGHT.
WELL, THANK YOU SO MUCH FOR WASTING MY TIME.
THEN AGAIN...
CHUT
SPAK
SPAK

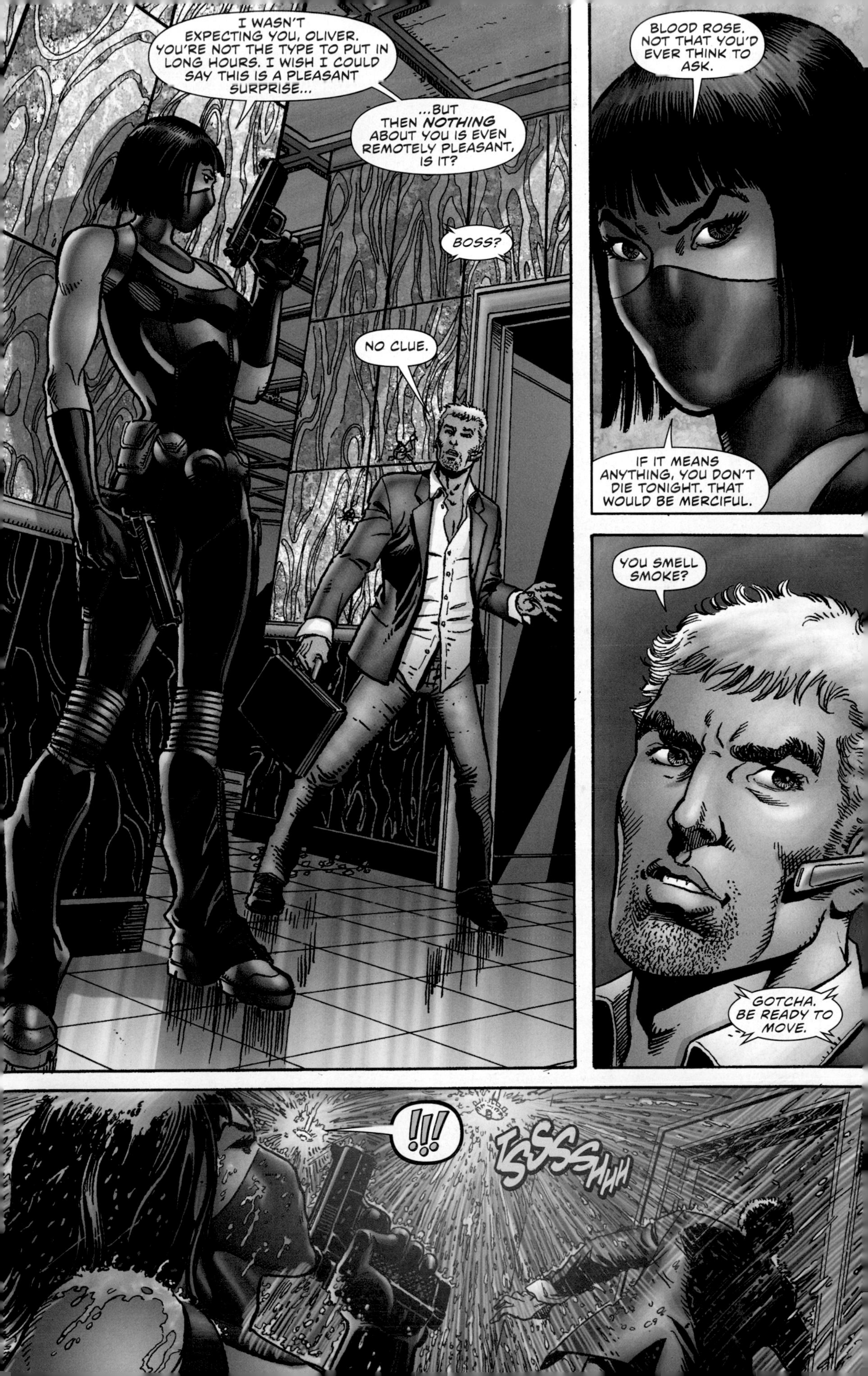
I WASN'T EXPECTING YOU, OLIVER. YOU'RE NOT THE TYPE TO PUT IN LONG HOURS. I WISH I COULD SAY THIS IS A PLEASANT SURPRISE...
...BUT THEN NOTHING ABOUT YOU IS EVEN REMOTELY PLEASANT, IS IT?
BOSS?
NO CLUE.
BLOOD ROSE. NOT THAT YOU'D EVER THINK TO ASK.
IF IT MEANS ANYTHING, YOU DON'T DIE TONIGHT. THAT WOULD BE MERCIFUL.
YOU SMELL SMOKE?
GOTCHA. BE READY TO MOVE.
!!!
TSSSSHHH

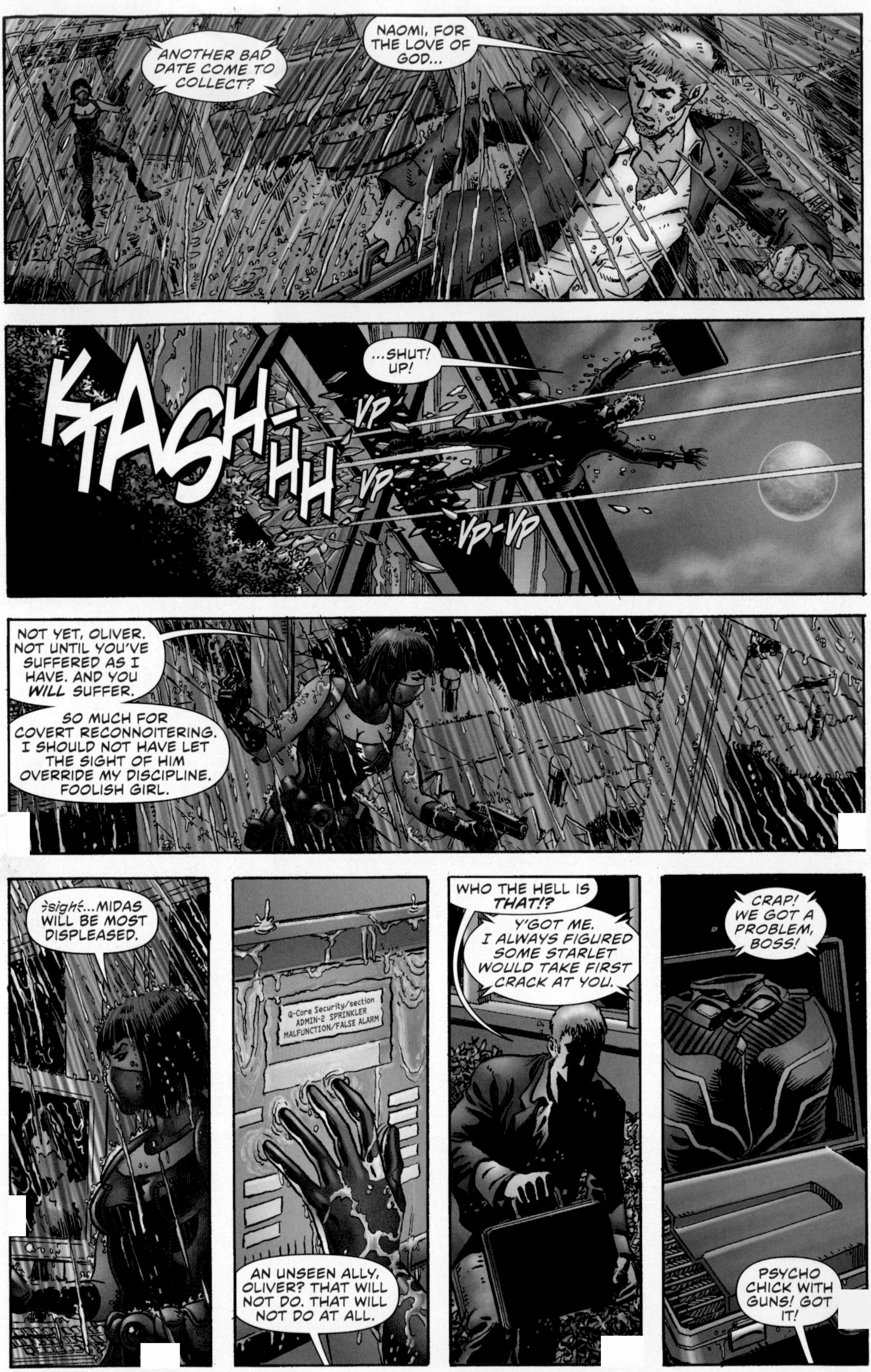
ANOTHER BAD DATE COME TO COLLECT?
NAOMI, FOR THE LOVE OF GOD...
KRASH-HH
...SHUT! UP!
VP
VP
VP-VP
NOT YET, OLIVER. NOT UNTIL YOU'VE SUFFERED AS I HAVE. AND YOU WILL SUFFER.
SO MUCH FOR COVERT RECONNOITERING. I SHOULD NOT HAVE LET THE SIGHT OF HIM OVERRIDE MY DISCIPLINE. FOOLISH GIRL.
sigh...MIDAS WILL BE MOST DISPLEASED.
Q-Core Security/section ADMIN-2 SPRINKLER MALFUNCTION/FALSE ALARM
AN UNSEEN ALLY, OLIVER? THAT WILL NOT DO. THAT WILL NOT DO AT ALL.
WHO THE HELL IS THAT!?
Y'GOT ME. I ALWAYS FIGURED SOME STARLET WOULD TAKE FIRST CRACK AT YOU.
CRAP! WE GOT A PROBLEM, BOSS!
PSYCHO CHICK WITH GUNS! GOT IT!

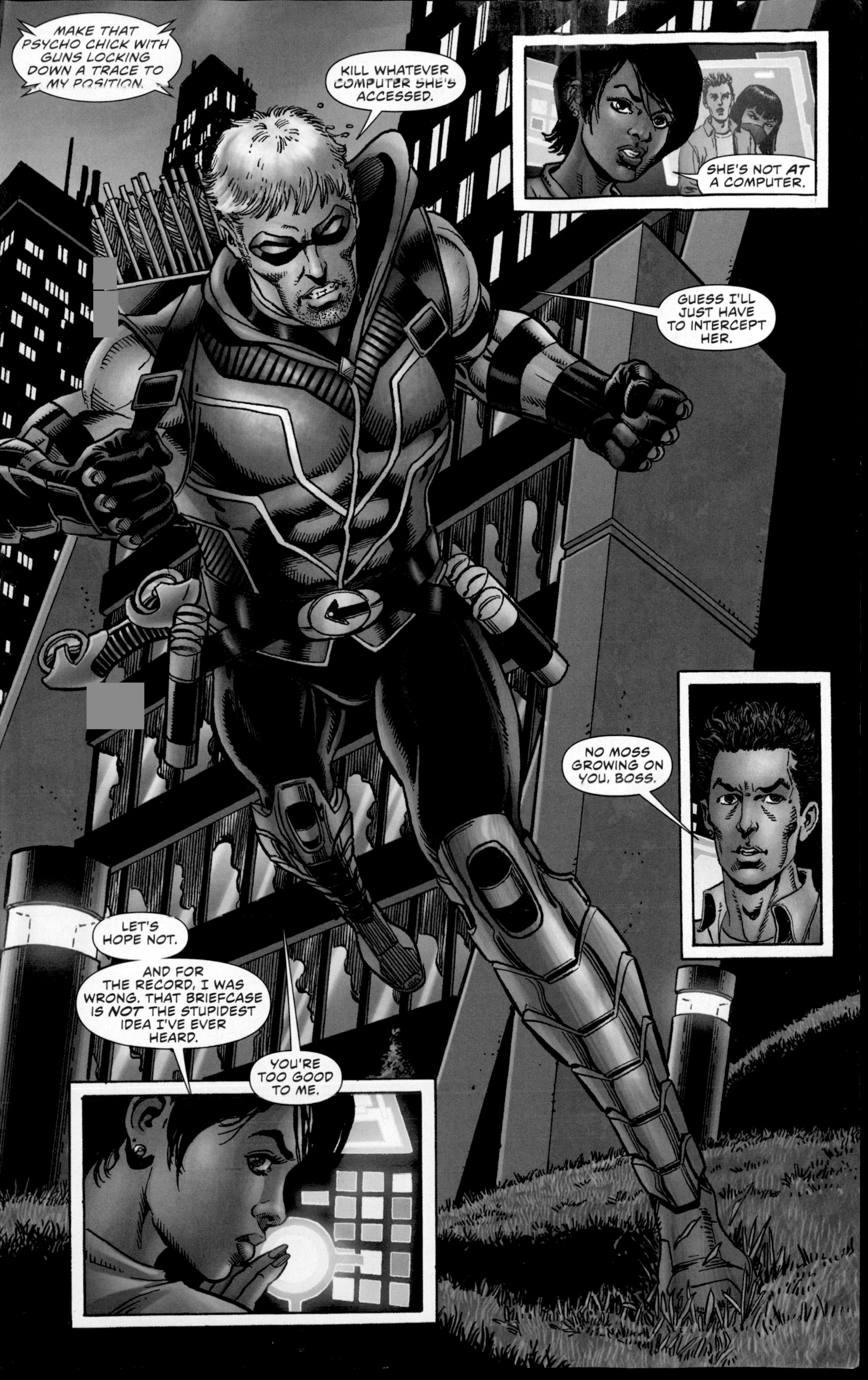
MAKE THAT PSYCHO CHICK WITH GUNS LOCKING DOWN A TRACE TO MY POSITION.
KILL WHATEVER COMPUTER SHE'S ACCESSED.
SHE'S NOT AT A COMPUTER.
GUESS I'LL JUST HAVE TO INTERCEPT HER.
NO MOSS GROWING ON YOU, BOSS.
LET'S HOPE NOT.
AND FOR THE RECORD, I WAS WRONG. THAT BRIEFCASE IS NOT THE STUPIDEST IDEA I'VE EVER HEARD.
YOU'RE TOO GOOD TO ME.

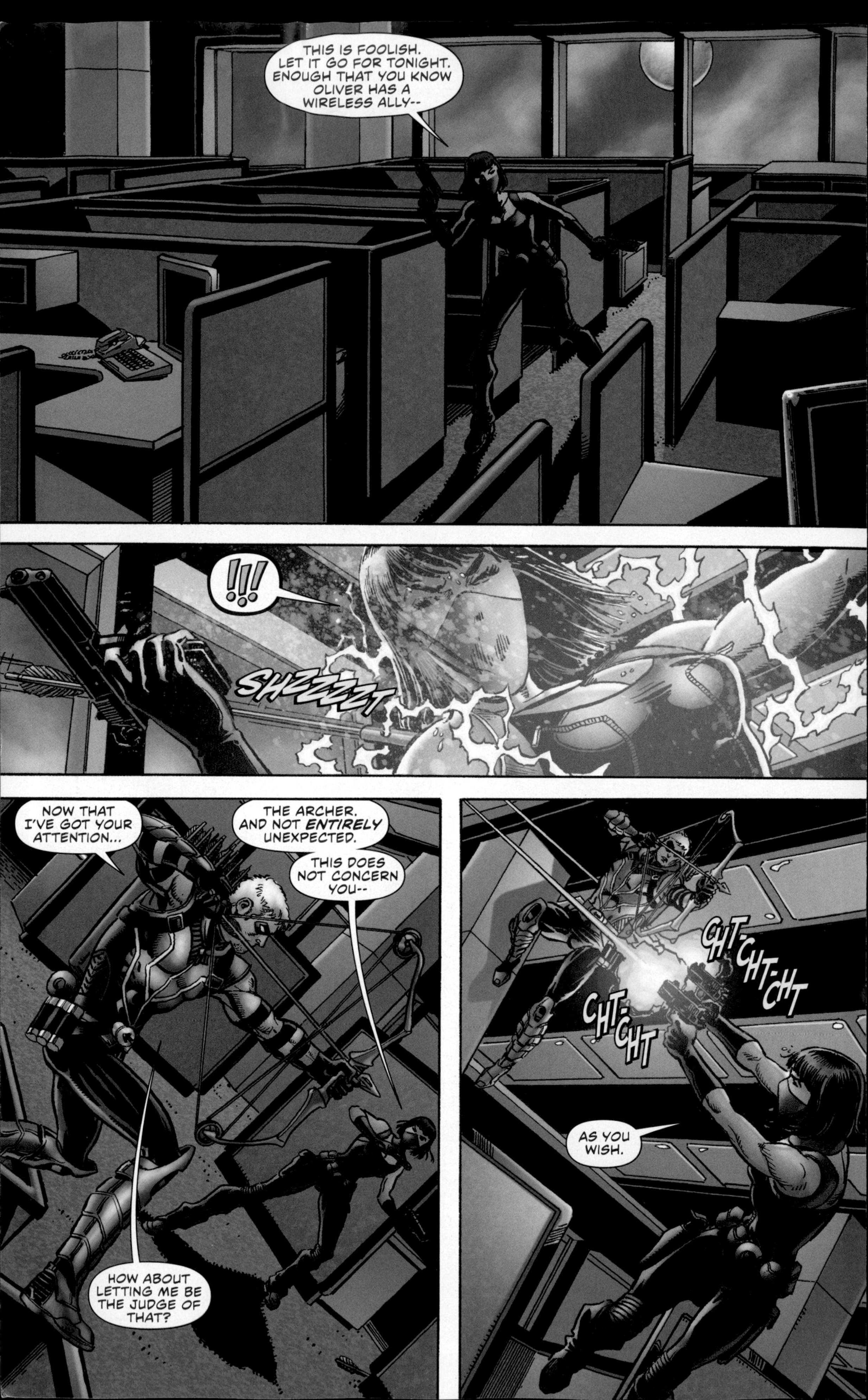
THIS IS FOOLISH. LET IT GO FOR TONIGHT. ENOUGH THAT YOU KNOW OLIVER HAS A WIRELESS ALLY--
!!!
SHZZZZZT
NOW THAT I'VE GOT YOUR ATTENTION...
THE ARCHER. AND NOT ENTIRELY UNEXPECTED.
THIS DOES NOT CONCERN YOU--
HOW ABOUT LETTING ME BE THE JUDGE OF THAT?
CHT-CHT-CHT-CHT
CHT-CHT
AS YOU WISH.

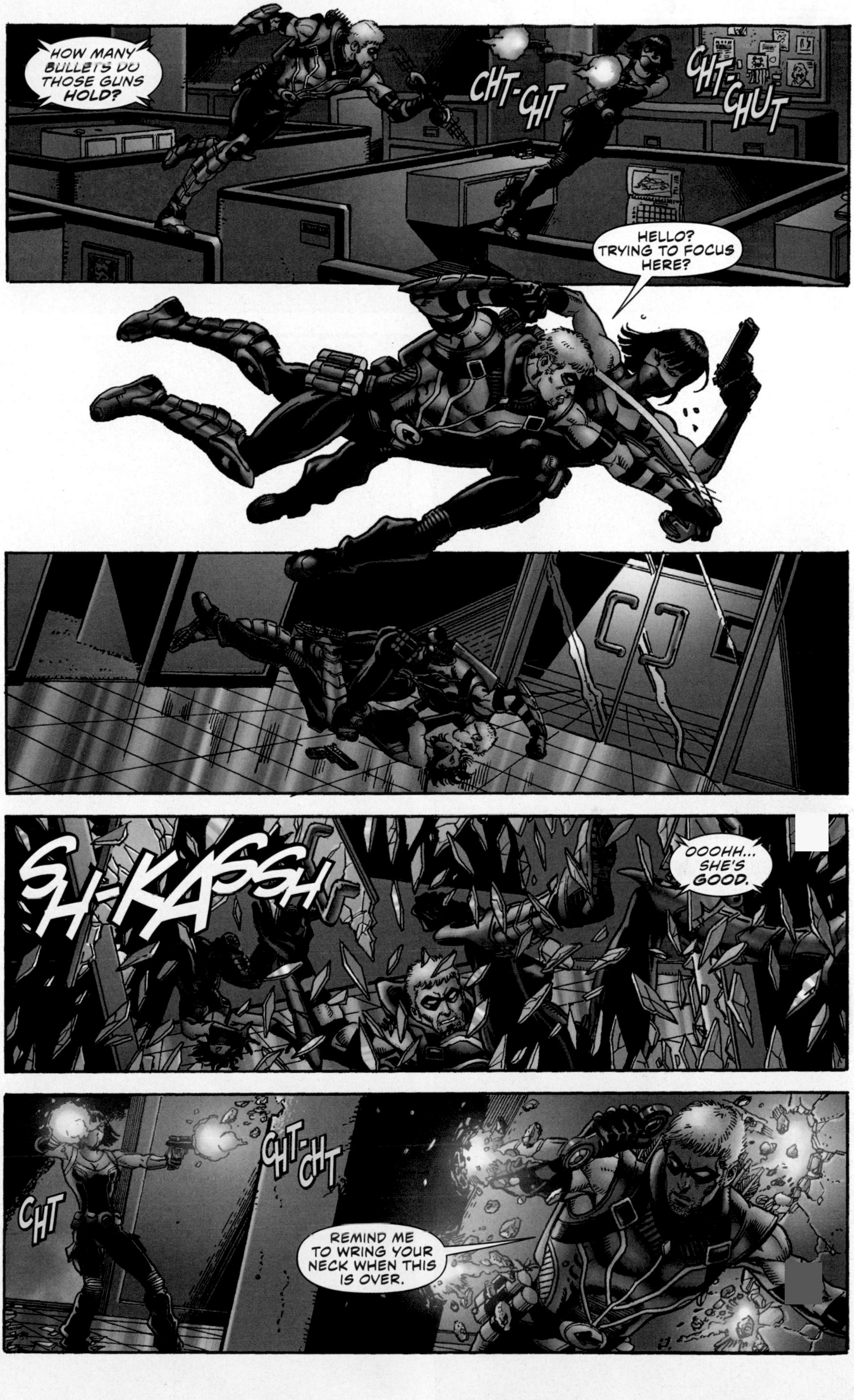
HOW MANY BULLETS DO THOSE GUNS HOLD?
CHT-CHT
CHT-CHUT
HELLO? TRYING TO FOCUS HERE?
SH-KASSH
OOOHH... SHE'S GOOD.
CHT
CHT-CHT
REMIND ME TO WRING YOUR NECK WHEN THIS IS OVER.

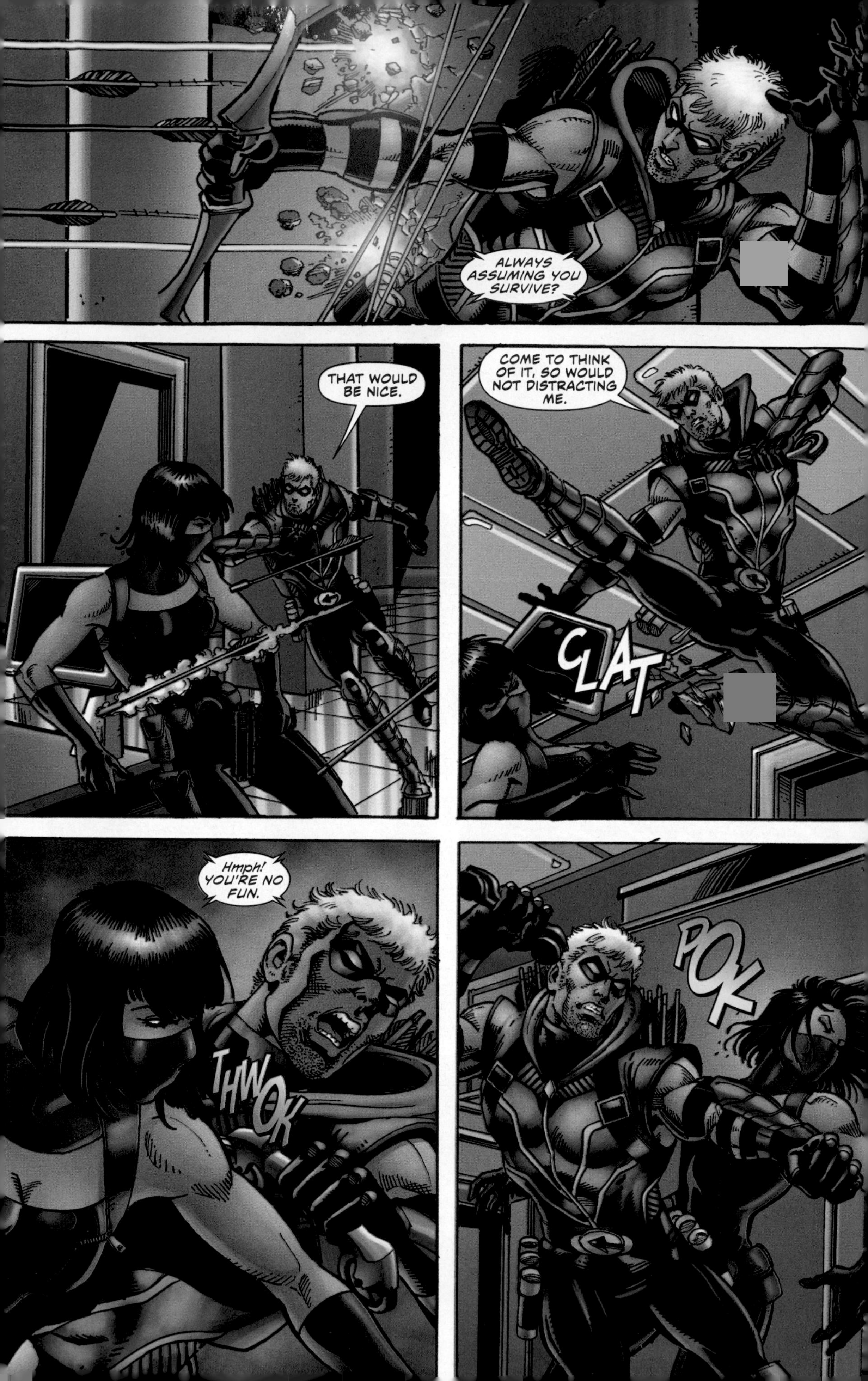
ALWAYS ASSUMING YOU SURVIVE?
THAT WOULD BE NICE.
COME TO THINK OF IT, SO WOULD NOT DISTRACTING ME.
CLAT
Hmph! YOU'RE NO FUN.
THWOK
POK

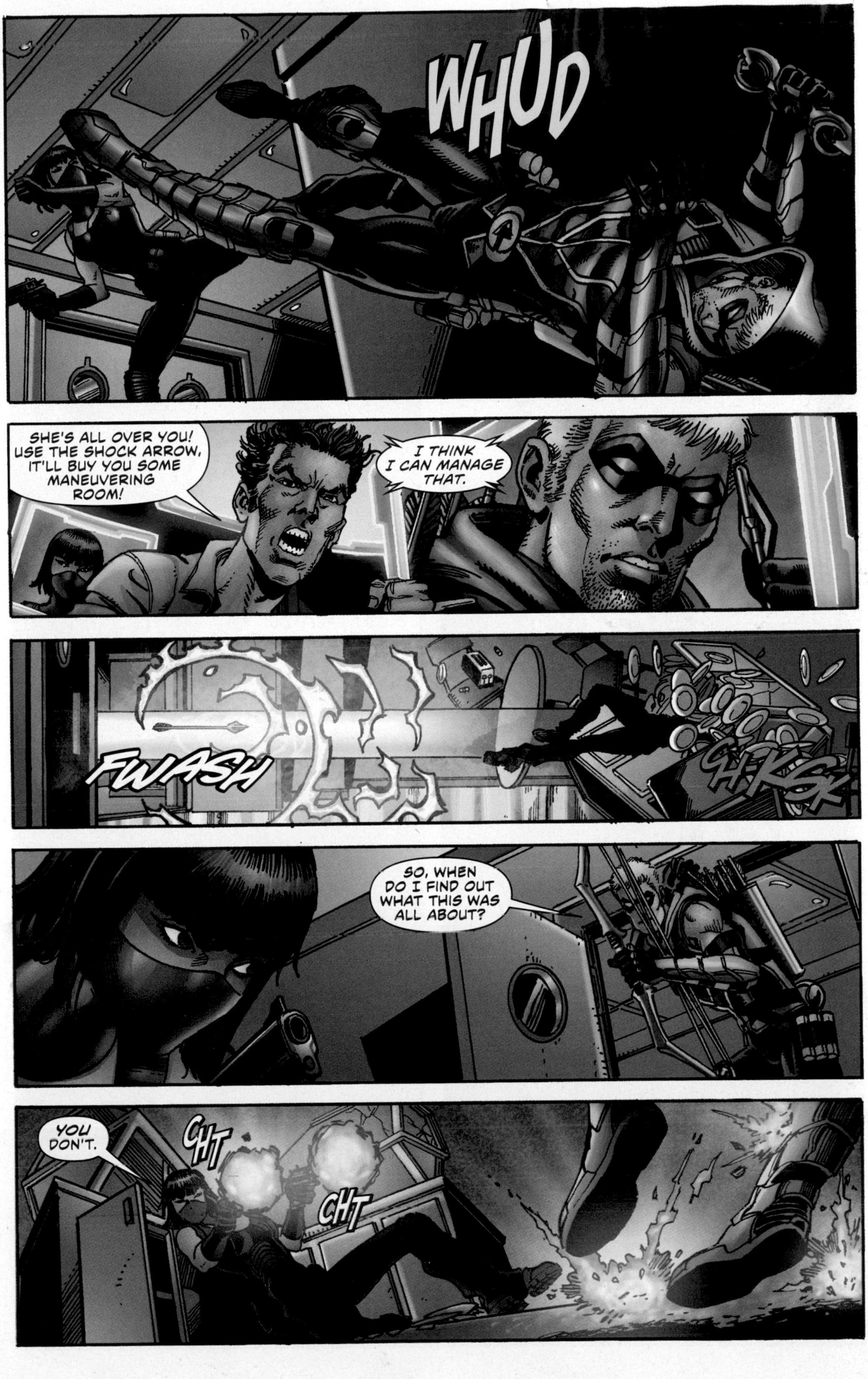
WHUD
SHE'S ALL OVER YOU! USE THE SHOCK ARROW, IT'LL BUY YOU SOME MANEUVERING ROOM!
I THINK I CAN MANAGE THAT.
FWASH
CHKSK
SO, WHEN DO I FIND OUT WHAT THIS WAS ALL ABOUT?
YOU DON'T.
CHT
CHT

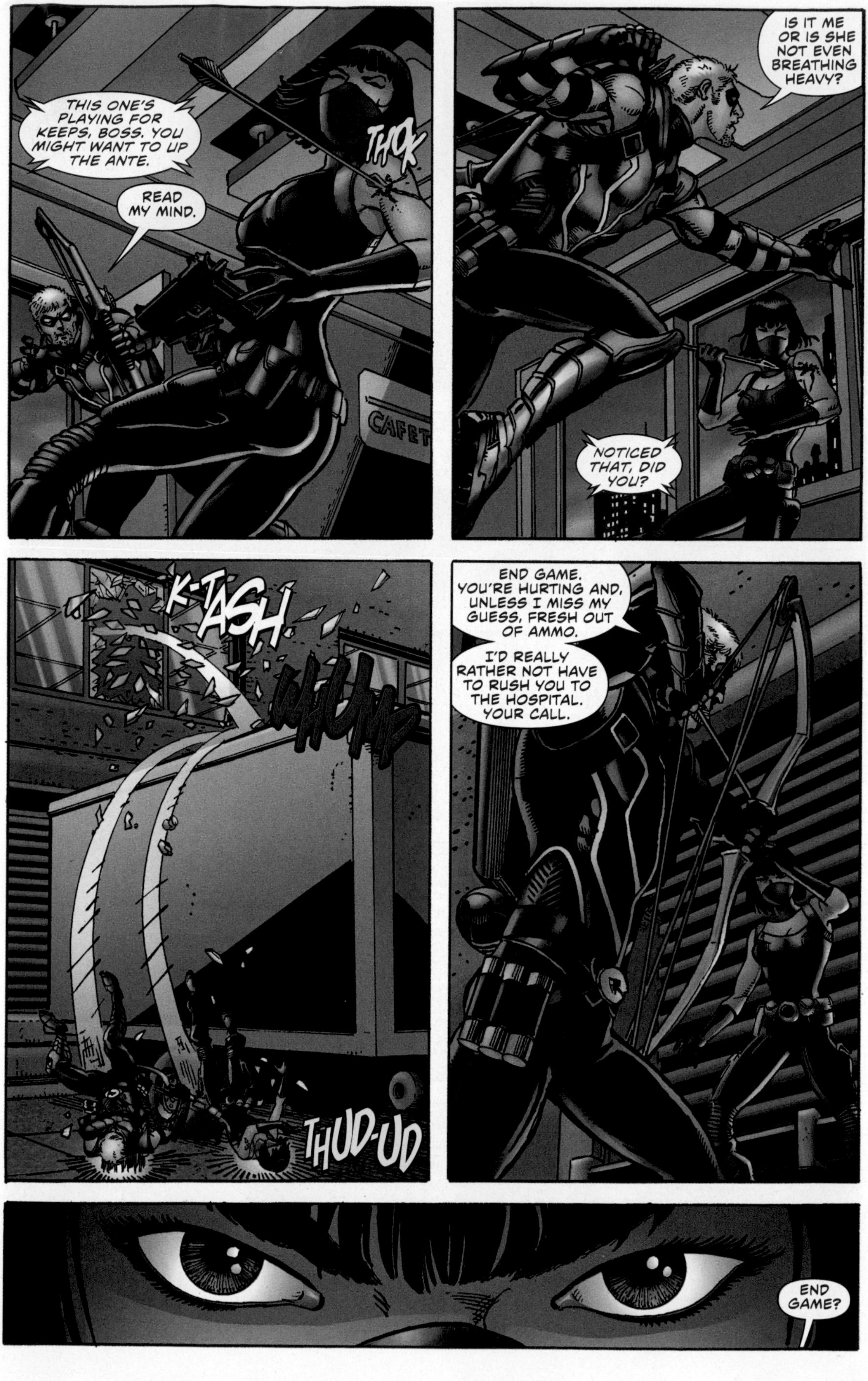
THIS ONE'S PLAYING FOR KEEPS, BOSS. YOU MIGHT WANT TO UP THE ANTE.
THOK
READ MY MIND.
CAFET
IS IT ME OR IS SHE NOT EVEN BREATHING HEAVY?
NOTICED THAT, DID YOU?
K-TASH
WHUMP
THUD-UD
END GAME. YOU'RE HURTING AND, UNLESS I MISS MY GUESS, FRESH OUT OF AMMO.
I'D REALLY RATHER NOT HAVE TO RUSH YOU TO THE HOSPITAL. YOUR CALL.
END GAME?

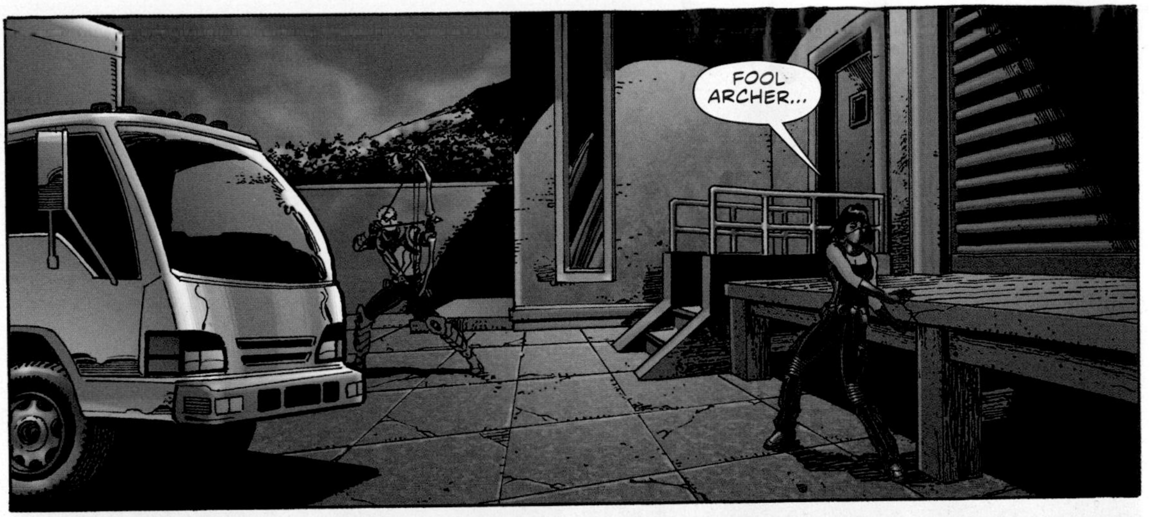
FOOL ARCHER...

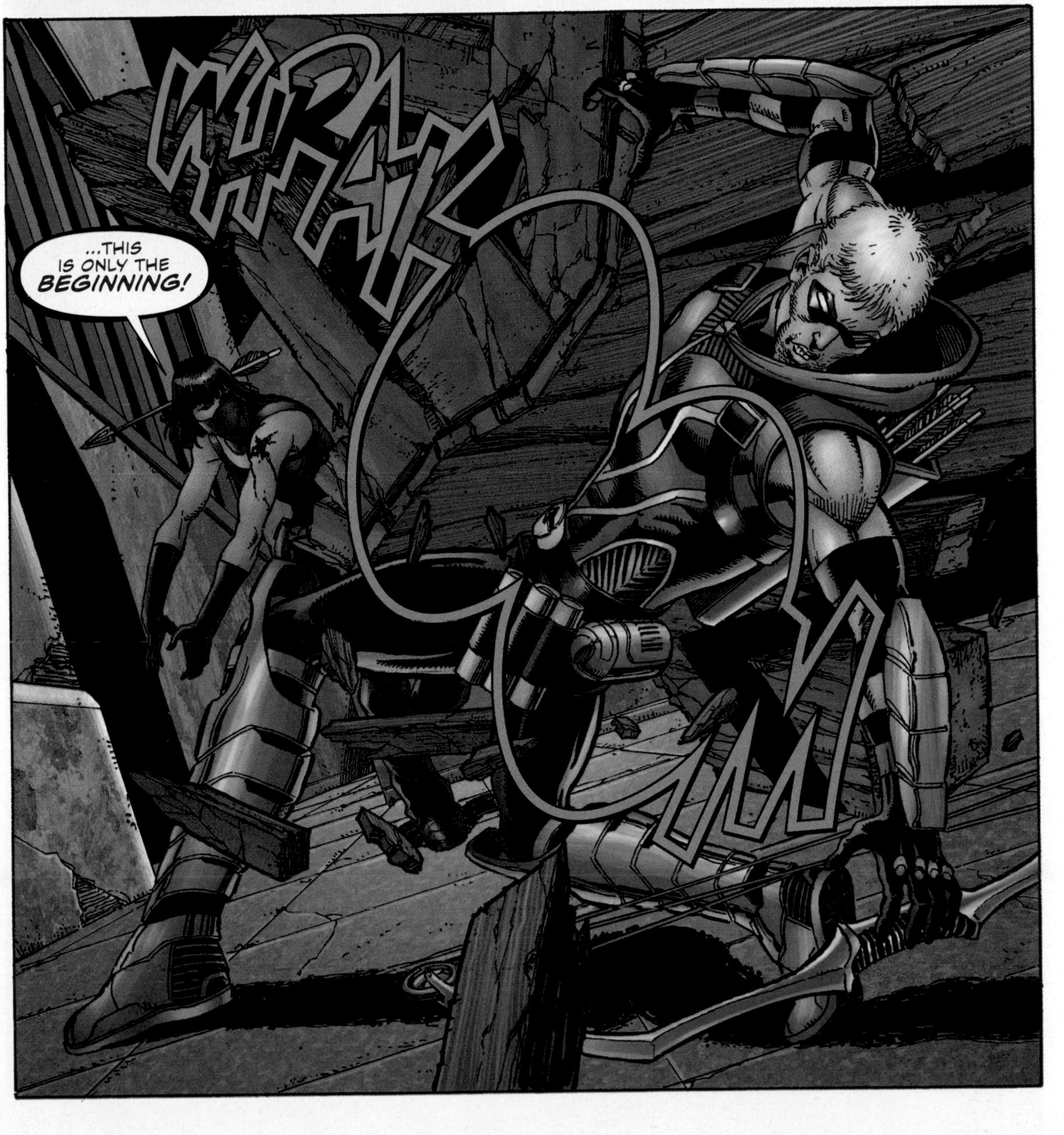
WHAK
...THIS IS ONLY THE BEGINNING!

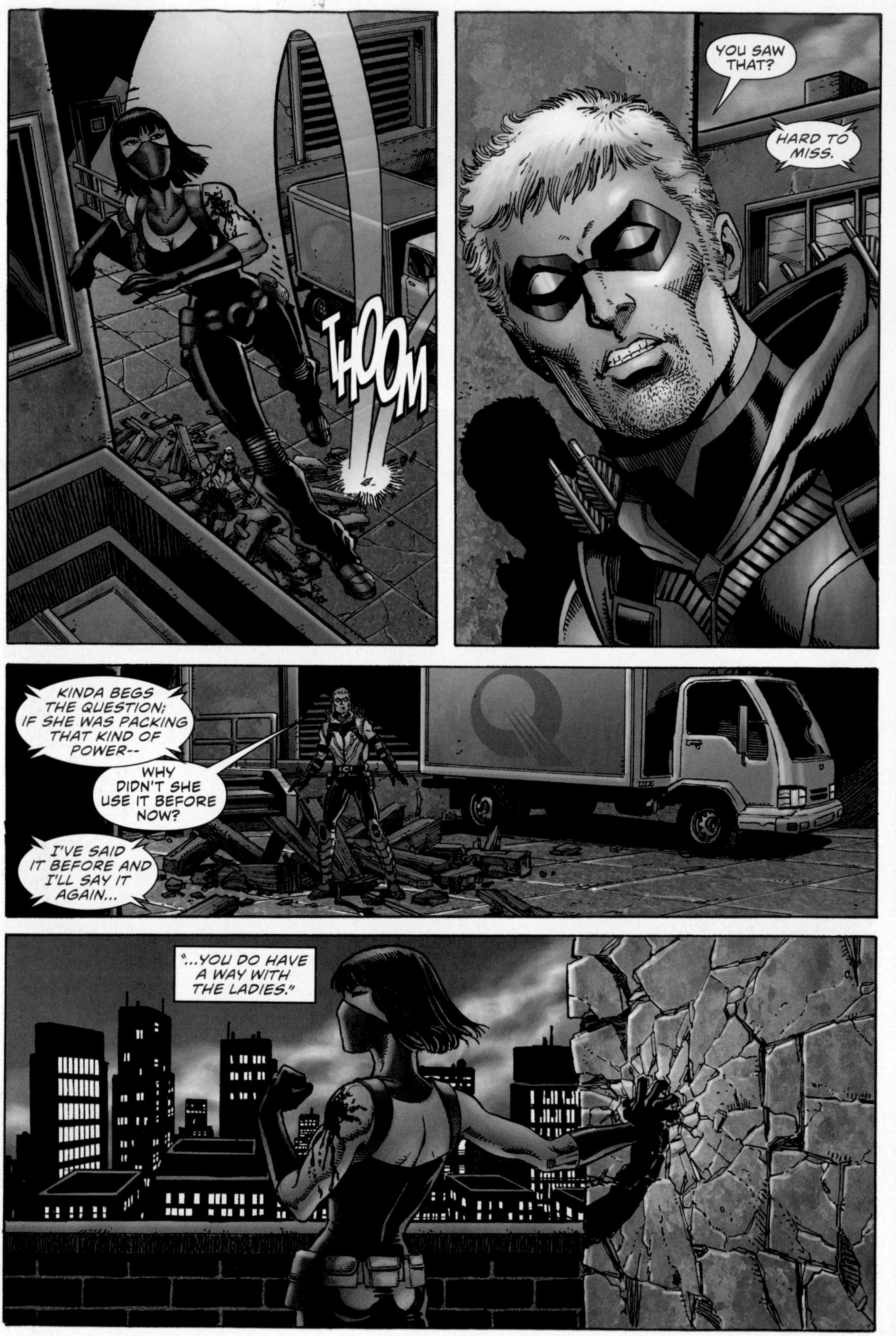
THOOM
YOU SAW THAT?
HARD TO MISS.
KINDA BEGS THE QUESTION; IF SHE WAS PACKING THAT KIND OF POWER--
WHY DIDN'T SHE USE IT BEFORE NOW?
I'VE SAID IT BEFORE AND I'LL SAY IT AGAIN...
"...YOU DO HAVE A WAY WITH THE LADIES."

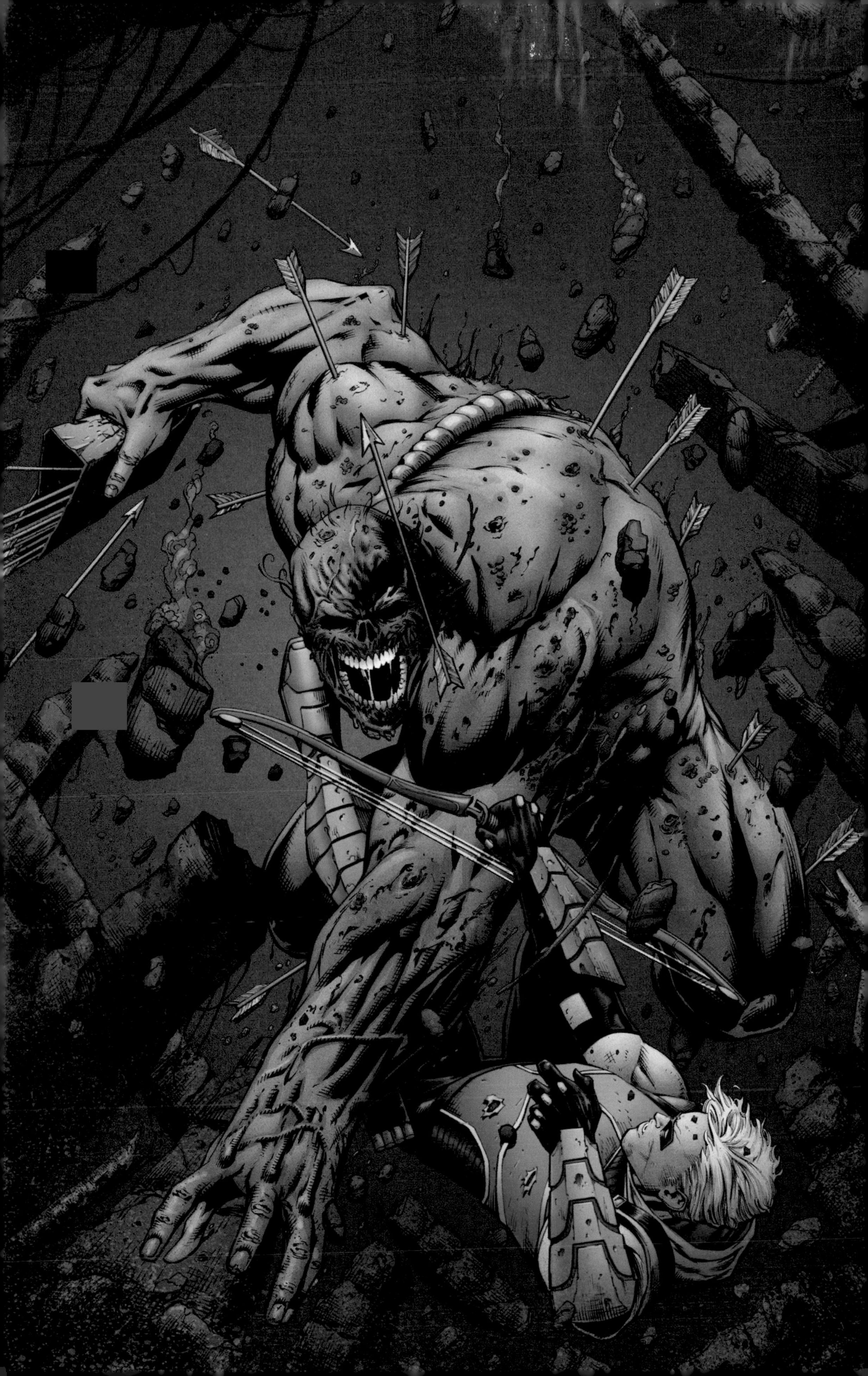

THE MIDAS TOUCH

KEITH GIFFEN
writer / co-plotter

DAN JURGENS
layouts / co-plotter

RAY McCARTHY
finishes

cover by JASON FABOK, RYAN WINN & ALLEN PASSALAQUA

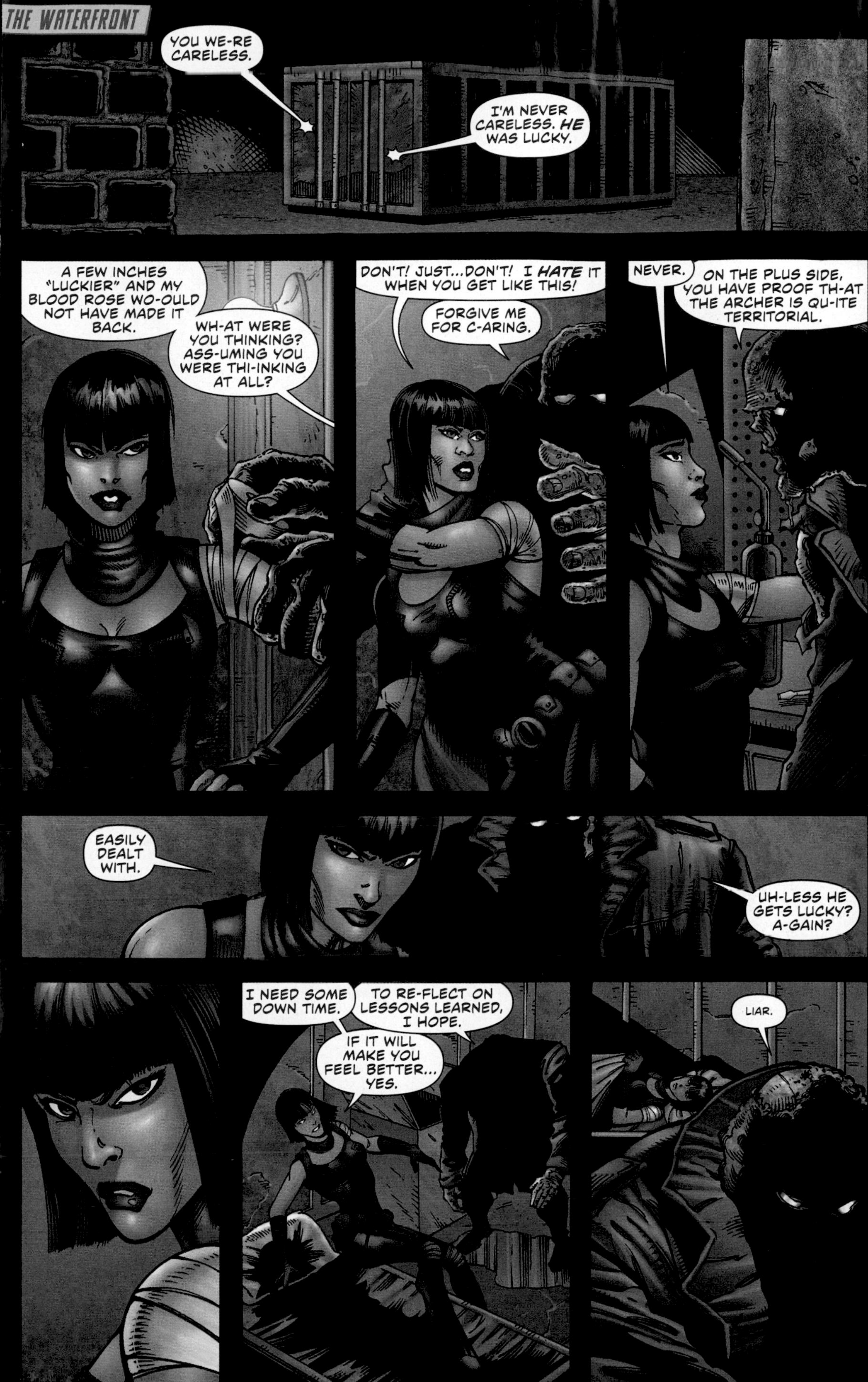
THE WATERFRONT
YOU WE-RE CARELESS.
I'M NEVER CARELESS. HE WAS LUCKY.
A FEW INCHES "LUCKIER" AND MY BLOOD ROSE WO-OULD NOT HAVE MADE IT BACK.
WH-AT WERE YOU THINKING? ASS-UMING YOU WERE THI-INKING AT ALL?
DON'T! JUST...DON'T! I HATE IT WHEN YOU GET LIKE THIS!
FORGIVE ME FOR C-ARING.
NEVER.
ON THE PLUS SIDE, YOU HAVE PROOF TH-AT THE ARCHER IS QU-ITE TERRITORIAL.
EASILY DEALT WITH.
UH-LESS HE GETS LUCKY? A-GAIN?
I NEED SOME DOWN TIME.
TO RE-FLECT ON LESSONS LEARNED, I HOPE.
IF IT WILL MAKE YOU FEEL BETTER... YES.
LIAR.

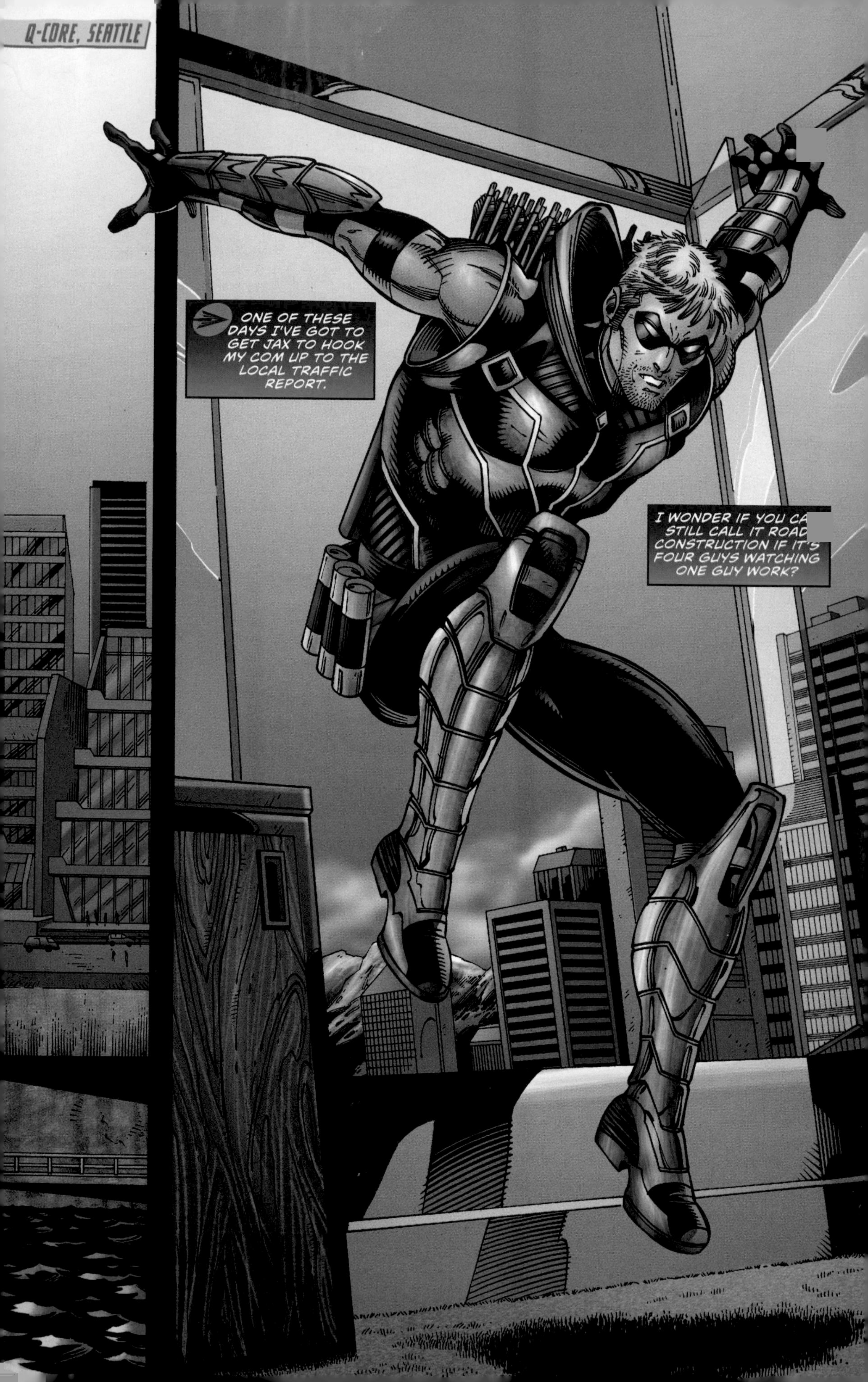
Q-CORE, SEATTLE
ONE OF THESE DAYS I'VE GOT TO GET JAX TO HOOK MY COM UP TO THE LOCAL TRAFFIC REPORT.
I WONDER IF YOU CA STILL CALL IT ROAD CONSTRUCTION IF IT'S FOUR GUYS WATCHING ONE GUY WORK?

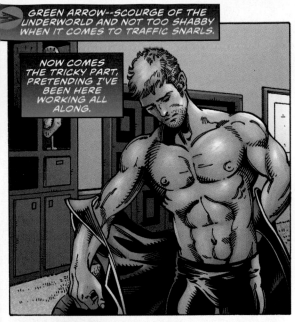

GREEN ARROW--SCOURGE OF THE UNDERWORLD AND NOT TOO SHABBY WHEN IT COMES TO TRAFFIC SNARLS.

NOW COMES THE TRICKY PART, PRETENDING I'VE BEEN HERE WORKING ALL ALONG.

I'LL SEE MYSELF IN.

BUT, MR. QUEEN LEFT EXPRESS INSTRUCTIONS THAT HE'S NOT TO BE DISTURBED.

LIKE I SAID, I'LL SEE MYSELF--

--IN?

WHAT'S WITH THE LOOK? IT'S NOT THE FIRST TIME YOU'VE SEEN ME LIKE THIS.

YES, BUT... USUALLY YOU'RE NOT ALONE.

USUALLY I'M NOT SECONDS OUT OF MY G.A. GEAR EITHER. TOO CLOSE.

OKAY, THEN, WHAT HAVE I NOT DONE OR DONE WRONG OR--

OLIVER... WE SHOULD TALK.

NOW THAT LOOK I KNOW.

⧽sigh⧽...YOU CAN SIGN THESE WHILE I...TRY TO EXPLAIN.

ADRIEN, PAPERWORK DOESN'T QUALIFY AS "SWEETENING THE PILL."

C'MON, OUT WITH IT. HOW BAD CAN IT BE?

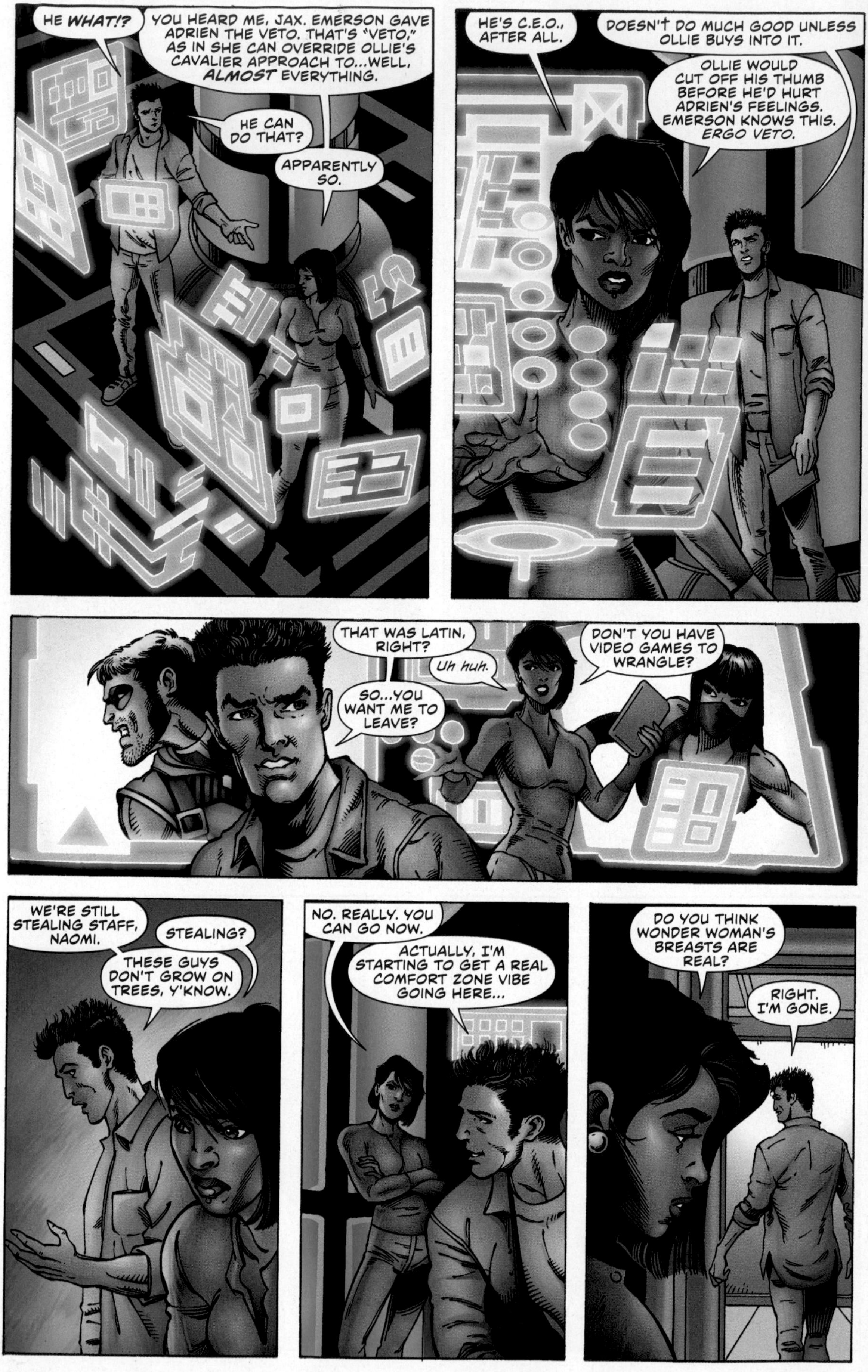

HE *WHAT!?*
YOU HEARD ME, JAX. EMERSON GAVE ADRIEN THE VETO. THAT'S "VETO," AS IN SHE CAN OVERRIDE OLLIE'S CAVALIER APPROACH TO...WELL, *ALMOST* EVERYTHING.
HE CAN DO THAT?
APPARENTLY SO.
HE'S C.E.O., AFTER ALL.
DOESN'T DO MUCH GOOD UNLESS OLLIE BUYS INTO IT.
OLLIE WOULD CUT OFF HIS THUMB BEFORE HE'D HURT ADRIEN'S FEELINGS. EMERSON KNOWS THIS. *ERGO VETO.*
THAT WAS LATIN, RIGHT?
Uh huh.
SO...YOU WANT ME TO LEAVE?
DON'T YOU HAVE VIDEO GAMES TO WRANGLE?
WE'RE STILL STEALING STAFF, NAOMI.
STEALING?
THESE GUYS DON'T GROW ON TREES, Y'KNOW.
NO. REALLY. YOU CAN GO NOW.
ACTUALLY, I'M STARTING TO GET A REAL COMFORT ZONE VIBE GOING HERE...
DO YOU THINK WONDER WOMAN'S BREASTS ARE REAL?
RIGHT. I'M GONE.

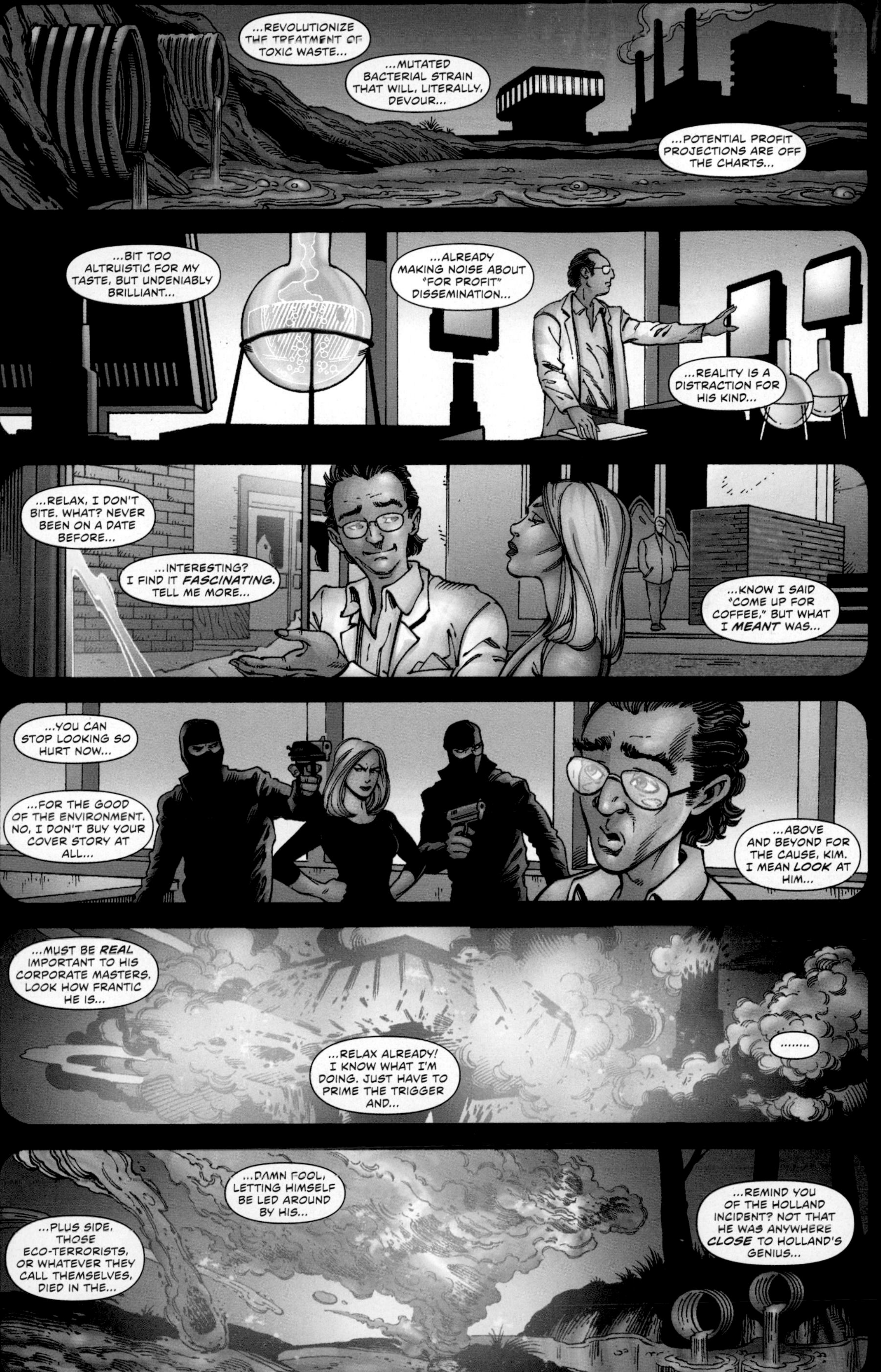
...REVOLUTIONIZE THE TREATMENT OF TOXIC WASTE...
...MUTATED BACTERIAL STRAIN THAT WILL, LITERALLY, DEVOUR...
...POTENTIAL PROFIT PROJECTIONS ARE OFF THE CHARTS...
...BIT TOO ALTRUISTIC FOR MY TASTE, BUT UNDENIABLY BRILLIANT...
...ALREADY MAKING NOISE ABOUT "FOR PROFIT" DISSEMINATION...
...REALITY IS A DISTRACTION FOR HIS KIND...
...RELAX, I DON'T BITE. WHAT? NEVER BEEN ON A DATE BEFORE...
...INTERESTING? I FIND IT *FASCINATING*. TELL ME MORE...
...KNOW I SAID "COME UP FOR COFFEE," BUT WHAT I *MEANT* WAS...
...YOU CAN STOP LOOKING SO HURT NOW...
...FOR THE GOOD OF THE ENVIRONMENT. NO, I DON'T BUY YOUR COVER STORY AT ALL...
...ABOVE AND BEYOND FOR THE CAUSE, KIM. I MEAN *LOOK* AT HIM...
...MUST BE *REAL* IMPORTANT TO HIS CORPORATE MASTERS. LOOK HOW FRANTIC HE IS...
...RELAX ALREADY! I KNOW WHAT I'M DOING. JUST HAVE TO PRIME THE TRIGGER AND...
....
...DAMN FOOL, LETTING HIMSELF BE LED AROUND BY HIS...
...PLUS SIDE, THOSE ECO-TERRORISTS, OR WHATEVER THEY CALL THEMSELVES, DIED IN THE...
...REMIND YOU OF THE HOLLAND INCIDENT? NOT THAT HE WAS ANYWHERE *CLOSE* TO HOLLAND'S GENIUS...

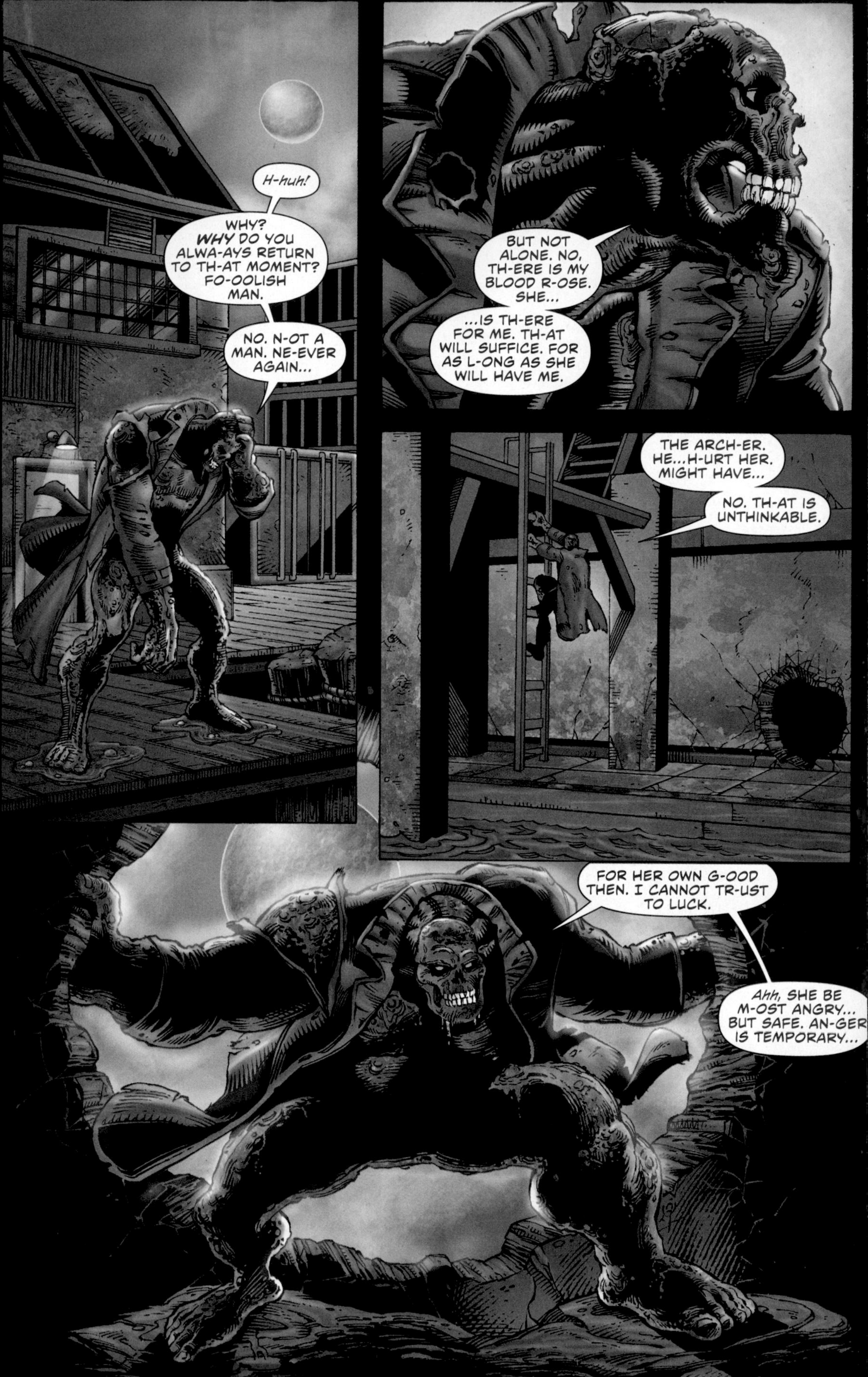
H-huh!
WHY? *WHY* DO YOU ALWA-AYS RETURN TO TH-AT MOMENT? FO-OOLISH MAN.
NO. N-OT A MAN. NE-EVER AGAIN...
BUT NOT ALONE. NO, TH-ERE IS MY BLOOD R-OSE. SHE...
...IS TH-ERE FOR ME. TH-AT WILL SUFFICE. FOR AS L-ONG AS SHE WILL HAVE ME.
THE ARCH-ER. HE...H-URT HER. MIGHT HAVE...
NO. TH-AT IS UNTHINKABLE.
FOR HER OWN G-OOD THEN. I CANNOT TR-UST TO LUCK.
Ahh, SHE BE M-OST ANGRY... BUT SAFE. AN-GER IS TEMPORARY...

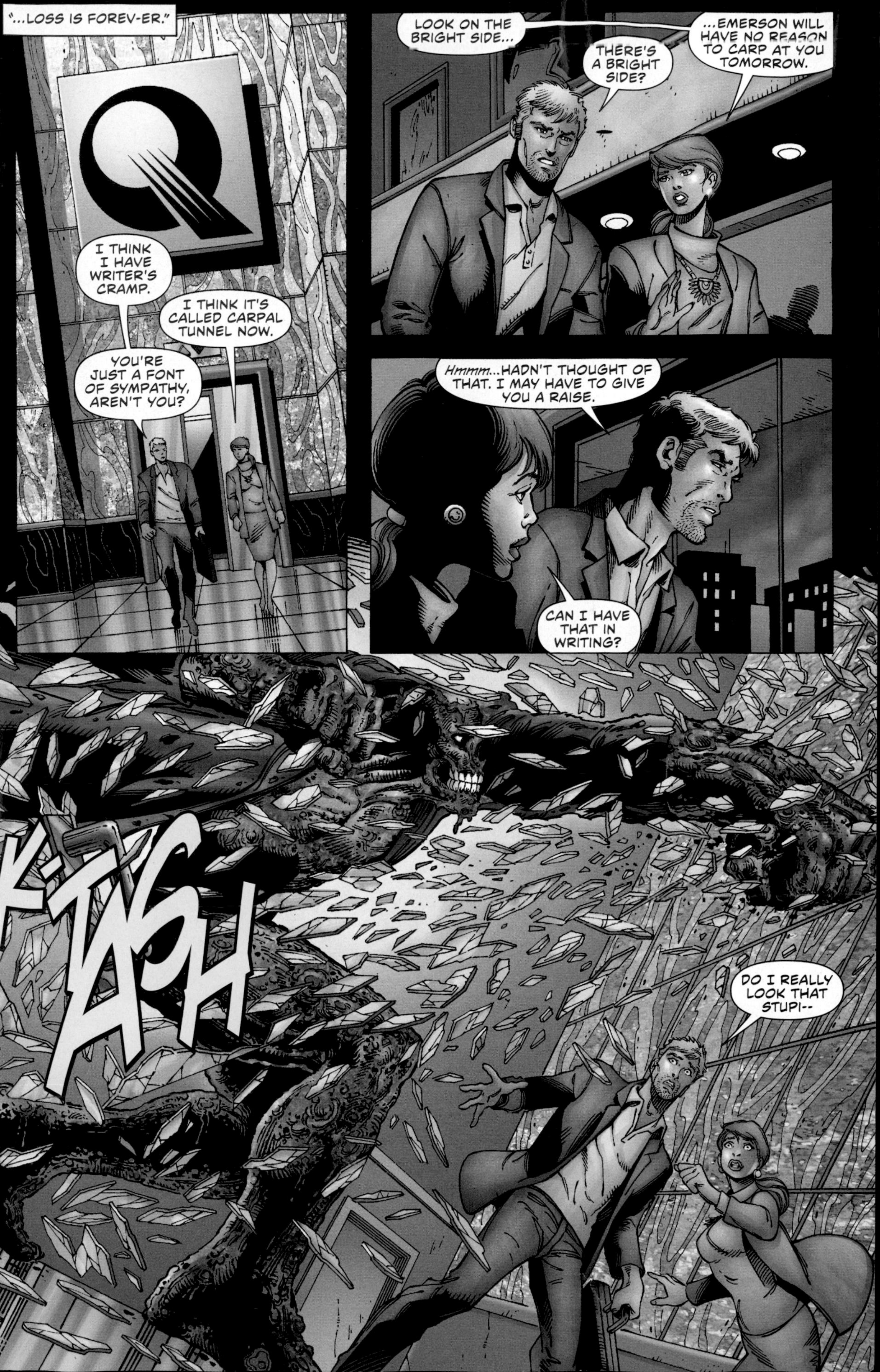
"...LOSS IS FOREV-ER."
I THINK I HAVE WRITER'S CRAMP.
I THINK IT'S CALLED CARPAL TUNNEL NOW.
YOU'RE JUST A FONT OF SYMPATHY, AREN'T YOU?
LOOK ON THE BRIGHT SIDE...
THERE'S A BRIGHT SIDE?
...EMERSON WILL HAVE NO REASON TO CARP AT YOU TOMORROW.
Hmmm...HADN'T THOUGHT OF THAT. I MAY HAVE TO GIVE YOU A RAISE.
CAN I HAVE THAT IN WRITING?
K-TASH
DO I REALLY LOOK THAT STUPI--

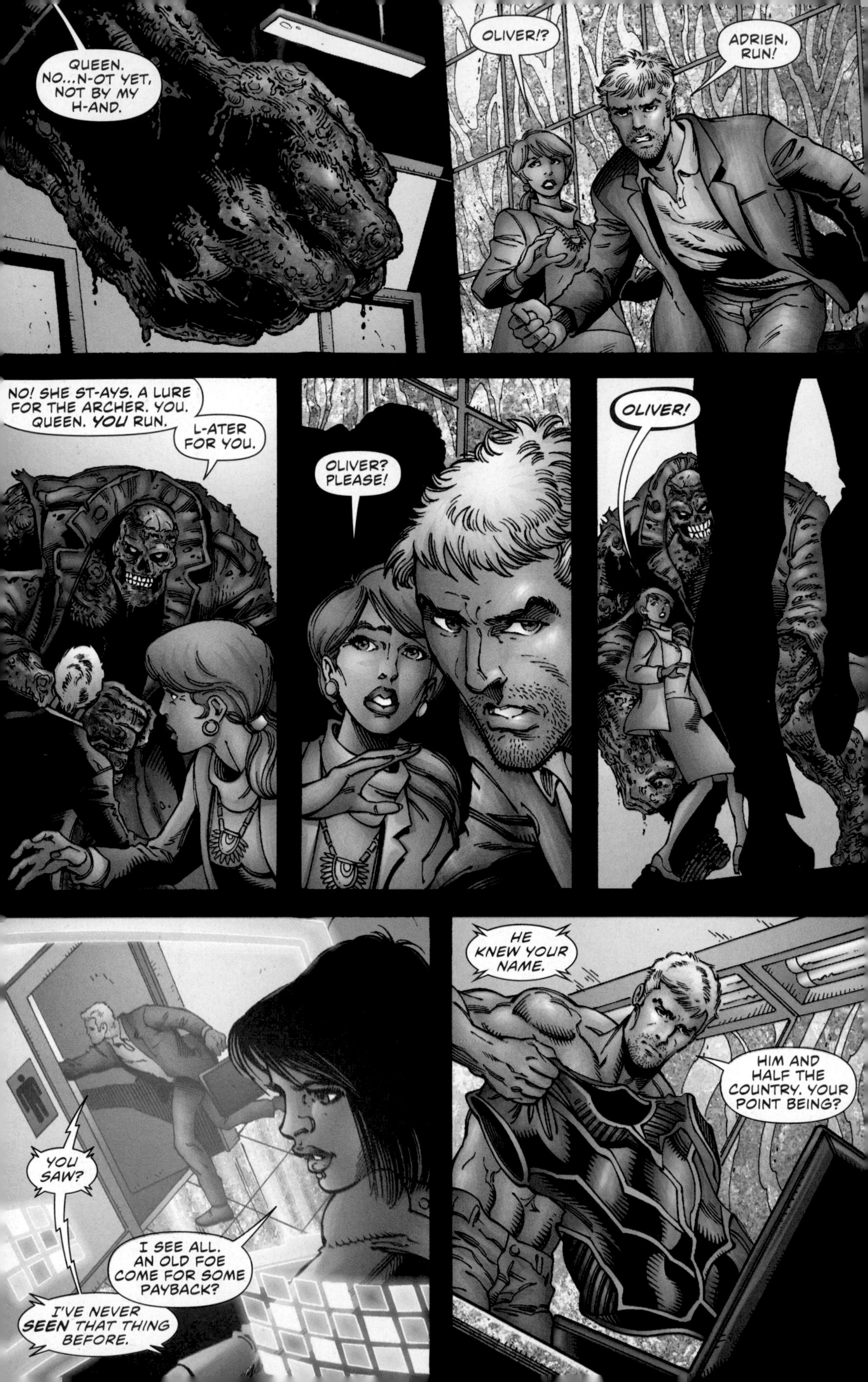
QUEEN. NO...N-OT YET, NOT BY MY H-AND.
OLIVER!?
ADRIEN, RUN!
NO! SHE ST-AYS. A LURE FOR THE ARCHER. YOU. QUEEN. *YOU* RUN.
L-ATER FOR YOU.
OLIVER? PLEASE!
OLIVER!
YOU SAW?
I SEE ALL. AN OLD FOE COME FOR SOME PAYBACK?
I'VE NEVER **SEEN** THAT THING BEFORE.
HE KNEW YOUR NAME.
HIM AND HALF THE COUNTRY. YOUR POINT BEING?

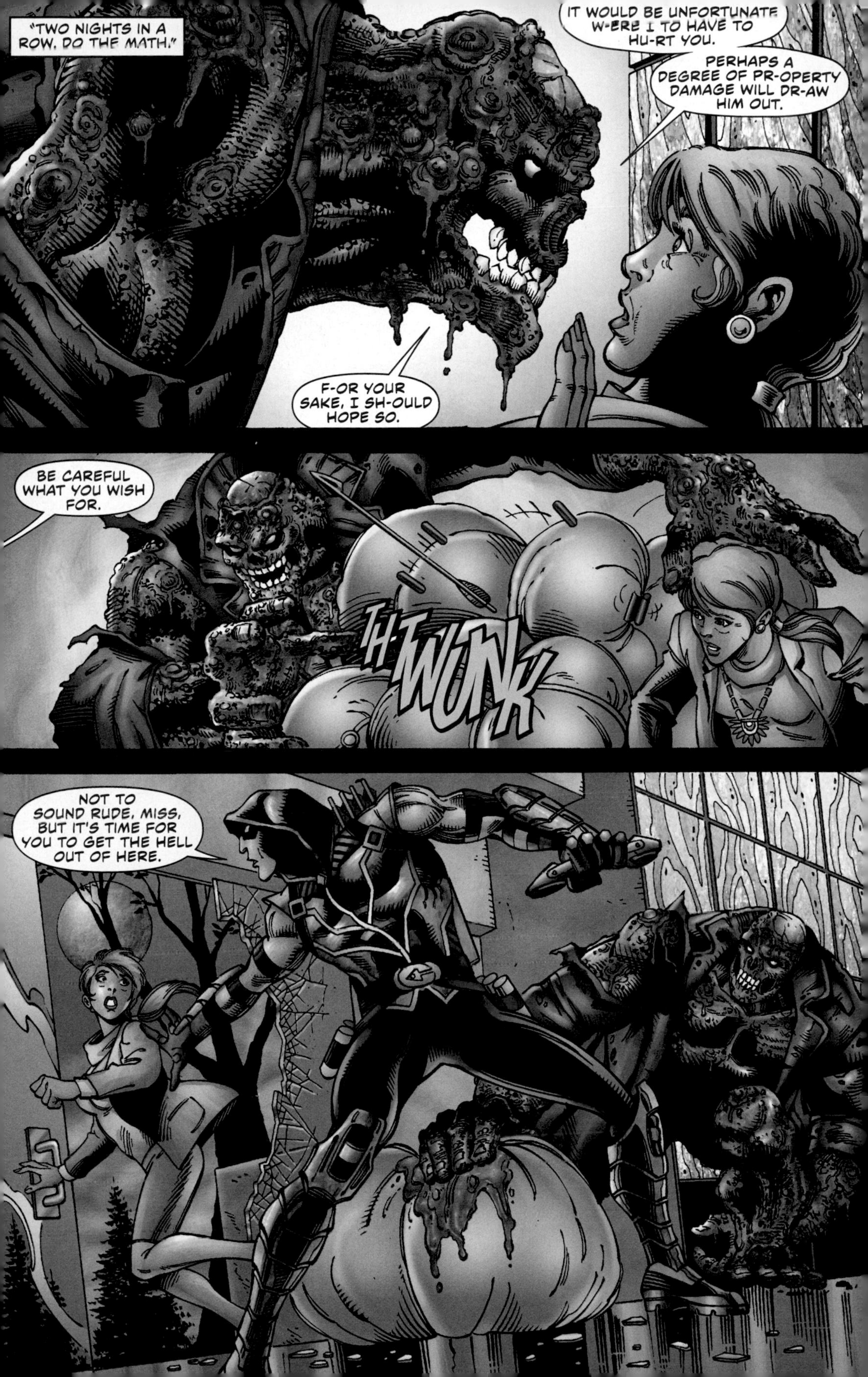
"TWO NIGHTS IN A ROW. DO THE MATH."
IT WOULD BE UNFORTUNATE W-ERE I TO HAVE TO HU-RT YOU.
PERHAPS A DEGREE OF PR-OPERTY DAMAGE WILL DR-AW HIM OUT.
F-OR YOUR SAKE, I SH-OULD HOPE SO.
BE CAREFUL WHAT YOU WISH FOR.
THTWUNK
NOT TO SOUND RUDE, MISS, BUT IT'S TIME FOR YOU TO GET THE HELL OUT OF HERE.

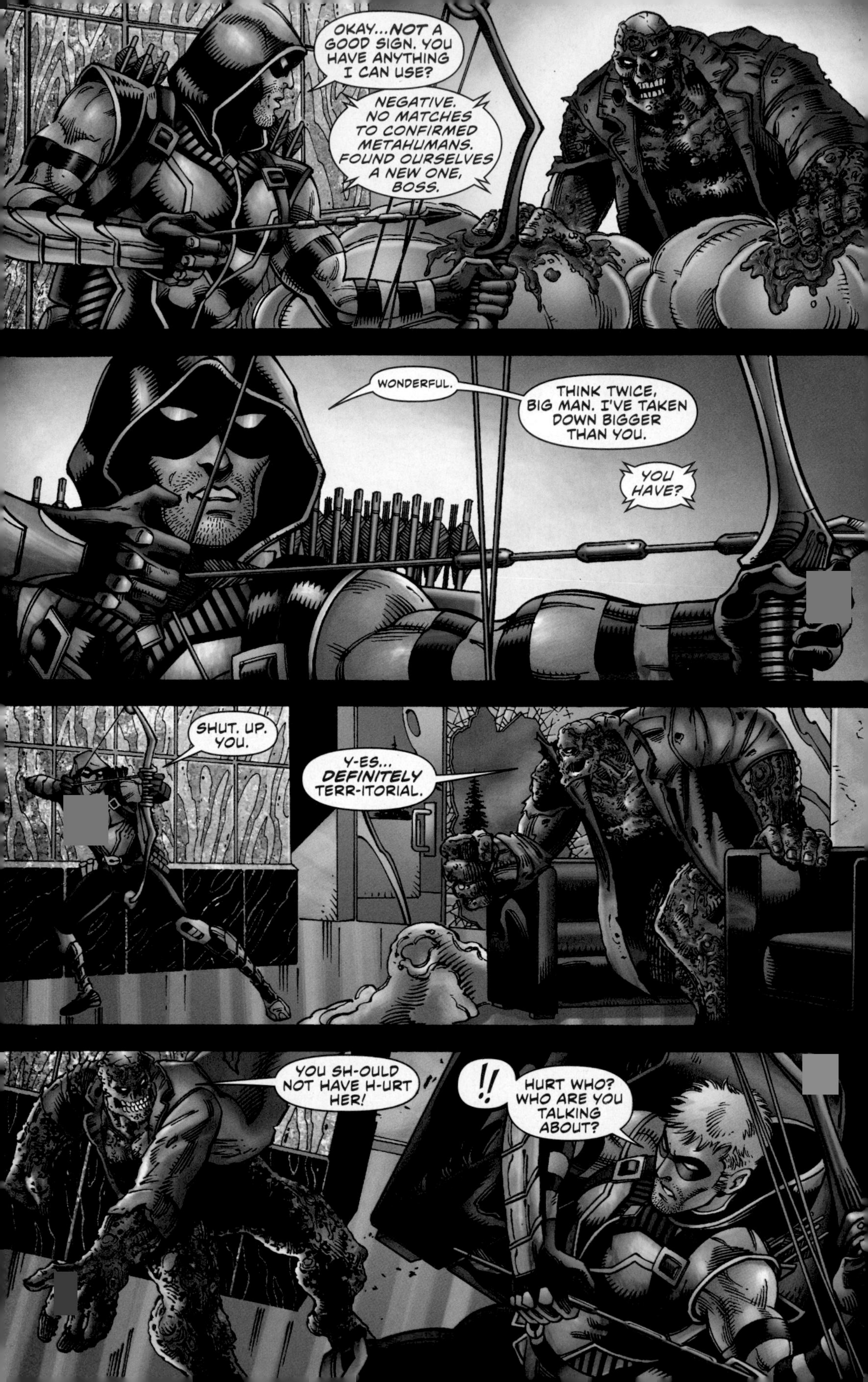
OKAY...NOT A GOOD SIGN. YOU HAVE ANYTHING I CAN USE?
NEGATIVE. NO MATCHES TO CONFIRMED METAHUMANS. FOUND OURSELVES A NEW ONE, BOSS.
WONDERFUL.
THINK TWICE, BIG MAN. I'VE TAKEN DOWN BIGGER THAN YOU.
YOU HAVE?
SHUT. UP. YOU.
Y-ES... DEFINITELY TERR-ITORIAL.
YOU SH-OULD NOT HAVE H-URT HER!
!!
HURT WHO? WHO ARE YOU TALKING ABOUT?

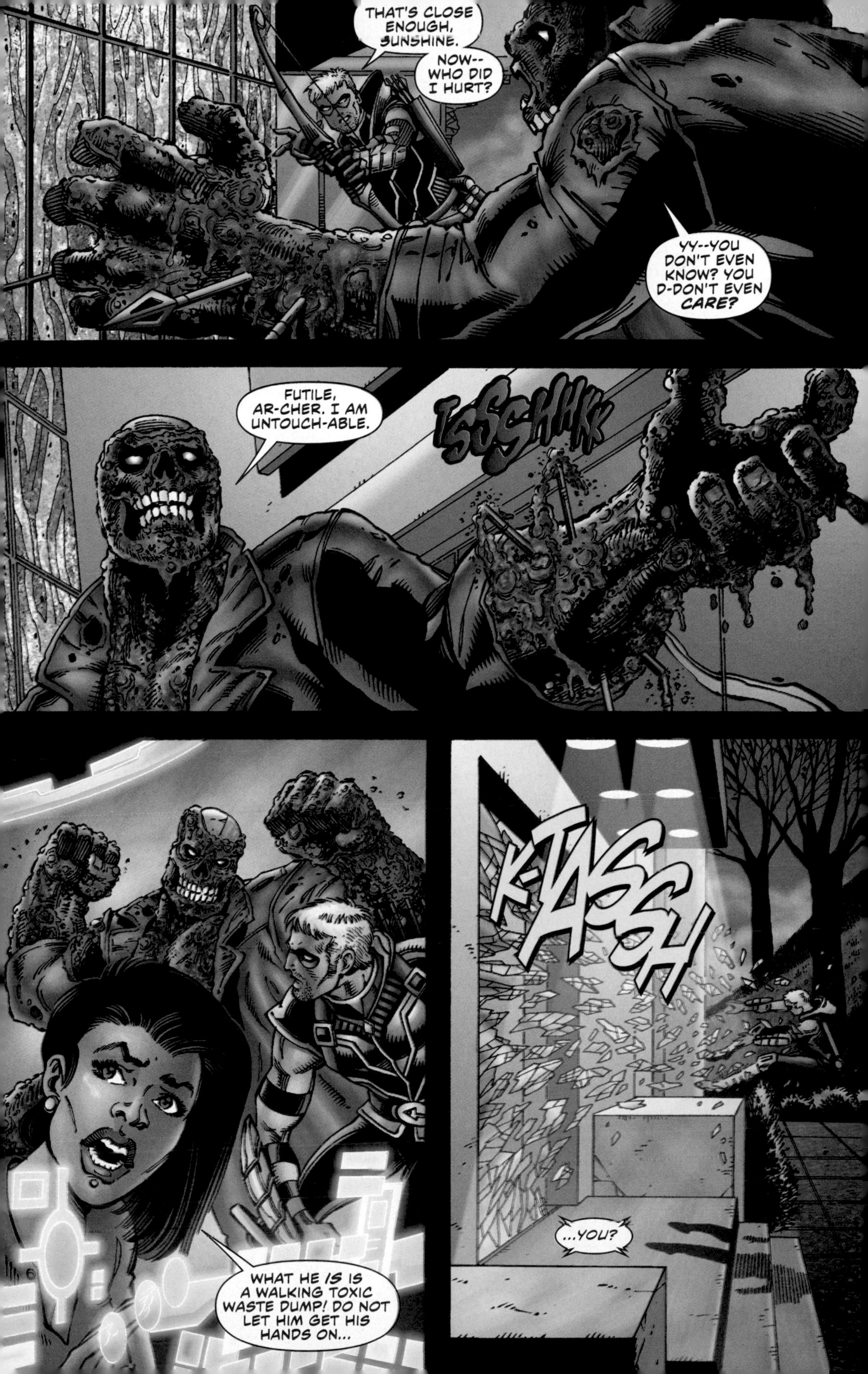
THAT'S CLOSE ENOUGH, SUNSHINE.
NOW-- WHO DID I HURT?
YY--YOU DON'T EVEN KNOW? YOU D-DON'T EVEN CARE?
FUTILE, AR-CHER. I AM UNTOUCH-ABLE.
TSSSHHKK
WHAT HE IS IS A WALKING TOXIC WASTE DUMP! DO NOT LET HIM GET HIS HANDS ON...
K-TASSH
...YOU?

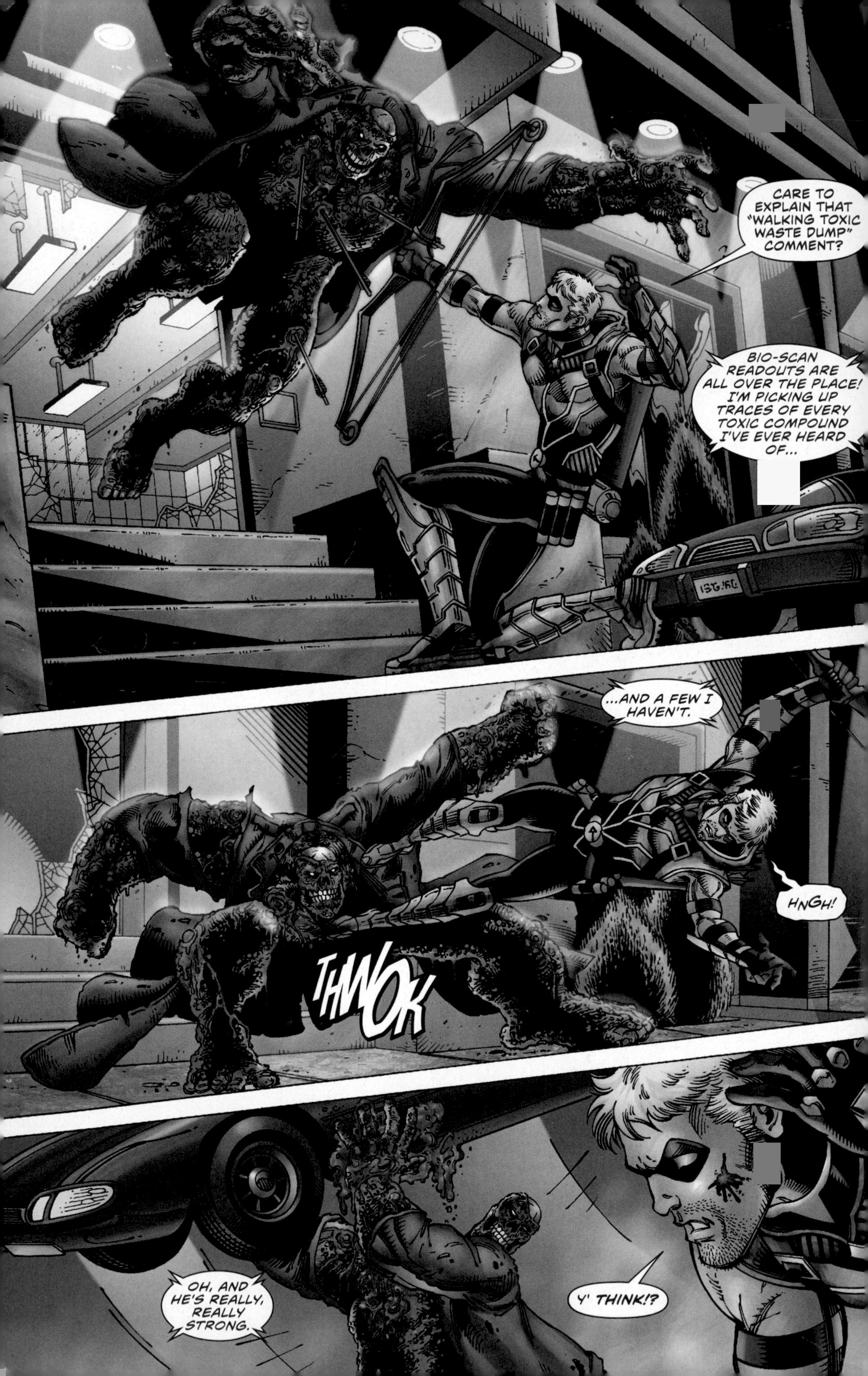
CARE TO EXPLAIN THAT "WALKING TOXIC WASTE DUMP" COMMENT?
BIO-SCAN READOUTS ARE ALL OVER THE PLACE! I'M PICKING UP TRACES OF EVERY TOXIC COMPOUND I'VE EVER HEARD OF...
...AND A FEW I HAVEN'T.
HNGH!
THWOK
OH, AND HE'S REALLY, REALLY STRONG.
Y' THINK!?

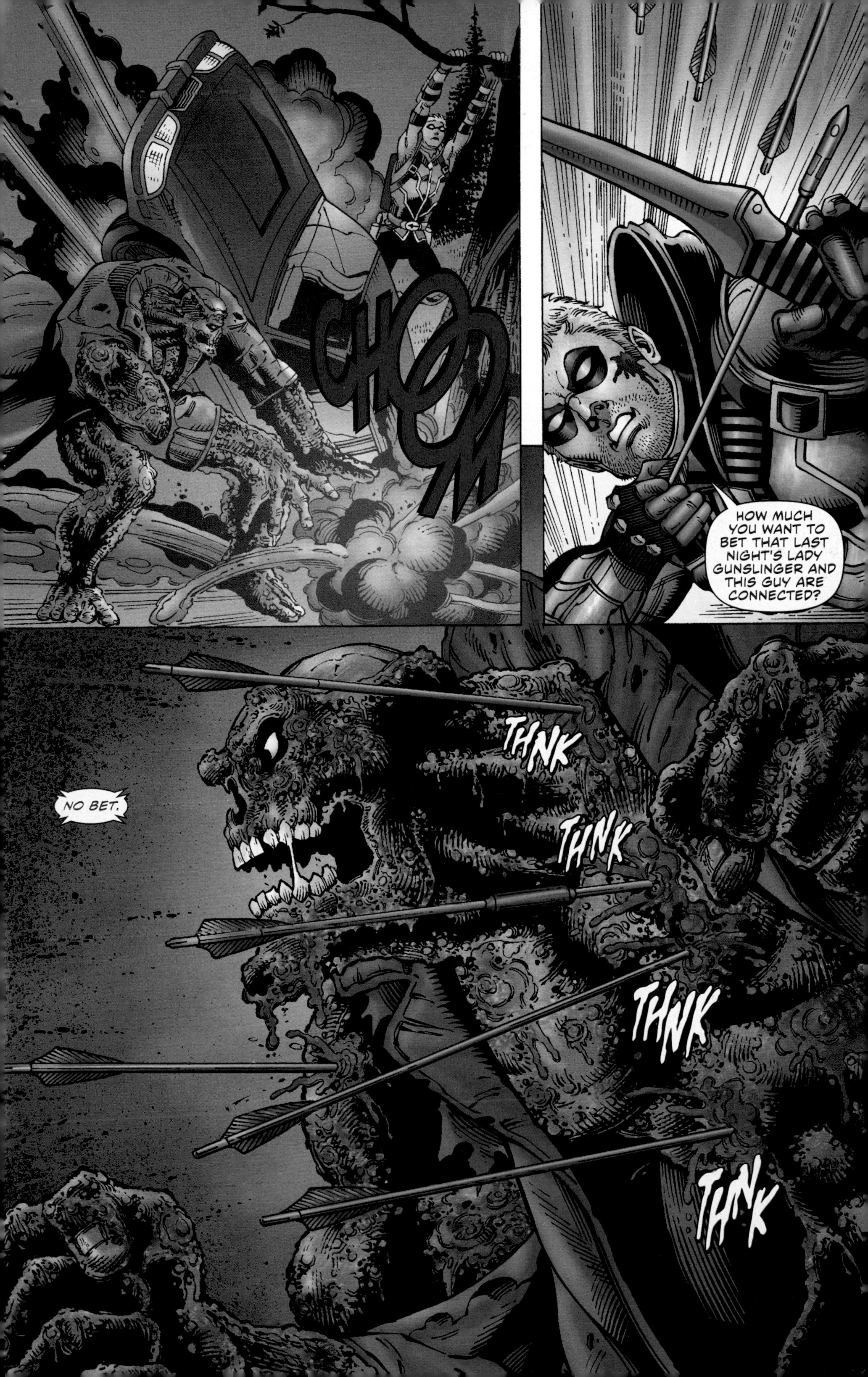
CHOOM
HOW MUCH YOU WANT TO BET THAT LAST NIGHT'S LADY GUNSLINGER AND THIS GUY ARE CONNECTED?
NO BET.
THNK
THNK
THNK
THNK

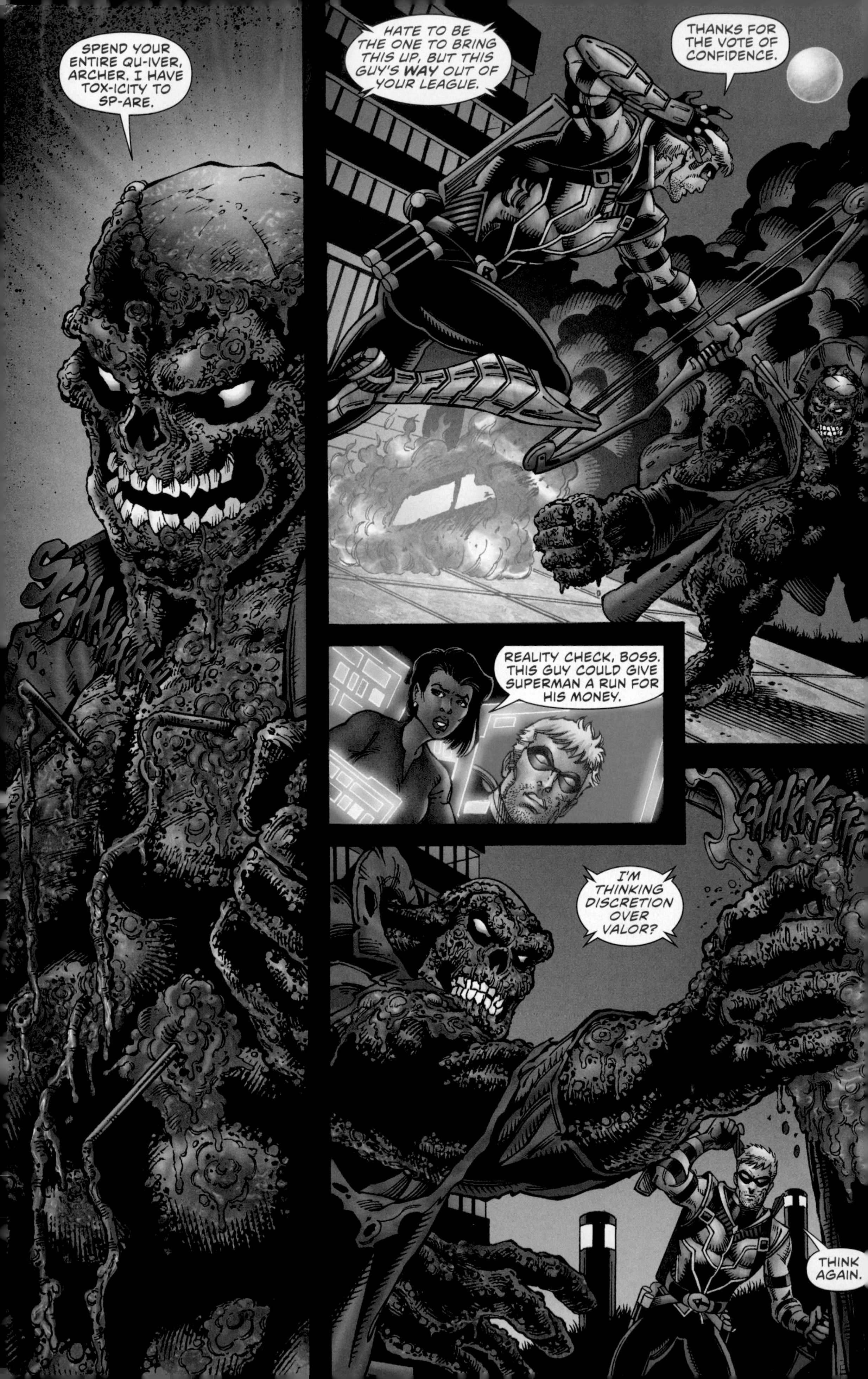
SPEND YOUR ENTIRE QU-IVER, ARCHER. I HAVE TOX-ICITY TO SP-ARE.
SSHHAKK
HATE TO BE THE ONE TO BRING THIS UP, BUT THIS GUY'S WAY OUT OF YOUR LEAGUE.
THANKS FOR THE VOTE OF CONFIDENCE.
REALITY CHECK, BOSS. THIS GUY COULD GIVE SUPERMAN A RUN FOR HIS MONEY.
I'M THINKING DISCRETION OVER VALOR?
THINK AGAIN.

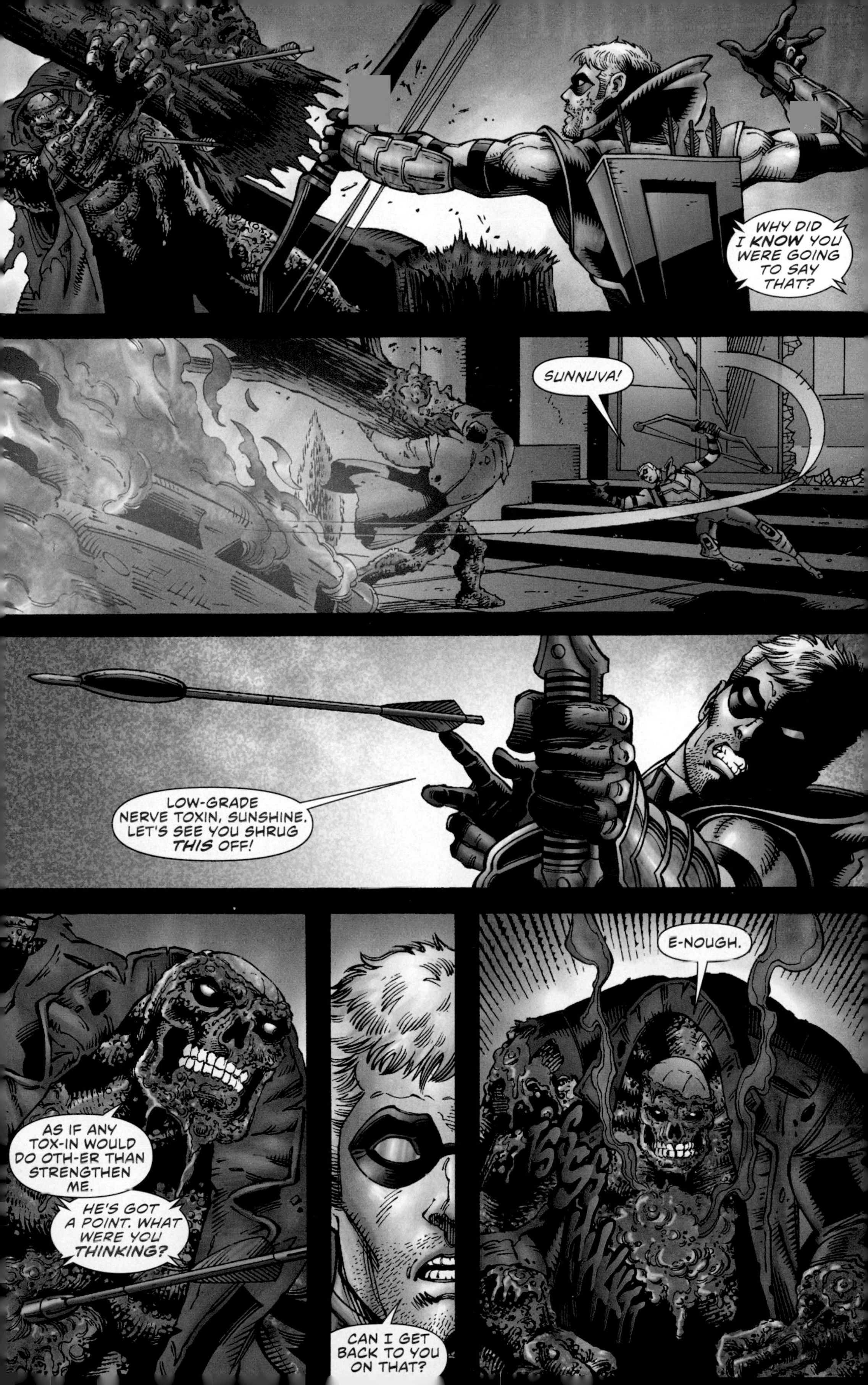
WHY DID I KNOW YOU WERE GOING TO SAY THAT?
SUNNUVA!
LOW-GRADE NERVE TOXIN, SUNSHINE. LET'S SEE YOU SHRUG THIS OFF!
AS IF ANY TOX-IN WOULD DO OTH-ER THAN STRENGTHEN ME.
HE'S GOT A POINT. WHAT WERE YOU THINKING?
CAN I GET BACK TO YOU ON THAT?
E-NOUGH.

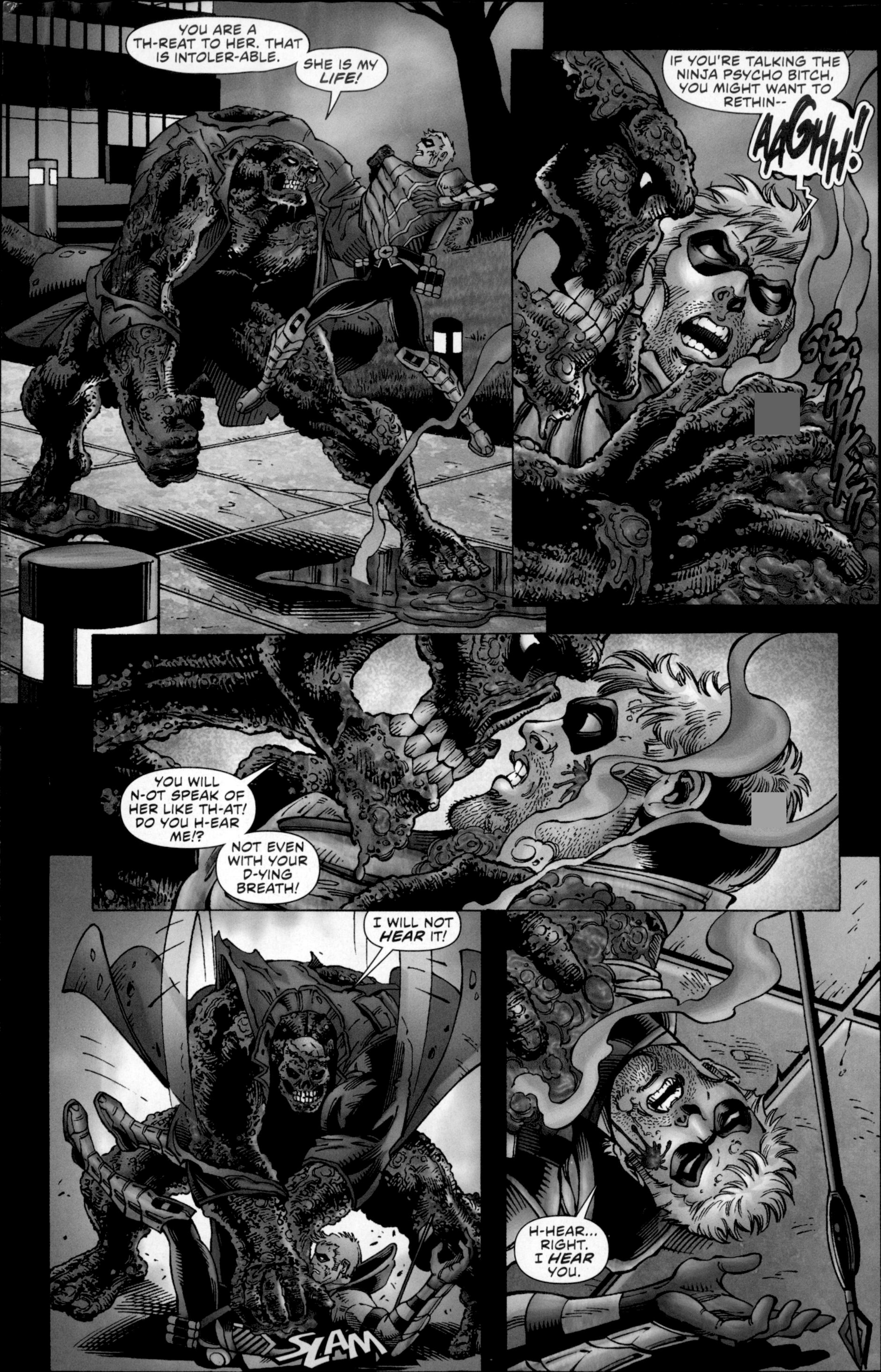
YOU ARE A TH-REAT TO HER. THAT IS INTOLER-ABLE.
SHE IS MY LIFE!
IF YOU'RE TALKING THE NINJA PSYCHO BITCH, YOU MIGHT WANT TO RETHIN--
AAGHH!
YOU WILL N-OT SPEAK OF HER LIKE TH-AT! DO YOU H-EAR ME!?
NOT EVEN WITH YOUR D-YING BREATH!
I WILL NOT HEAR IT!
SLAM
H-HEAR... RIGHT. I HEAR YOU.

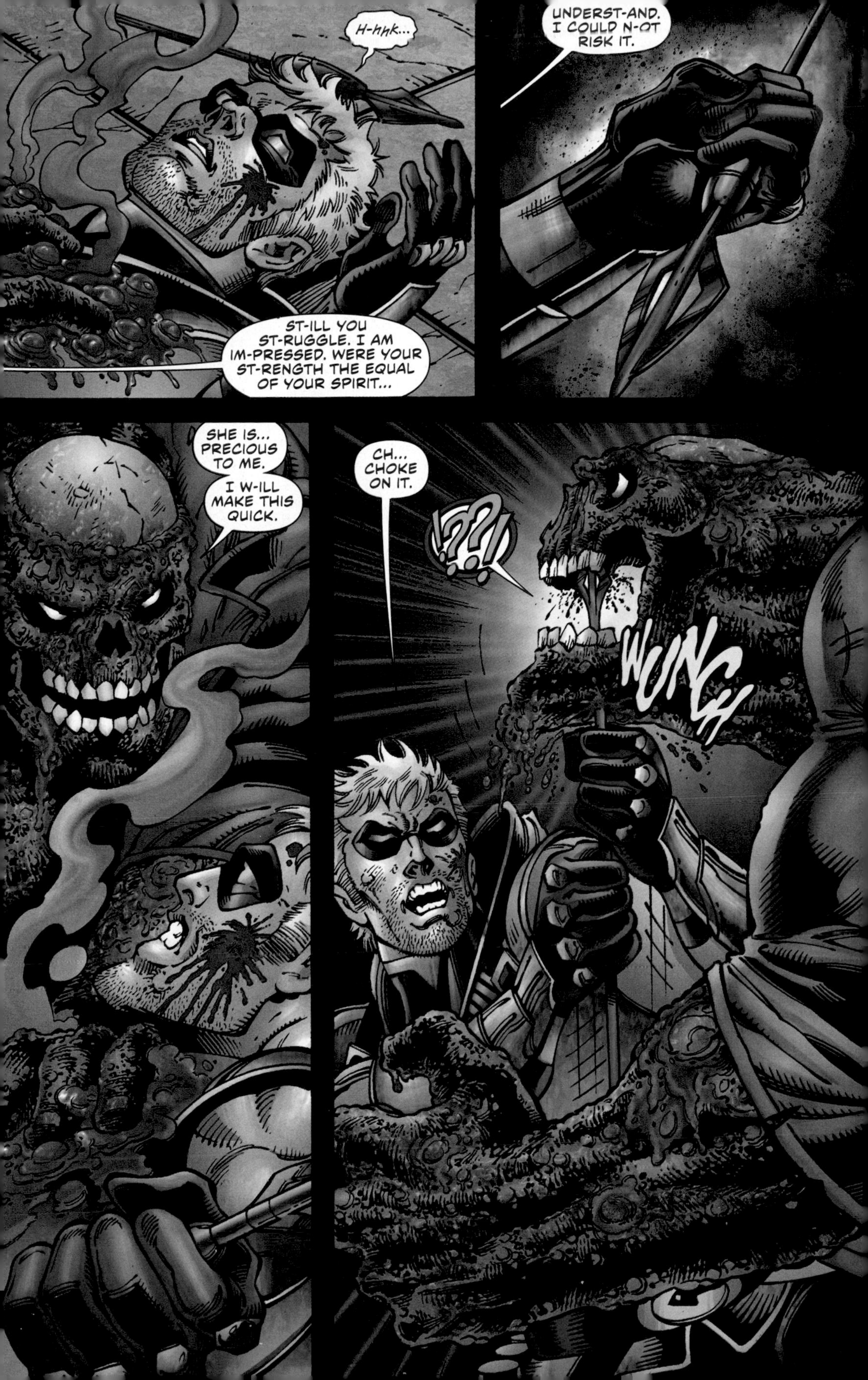
H-HNK...
UNDERST-AND. I COULD N-OT RISK IT.
ST-ILL YOU ST-RUGGLE. I AM IM-PRESSED. WERE YOUR ST-RENGTH THE EQUAL OF YOUR SPIRIT...
SHE IS... PRECIOUS TO ME.
I W-ILL MAKE THIS QUICK.
CH... CHOKE ON IT.
!??!
WUNCH

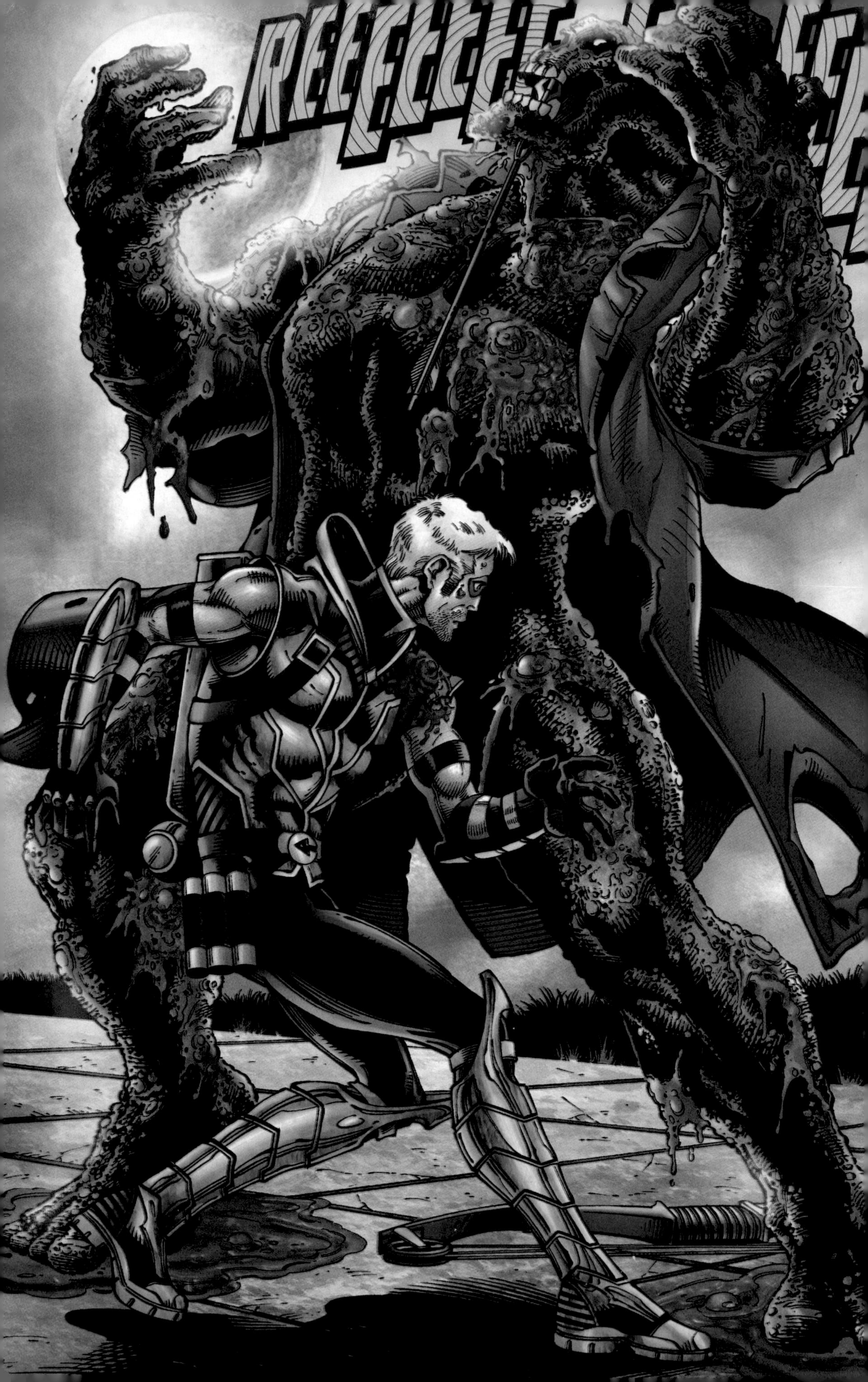

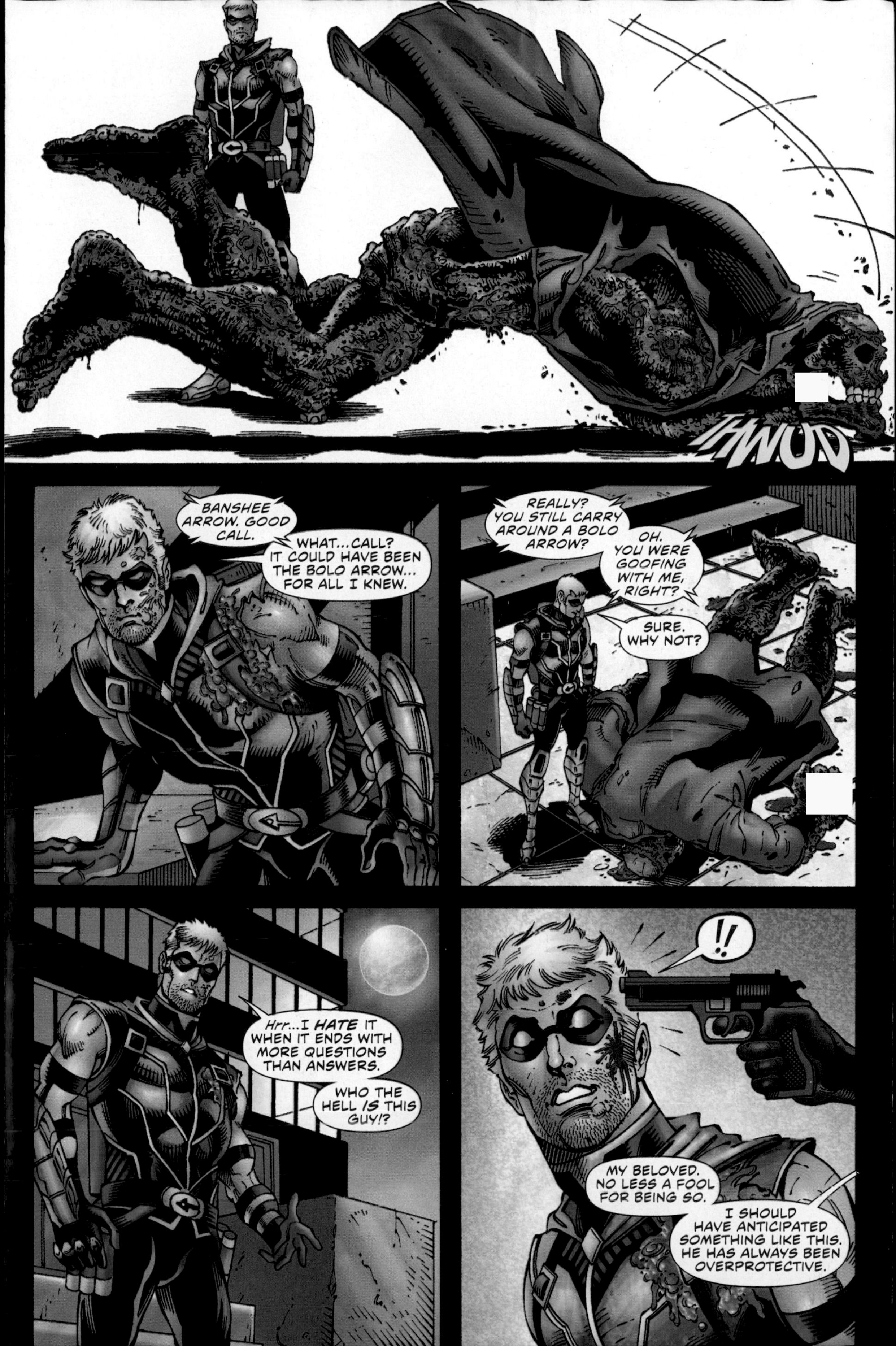
THWUD
BANSHEE ARROW. GOOD CALL.
WHAT...CALL? IT COULD HAVE BEEN THE BOLO ARROW... FOR ALL I KNEW.
REALLY? YOU STILL CARRY AROUND A BOLO ARROW?
OH. YOU WERE GOOFING WITH ME, RIGHT?
SURE. WHY NOT?
Hrr...I HATE IT WHEN IT ENDS WITH MORE QUESTIONS THAN ANSWERS.
WHO THE HELL IS THIS GUY!?
!!
MY BELOVED. NO LESS A FOOL FOR BEING SO.
I SHOULD HAVE ANTICIPATED SOMETHING LIKE THIS. HE HAS ALWAYS BEEN OVERPROTECTIVE.

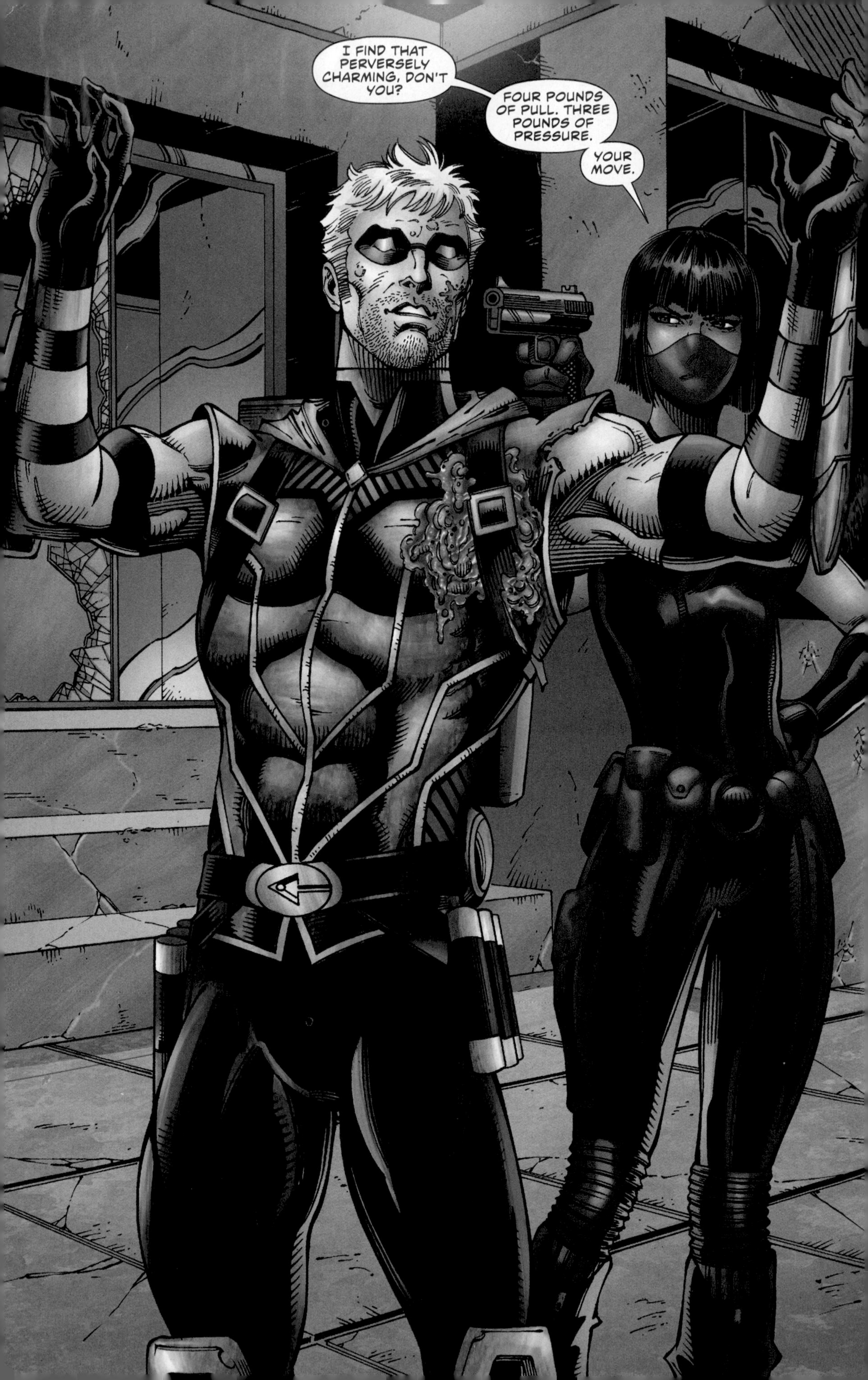
I FIND THAT PERVERSELY CHARMING, DON'T YOU?
FOUR POUNDS OF PULL. THREE POUNDS OF PRESSURE.
YOUR MOVE.

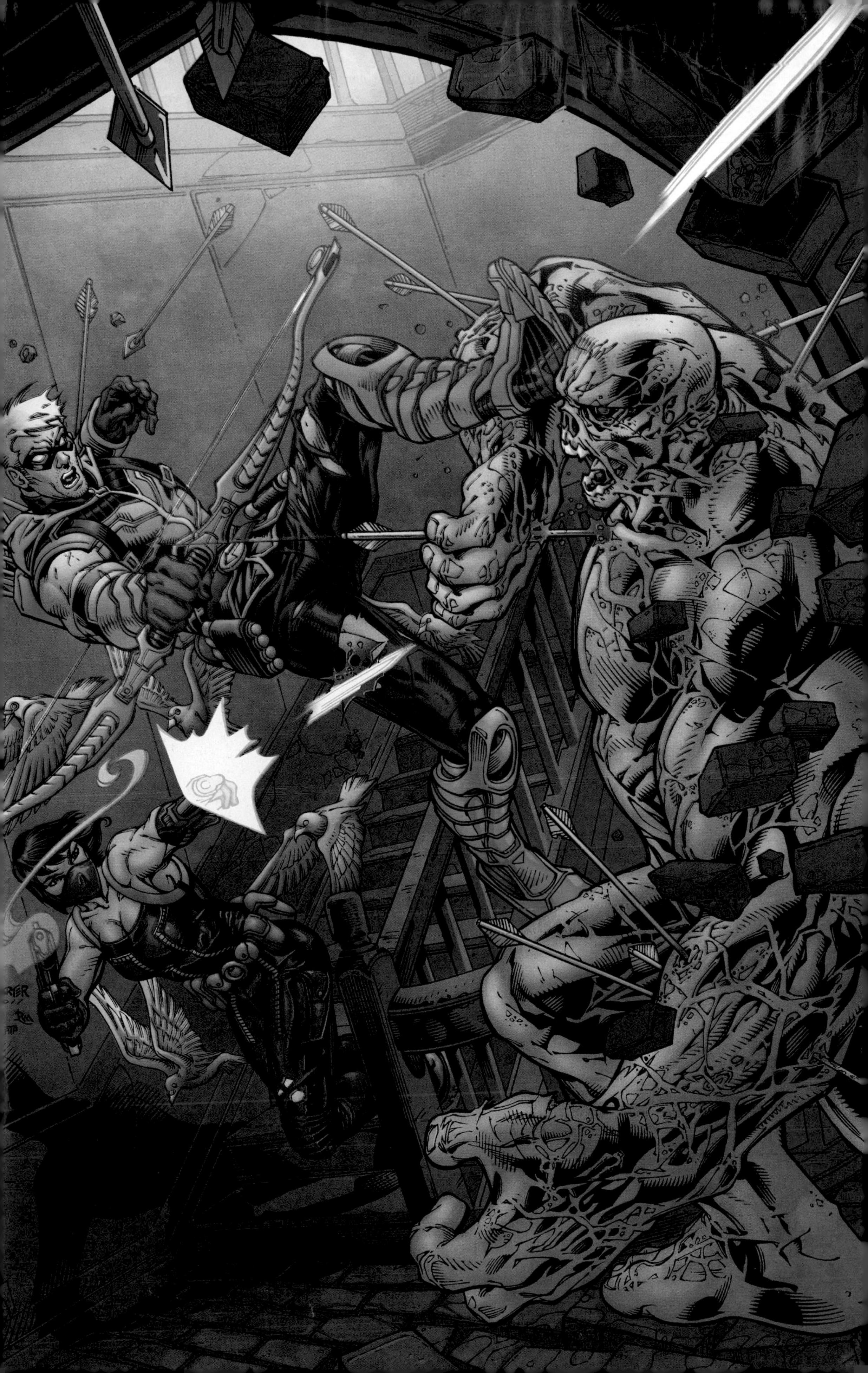

LOVERS & OTHER DANGERS

KEITH GIFFEN
writer / co-plotter

DAN JURGENS
layouts / co-plotter

IGNACIO CALERO
penciller

RAY McCARTHY
inker

cover by HOWARD PORTER, RAY McCARTHY & ALLEN PASSALAQUA

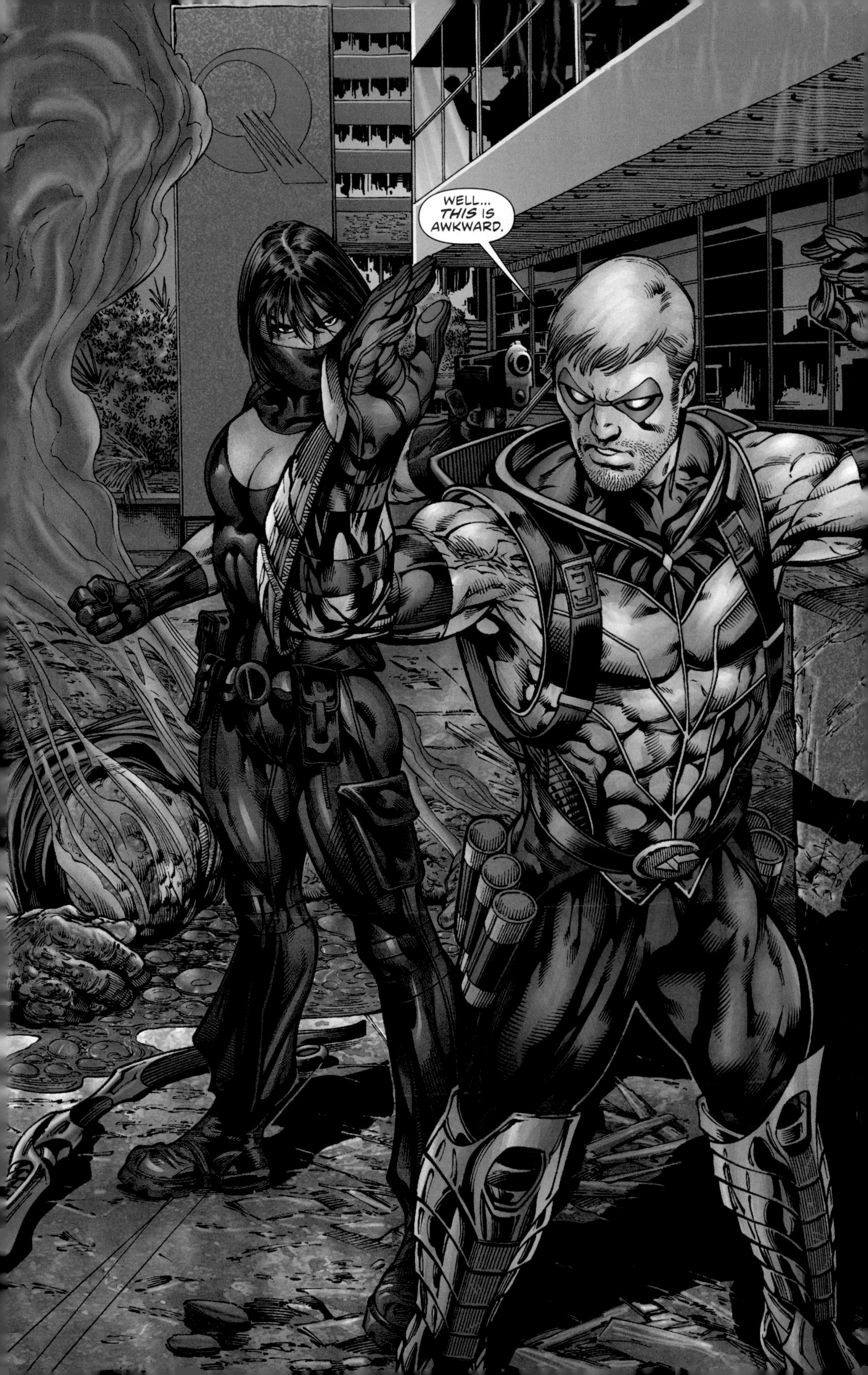
WELL... *THIS* IS AWKWARD.

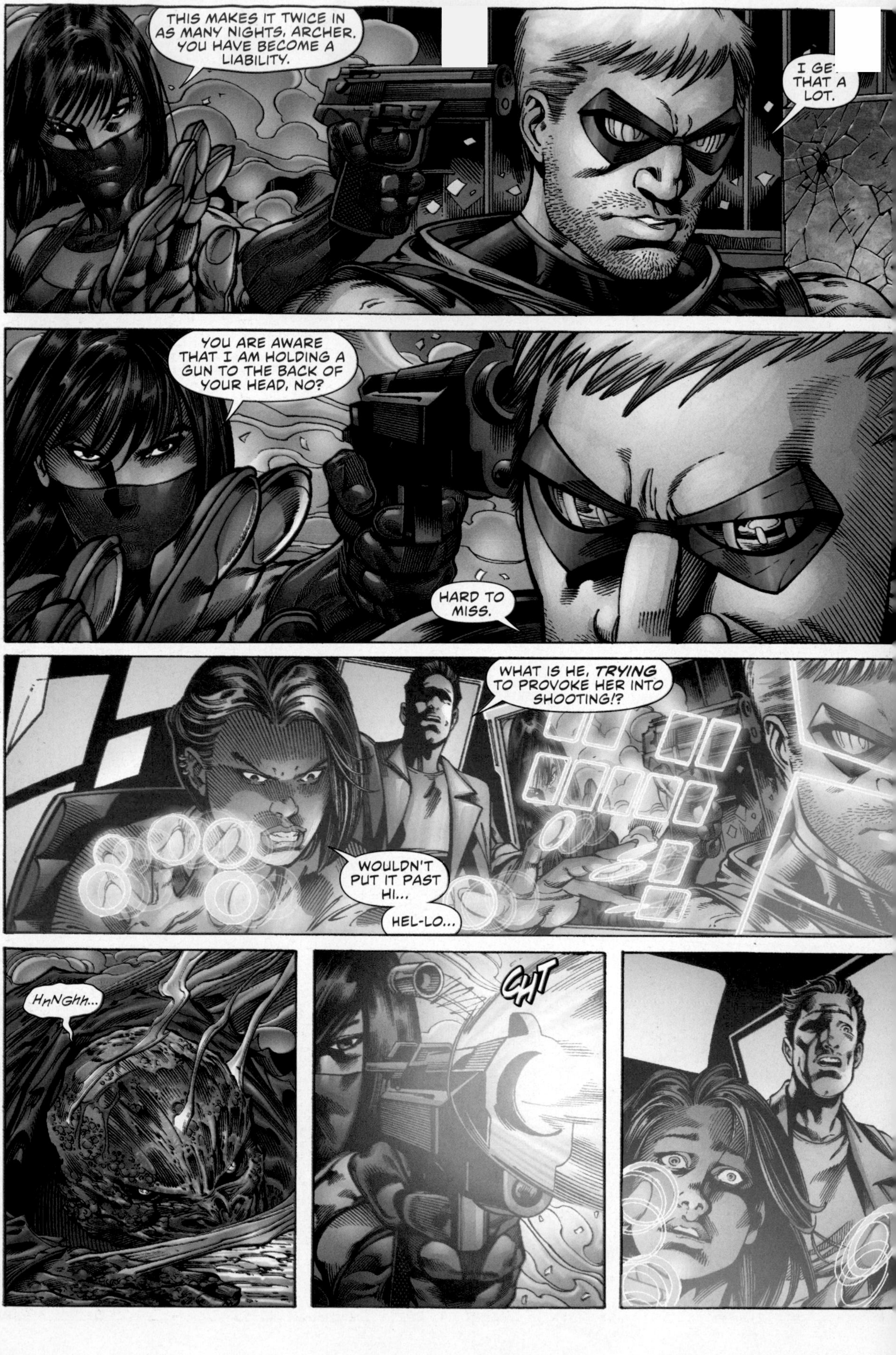
THIS MAKES IT TWICE IN AS MANY NIGHTS, ARCHER. YOU HAVE BECOME A LIABILITY.
THAT A LOT.
YOU ARE AWARE THAT I AM HOLDING A GUN TO THE BACK OF YOUR HEAD, NO?
HARD TO MISS.
WHAT IS HE, TRYING TO PROVOKE HER INTO SHOOTING!?
WOULDN'T PUT IT PAST HI...
HEL-LO...
HnNGhh...
CHT

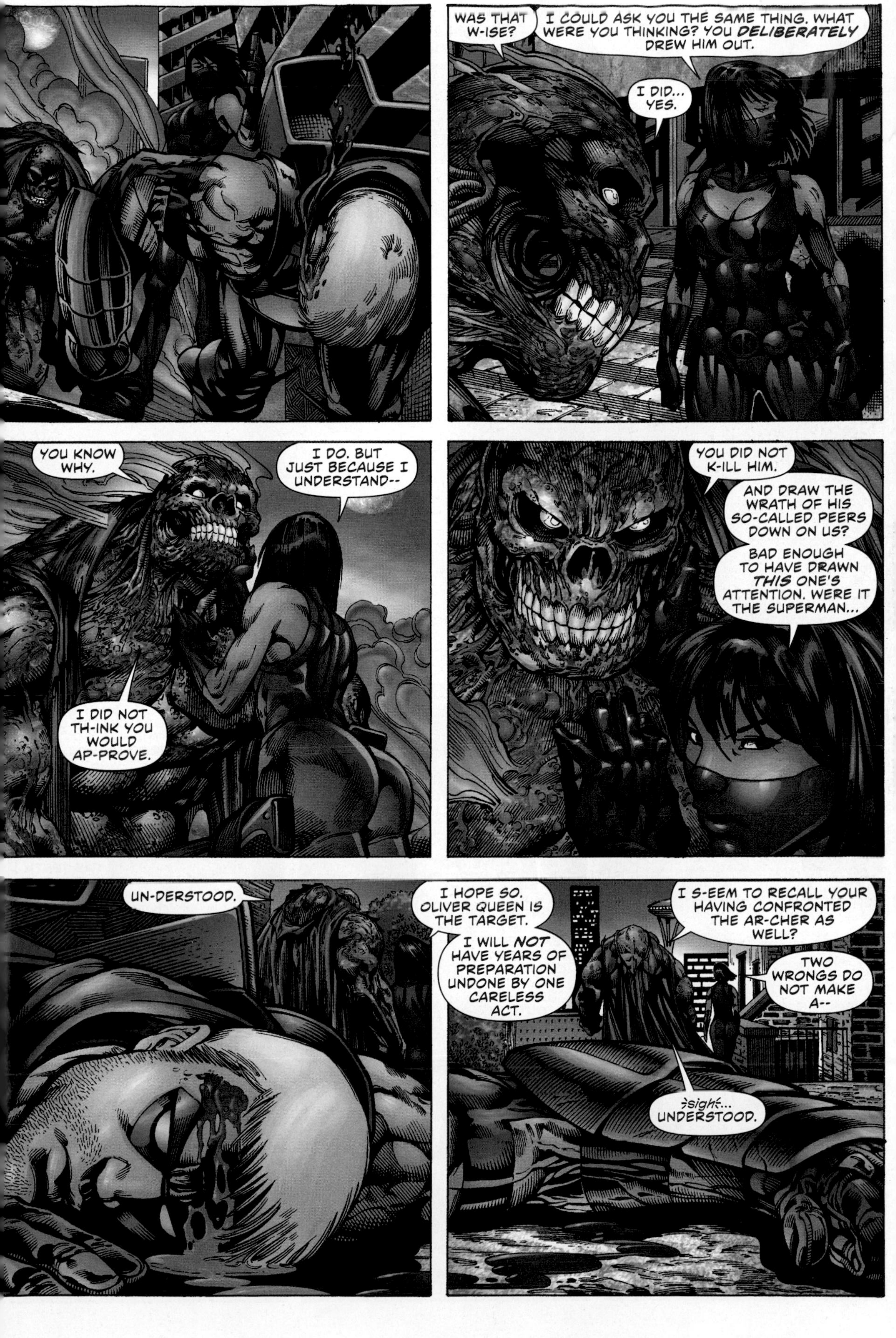
WAS THAT W-ISE?
I COULD ASK YOU THE SAME THING. WHAT WERE YOU THINKING? YOU DELIBERATELY DREW HIM OUT.
I DID... YES.
YOU KNOW WHY.
I DO. BUT JUST BECAUSE I UNDERSTAND--
I DID NOT TH-INK YOU WOULD AP-PROVE.
YOU DID NOT K-ILL HIM.
AND DRAW THE WRATH OF HIS SO-CALLED PEERS DOWN ON US?
BAD ENOUGH TO HAVE DRAWN THIS ONE'S ATTENTION. WERE IT THE SUPERMAN...
UN-DERSTOOD.
I HOPE SO. OLIVER QUEEN IS THE TARGET.
I WILL NOT HAVE YEARS OF PREPARATION UNDONE BY ONE CARELESS ACT.
I S-EEM TO RECALL YOUR HAVING CONFRONTED THE AR-CHER AS WELL?
TWO WRONGS DO NOT MAKE A--
sigh... UNDERSTOOD.

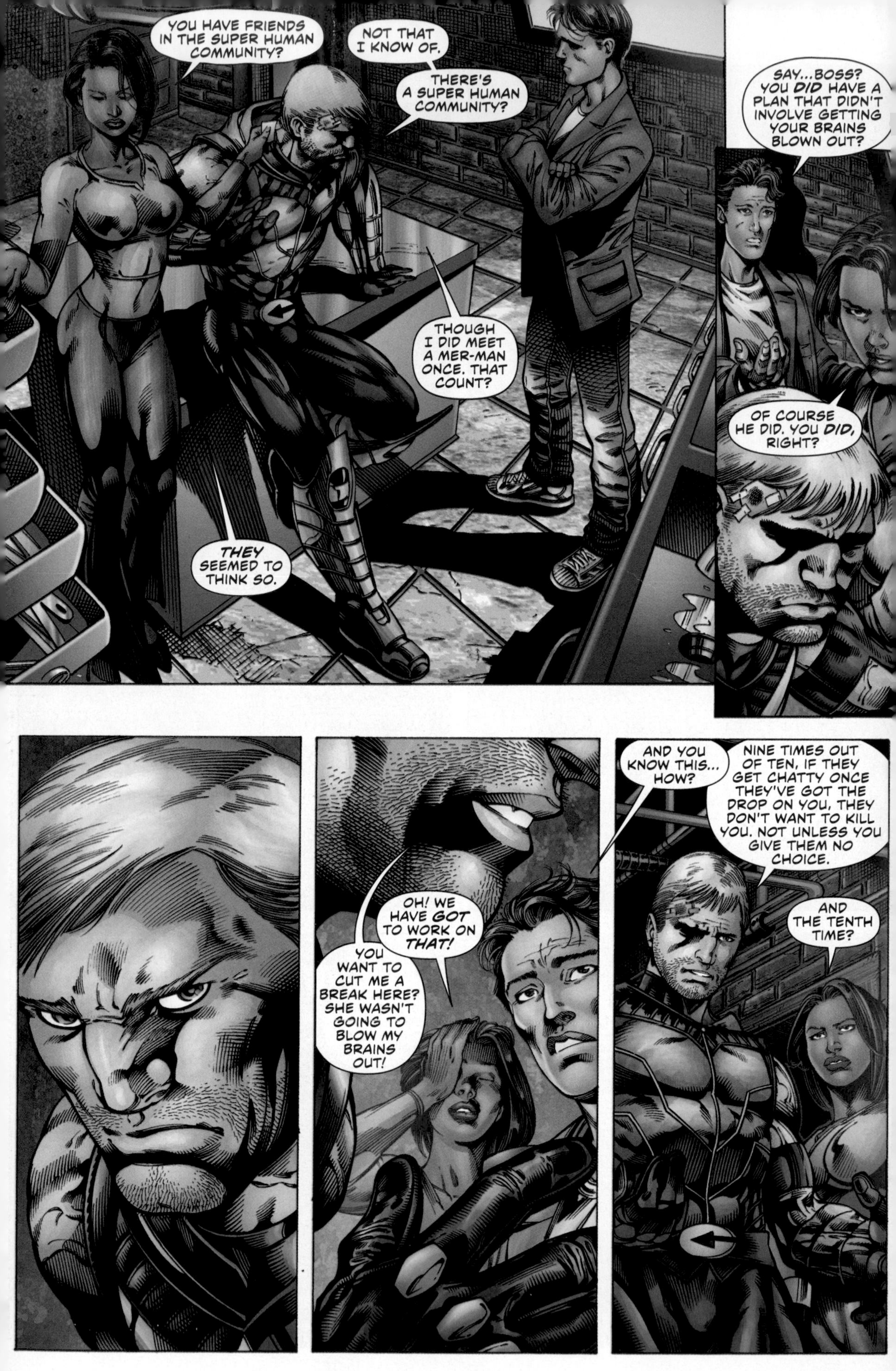
YOU HAVE FRIENDS IN THE SUPER HUMAN COMMUNITY?
NOT THAT I KNOW OF.
THERE'S A SUPER HUMAN COMMUNITY?
THOUGH I DID MEET A MER-MAN ONCE. THAT COUNT?
THEY SEEMED TO THINK SO.
SAY...BOSS? YOU *DID* HAVE A PLAN THAT DIDN'T INVOLVE GETTING YOUR BRAINS BLOWN OUT?
OF COURSE HE DID. YOU *DID*, RIGHT?
OH! WE HAVE *GOT* TO WORK ON *THAT!*
YOU WANT TO CUT ME A BREAK HERE? SHE WASN'T GOING TO BLOW MY BRAINS OUT!
AND YOU KNOW THIS... HOW?
NINE TIMES OUT OF TEN, IF THEY GET CHATTY ONCE THEY'VE GOT THE DROP ON YOU, THEY DON'T WANT TO KILL YOU. NOT UNLESS YOU GIVE THEM NO CHOICE.
AND THE TENTH TIME?

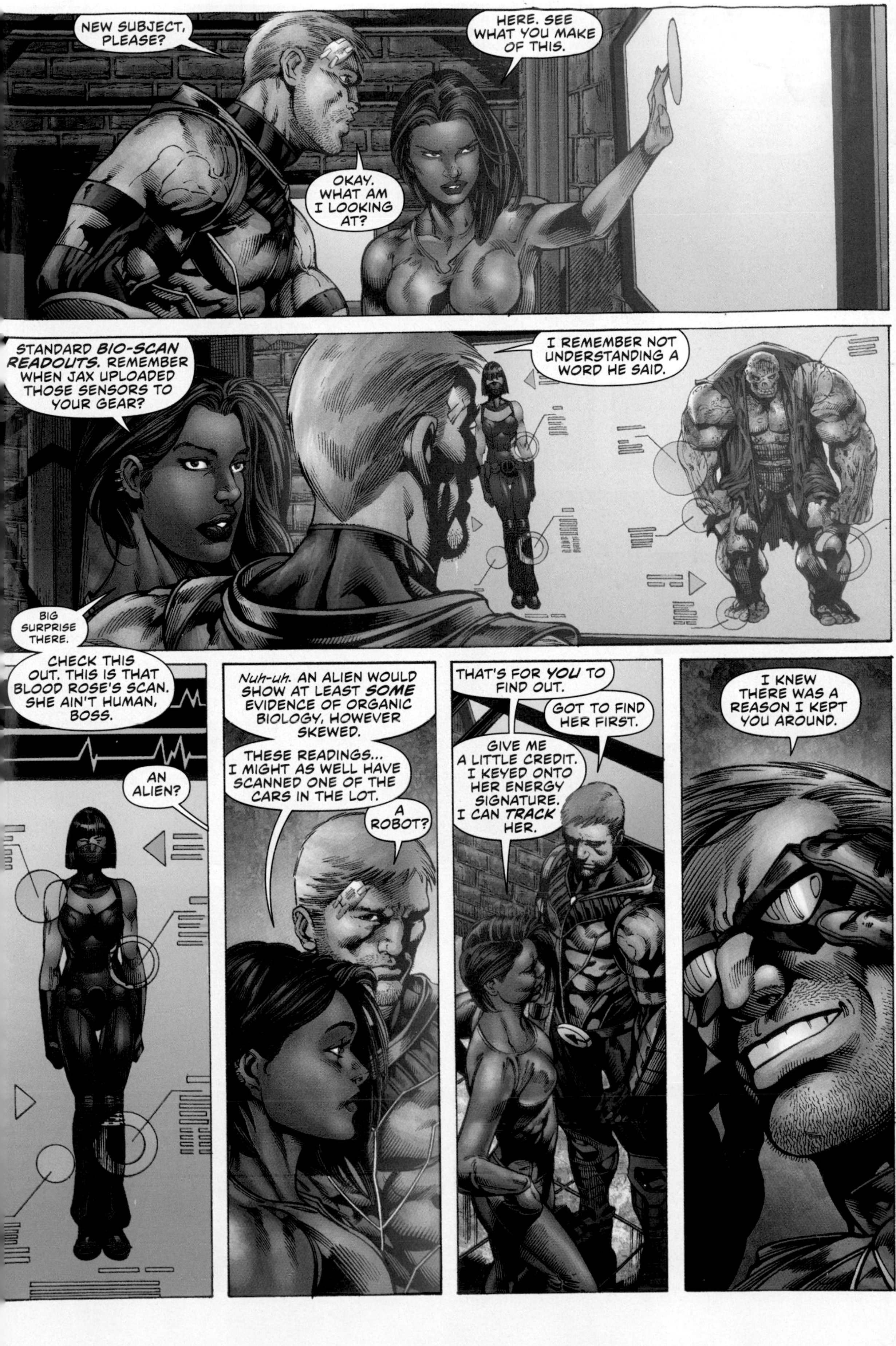
NEW SUBJECT, PLEASE?
HERE. SEE WHAT YOU MAKE OF THIS.
OKAY. WHAT AM I LOOKING AT?
STANDARD *BIO-SCAN READOUTS.* REMEMBER WHEN JAX UPLOADED THOSE SENSORS TO YOUR GEAR?
I REMEMBER NOT UNDERSTANDING A WORD HE SAID.
BIG SURPRISE THERE.
CHECK THIS OUT. THIS IS THAT BLOOD ROSE'S SCAN. SHE AIN'T HUMAN, BOSS.
AN ALIEN?
Nuh-uh. AN ALIEN WOULD SHOW AT LEAST *SOME* EVIDENCE OF ORGANIC BIOLOGY, HOWEVER SKEWED.
THESE READINGS... I MIGHT AS WELL HAVE SCANNED ONE OF THE CARS IN THE LOT.
A ROBOT?
THAT'S FOR *YOU* TO FIND OUT.
GOT TO FIND HER FIRST.
GIVE ME A LITTLE CREDIT. I KEYED ONTO HER ENERGY SIGNATURE. I CAN *TRACK* HER.
I KNEW THERE WAS A REASON I KEPT YOU AROUND.

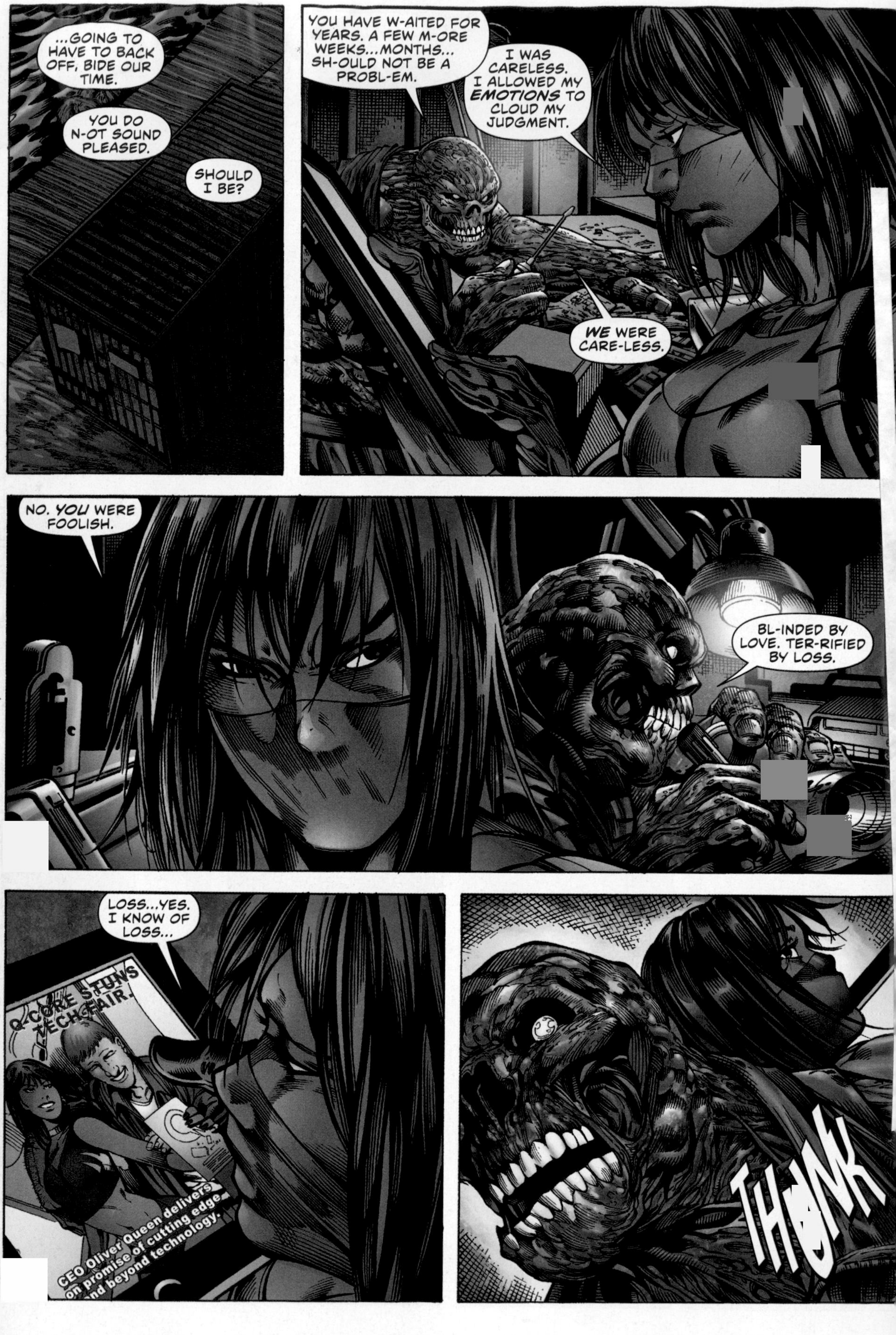
...GOING TO HAVE TO BACK OFF, BIDE OUR TIME.
YOU DO N-OT SOUND PLEASED.
SHOULD I BE?
YOU HAVE W-AITED FOR YEARS. A FEW M-ORE WEEKS...MONTHS... SH-OULD NOT BE A PROBL-EM.
I WAS CARELESS. I ALLOWED MY EMOTIONS TO CLOUD MY JUDGMENT.
WE WERE CARE-LESS.
NO. YOU WERE FOOLISH.
BL-INDED BY LOVE. TER-RIFIED BY LOSS.
LOSS...YES. I KNOW OF LOSS...
Q-CORE STUNS TECH FAIR.
CEO Oliver Queen delivers on promise of cutting edge and beyond technology.
THUNK

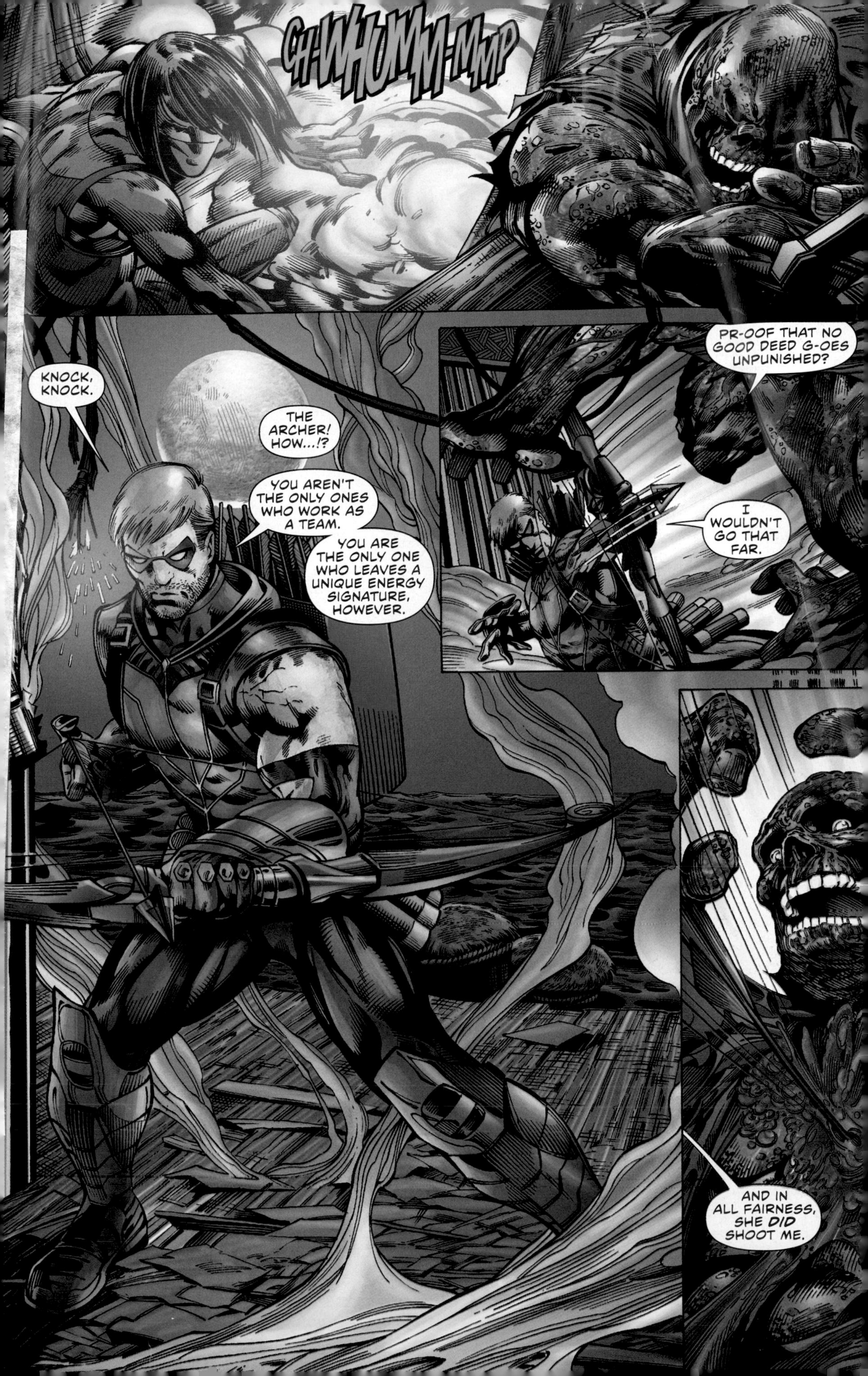
CH-WHUMM-MMP
KNOCK, KNOCK.
THE ARCHER! HOW...!?
YOU AREN'T THE ONLY ONES WHO WORK AS A TEAM.
YOU ARE THE ONLY ONE WHO LEAVES A UNIQUE ENERGY SIGNATURE, HOWEVER.
PR-OOF THAT NO GOOD DEED G-OES UNPUNISHED?
I WOULDN'T GO THAT FAR.
AND IN ALL FAIRNESS, SHE *DID* SHOOT ME.

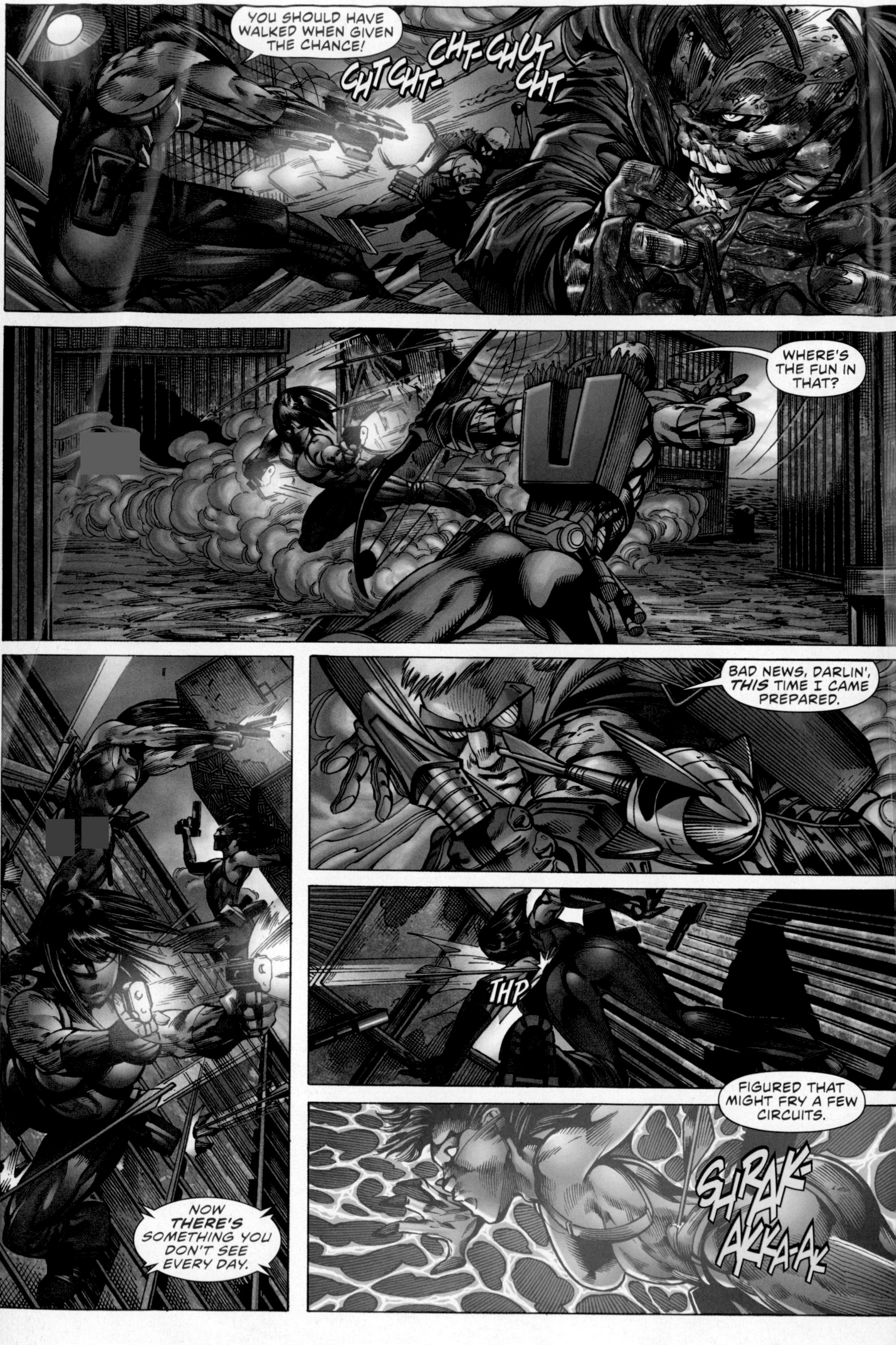
YOU SHOULD HAVE WALKED WHEN GIVEN THE CHANCE!
CHT CHT-
CHT-CHUT
CHT
WHERE'S THE FUN IN THAT?
NOW *THERE'S* SOMETHING YOU DON'T SEE EVERY DAY.
BAD NEWS, DARLIN', *THIS* TIME I CAME PREPARED.
THP
FIGURED THAT MIGHT FRY A FEW CIRCUITS.
SHRAK-
AKKA-AK

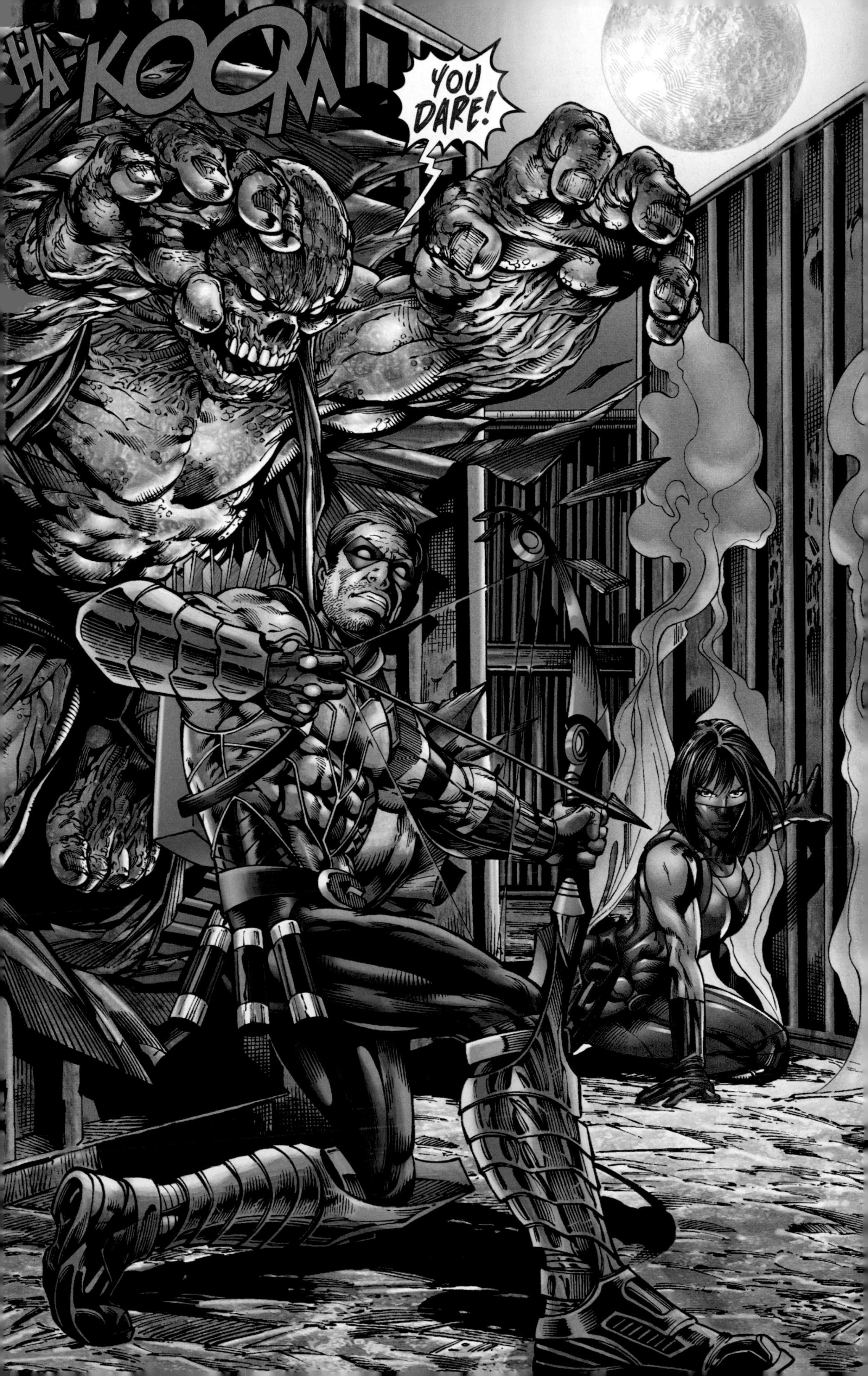
HA-KOOM!
YOU DARE!

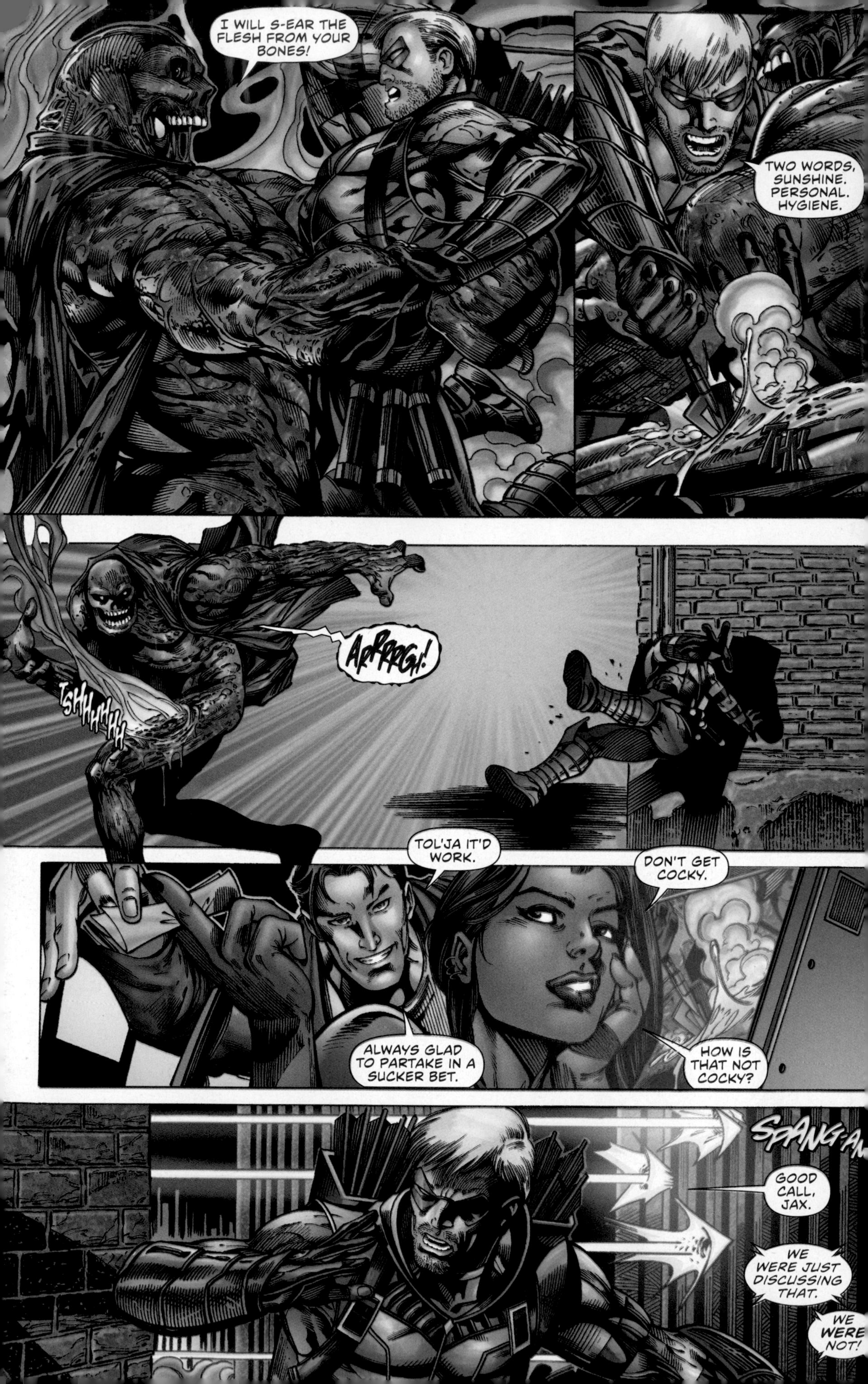
I WILL S-EAR THE FLESH FROM YOUR BONES!
TWO WORDS, SUNSHINE. PERSONAL. HYGIENE.
TCK
TSHHHHHH
ARRRRGH!
TOL'JA IT'D WORK.
DON'T GET COCKY.
ALWAYS GLAD TO PARTAKE IN A SUCKER BET.
HOW IS THAT NOT COCKY?
GOOD CALL, JAX.
WE WERE JUST DISCUSSING THAT.
WE WERE NOT!

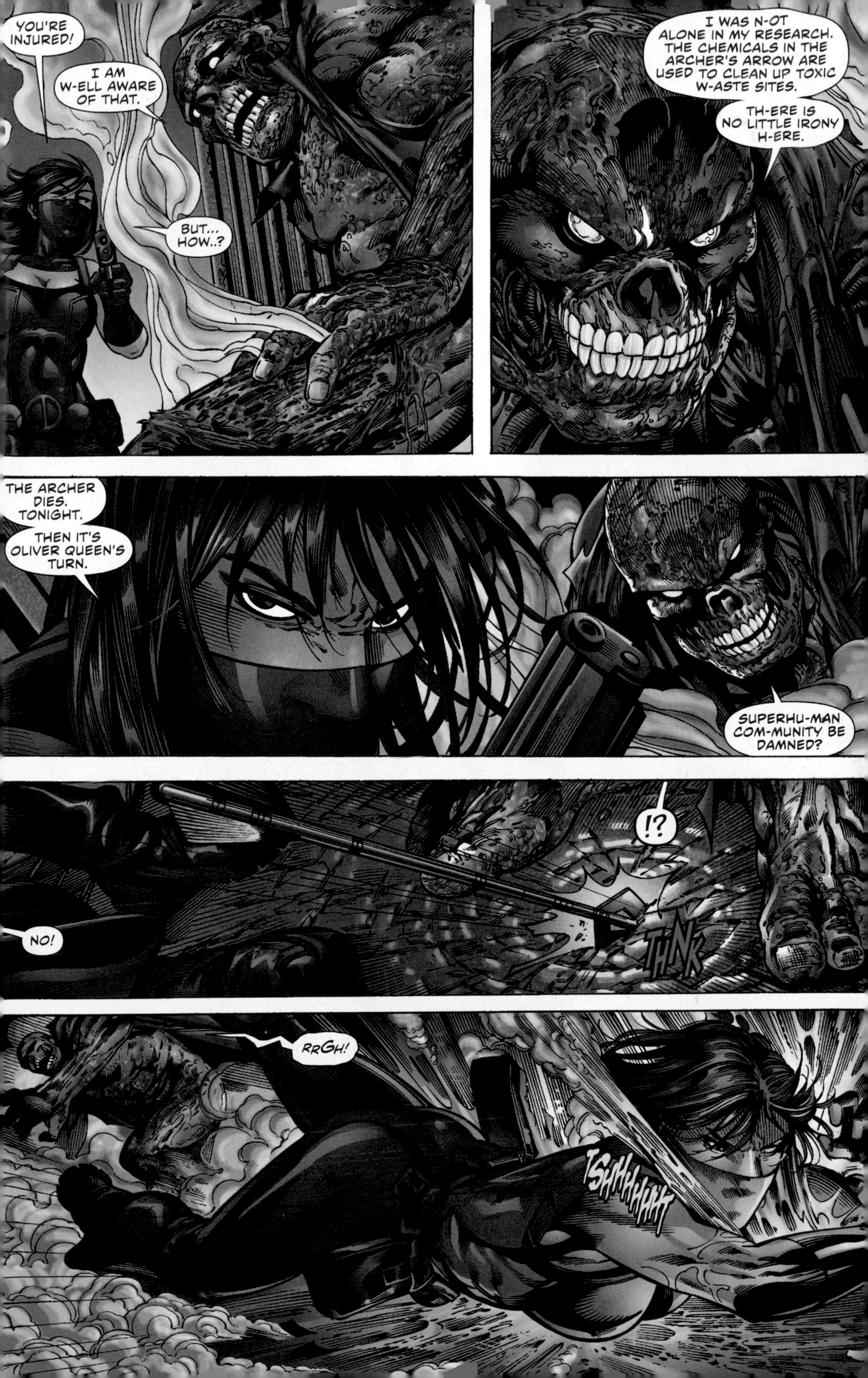
YOU'RE INJURED!
I AM W-ELL AWARE OF THAT.
BUT... HOW..?
I WAS N-OT ALONE IN MY RESEARCH. THE CHEMICALS IN THE ARCHER'S ARROW ARE USED TO CLEAN UP TOXIC W-ASTE SITES.
TH-ERE IS NO LITTLE IRONY H-ERE.
THE ARCHER DIES. TONIGHT.
THEN IT'S OLIVER QUEEN'S TURN.
SUPERHU-MAN COM-MUNITY BE DAMNED?
!?
NO!
THNK
RRGH!
TSHHHHHH

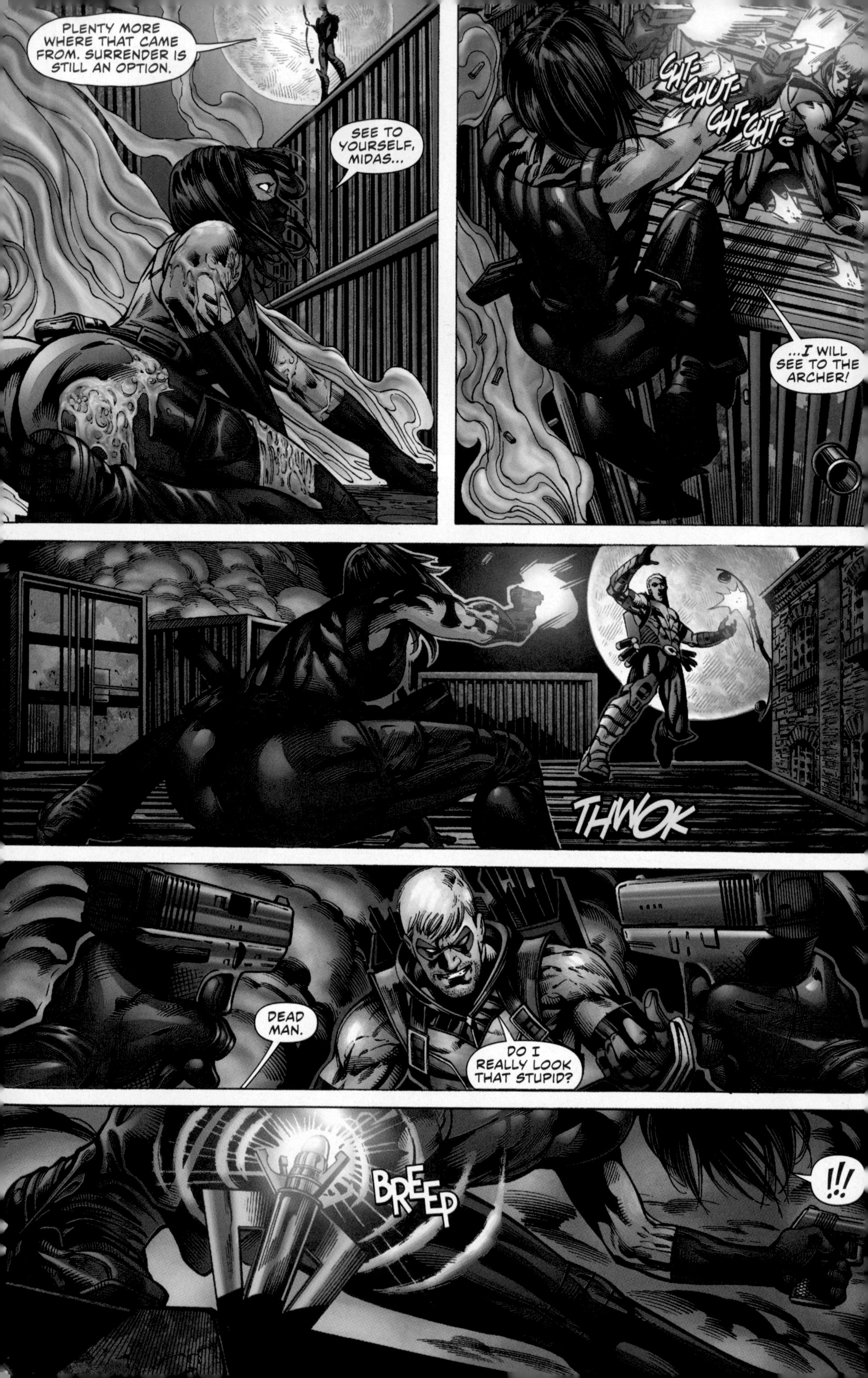
PLENTY MORE WHERE THAT CAME FROM. SURRENDER IS STILL AN OPTION.
SEE TO YOURSELF, MIDAS...
CHT-CHUT-CHT-CHT
...I WILL SEE TO THE ARCHER!
THWOK
DEAD MAN.
DO I REALLY LOOK THAT STUPID?
BREEEP
!!!

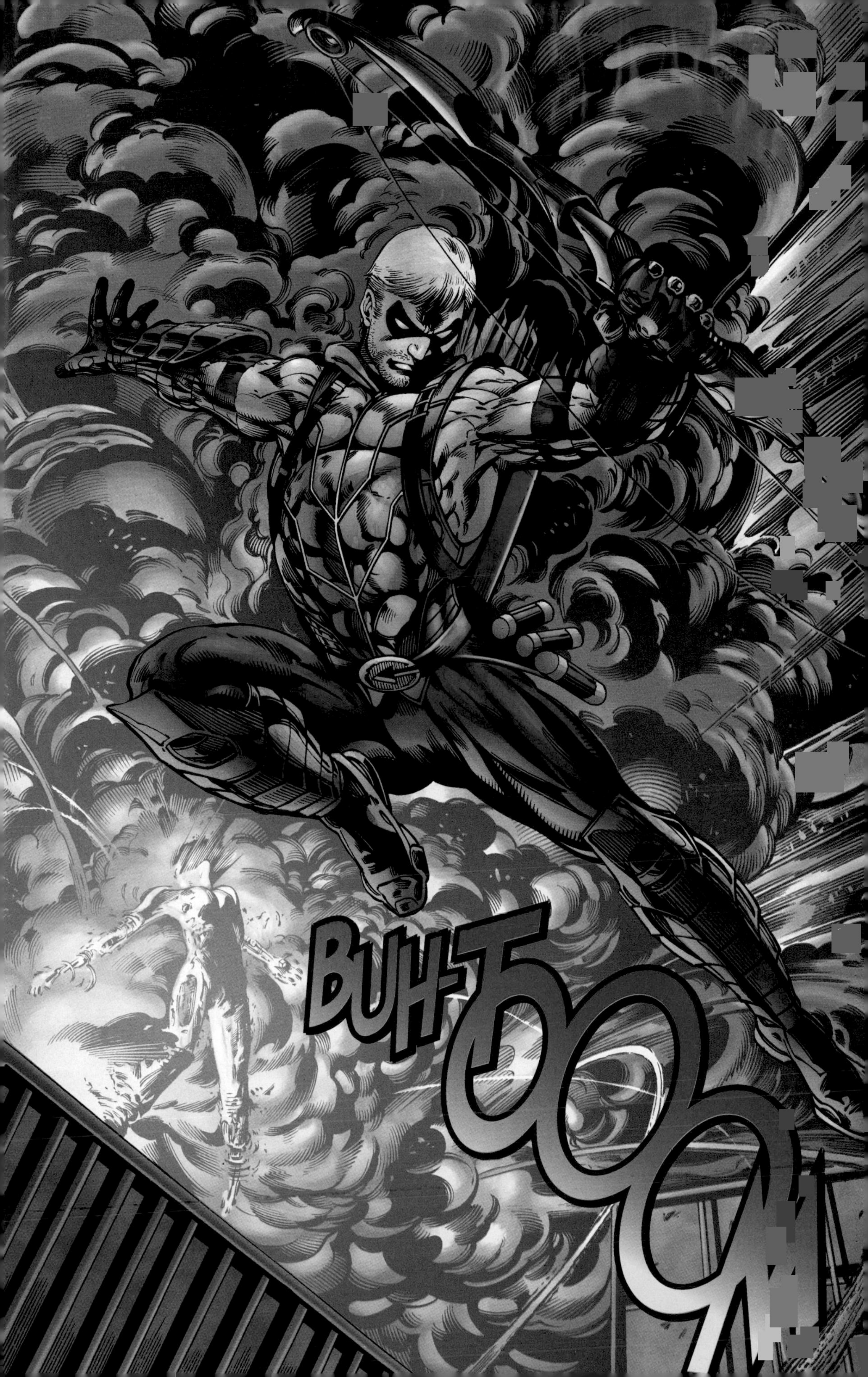
BUH-TOOOM

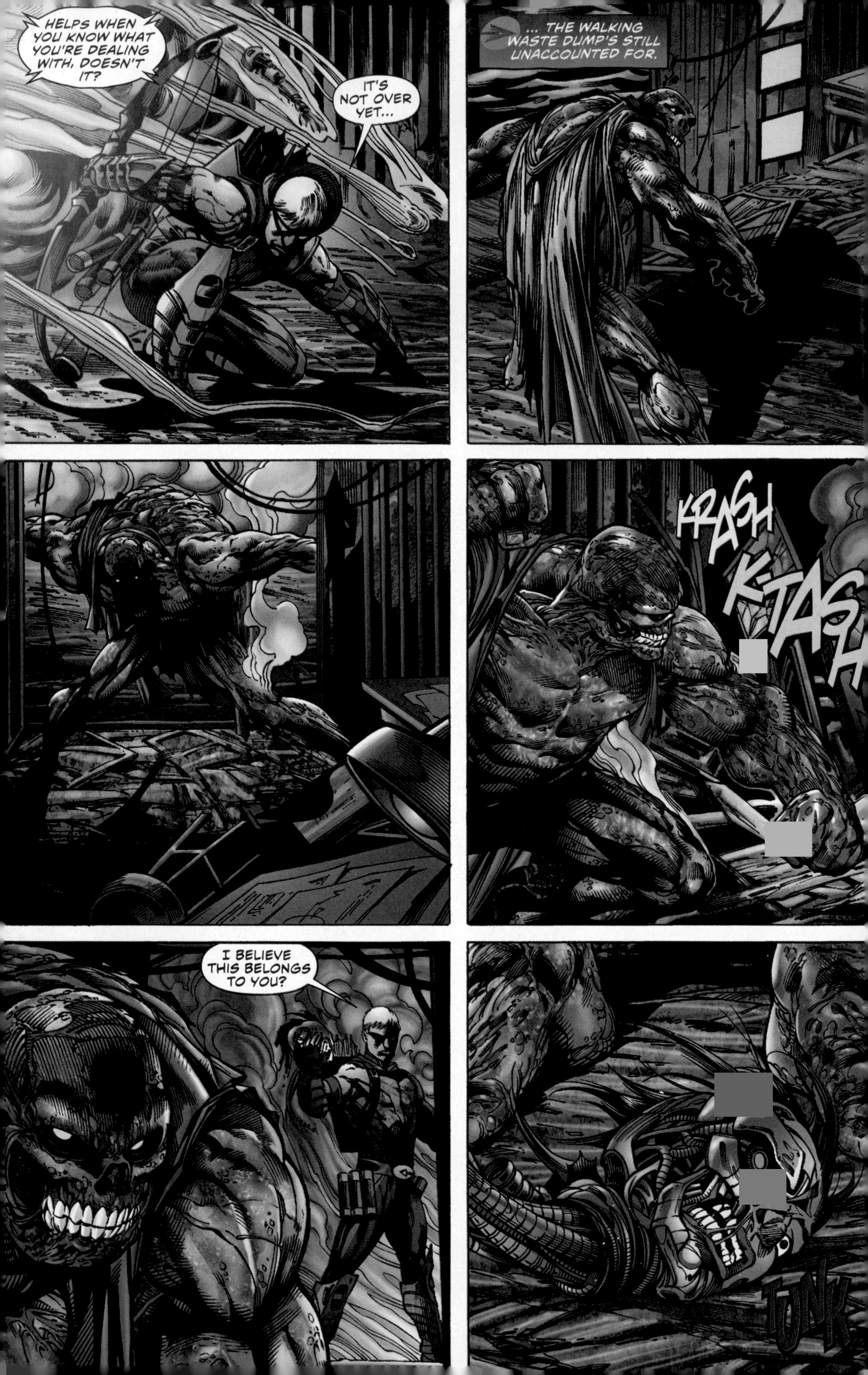
HELPS WHEN YOU KNOW WHAT YOU'RE DEALING WITH, DOESN'T IT?
IT'S NOT OVER YET...
... THE WALKING WASTE DUMP'S STILL UNACCOUNTED FOR.
KRASH
K-TASH
I BELIEVE THIS BELONGS TO YOU?
TUNK

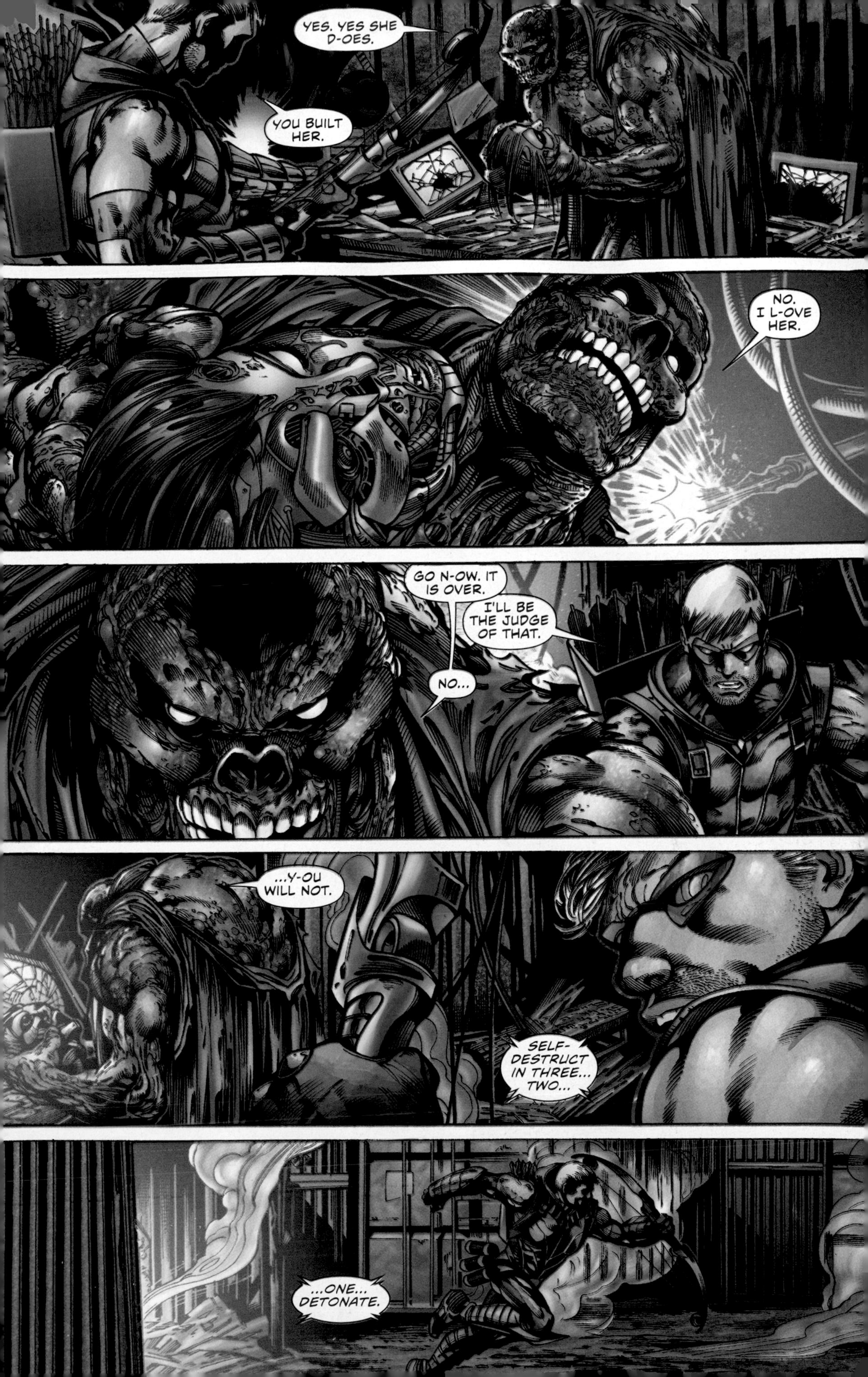
YES. YES SHE D-OES.
YOU BUILT HER.
NO. I L-OVE HER.
GO N-OW. IT IS OVER.
I'LL BE THE JUDGE OF THAT.
NO...
...Y-OU WILL NOT.
SELF-DESTRUCT IN THREE... TWO...
...ONE... DETONATE.

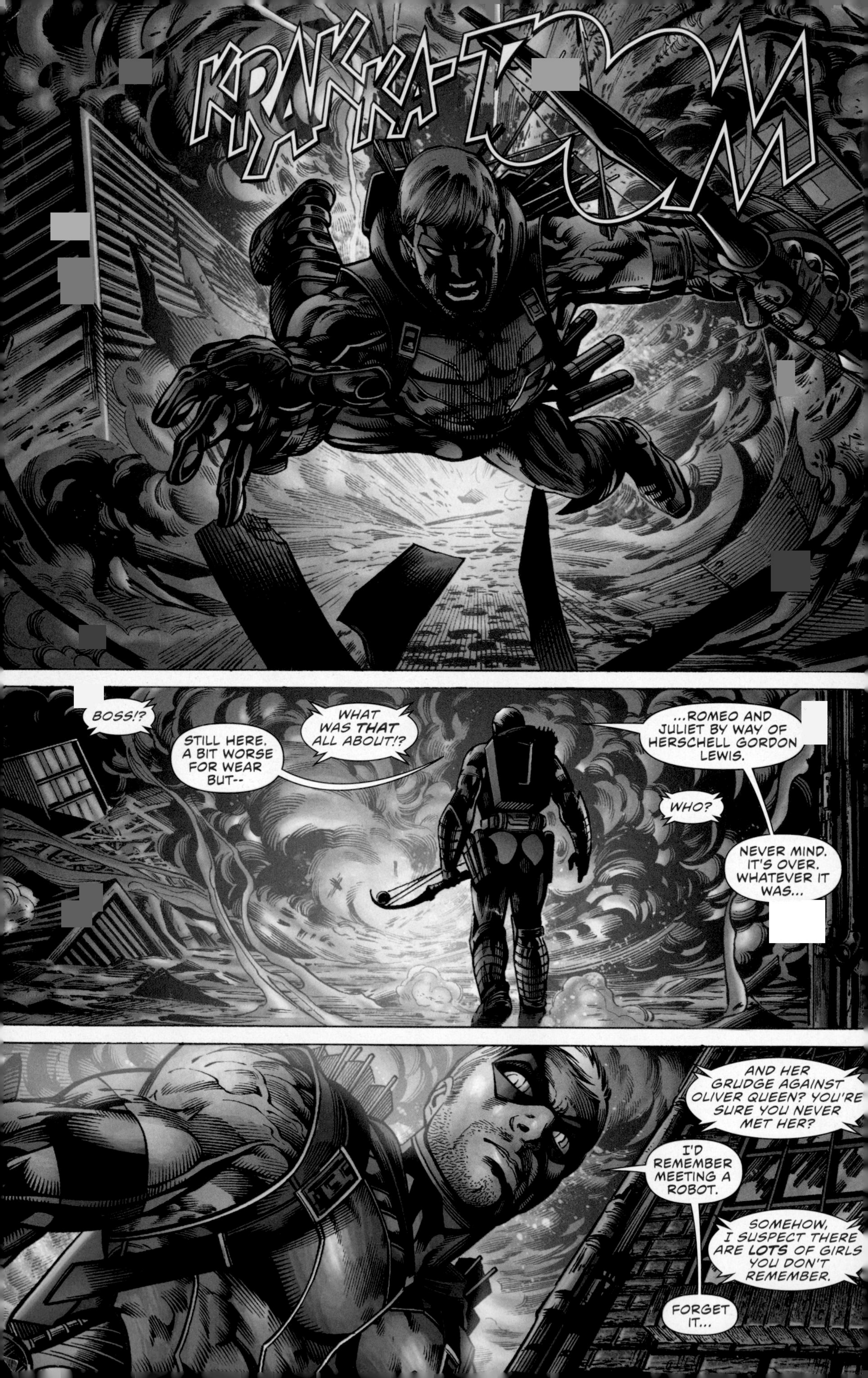
KRAKKA-TOOM
BOSS!?
STILL HERE. A BIT WORSE FOR WEAR BUT--
WHAT WAS **THAT** ALL ABOUT!?
...ROMEO AND JULIET BY WAY OF HERSCHELL GORDON LEWIS.
WHO?
NEVER MIND. IT'S OVER. WHATEVER IT WAS...
AND HER GRUDGE AGAINST OLIVER QUEEN? YOU'RE SURE YOU NEVER MET HER?
I'D REMEMBER MEETING A ROBOT.
SOMEHOW, I SUSPECT THERE ARE **LOTS** OF GIRLS YOU DON'T REMEMBER.
FORGET IT...

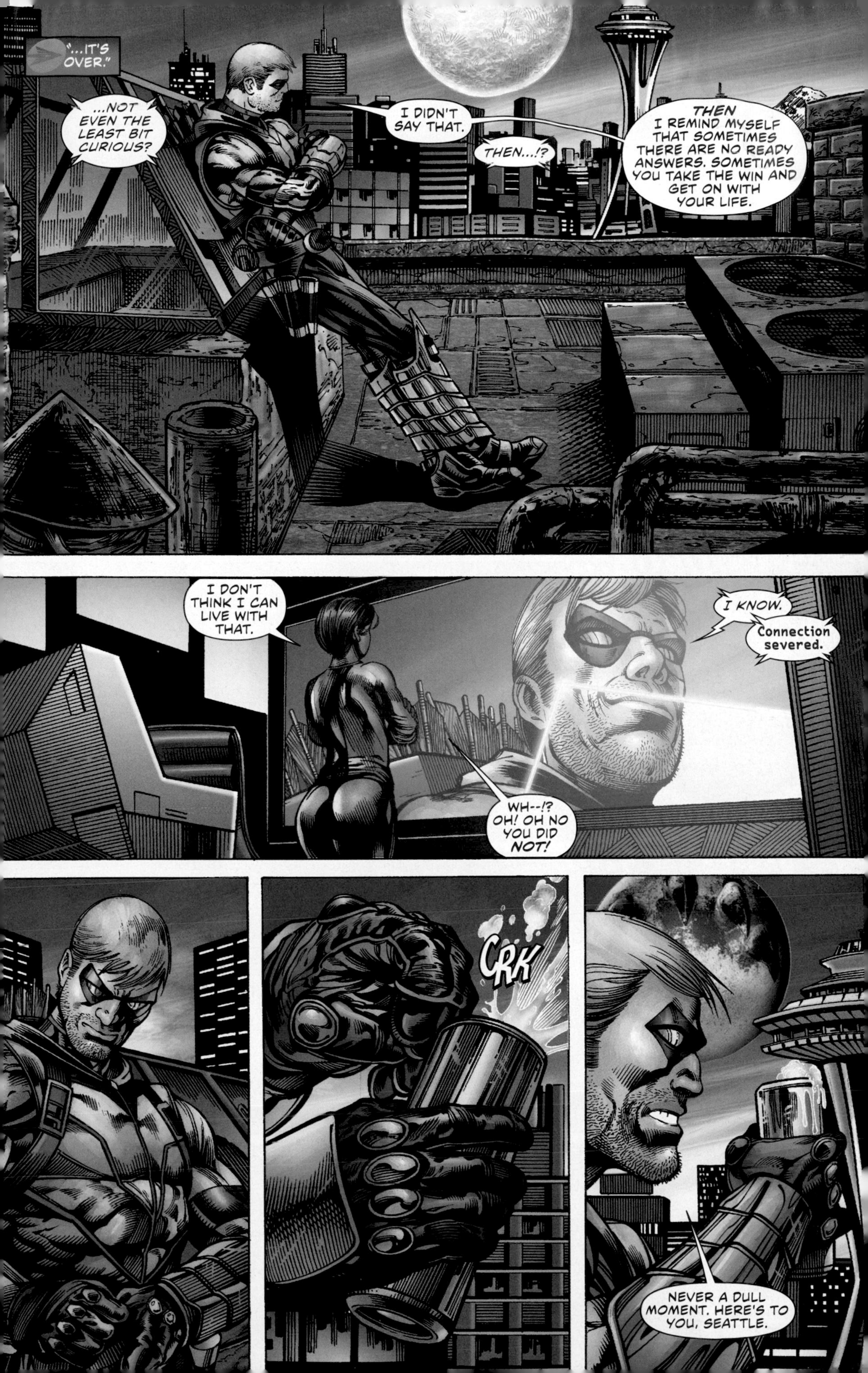
"...IT'S OVER."
...NOT EVEN THE LEAST BIT CURIOUS?
I DIDN'T SAY THAT.
THEN...!?
THEN I REMIND MYSELF THAT SOMETIMES THERE ARE NO READY ANSWERS. SOMETIMES YOU TAKE THE WIN AND GET ON WITH YOUR LIFE.
I DON'T THINK I CAN LIVE WITH THAT.
I KNOW.
Connection severed.
WH--!? OH! OH NO YOU DID NOT!
CRK
NEVER A DULL MOMENT. HERE'S TO YOU, SEATTLE.

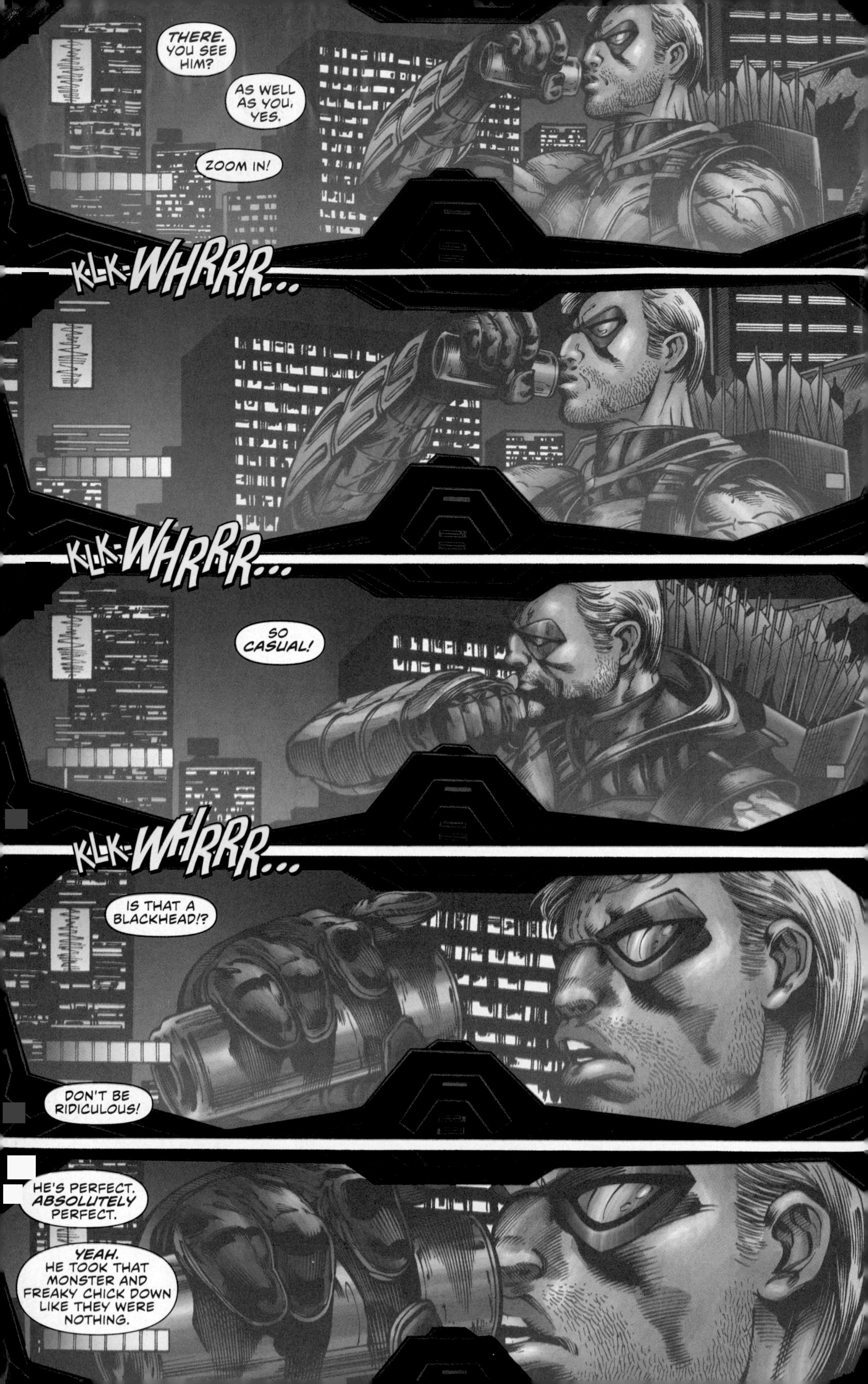
THERE. YOU SEE HIM?
AS WELL AS YOU, YES.
ZOOM IN!
K-LK-WHRRR...
K-LK-WHRRR...
SO CASUAL!
K-LK-WHRRR...
IS THAT A BLACKHEAD!?
DON'T BE RIDICULOUS!
HE'S PERFECT. ABSOLUTELY PERFECT.
YEAH. HE TOOK THAT MONSTER AND FREAKY CHICK DOWN LIKE THEY WERE NOTHING.

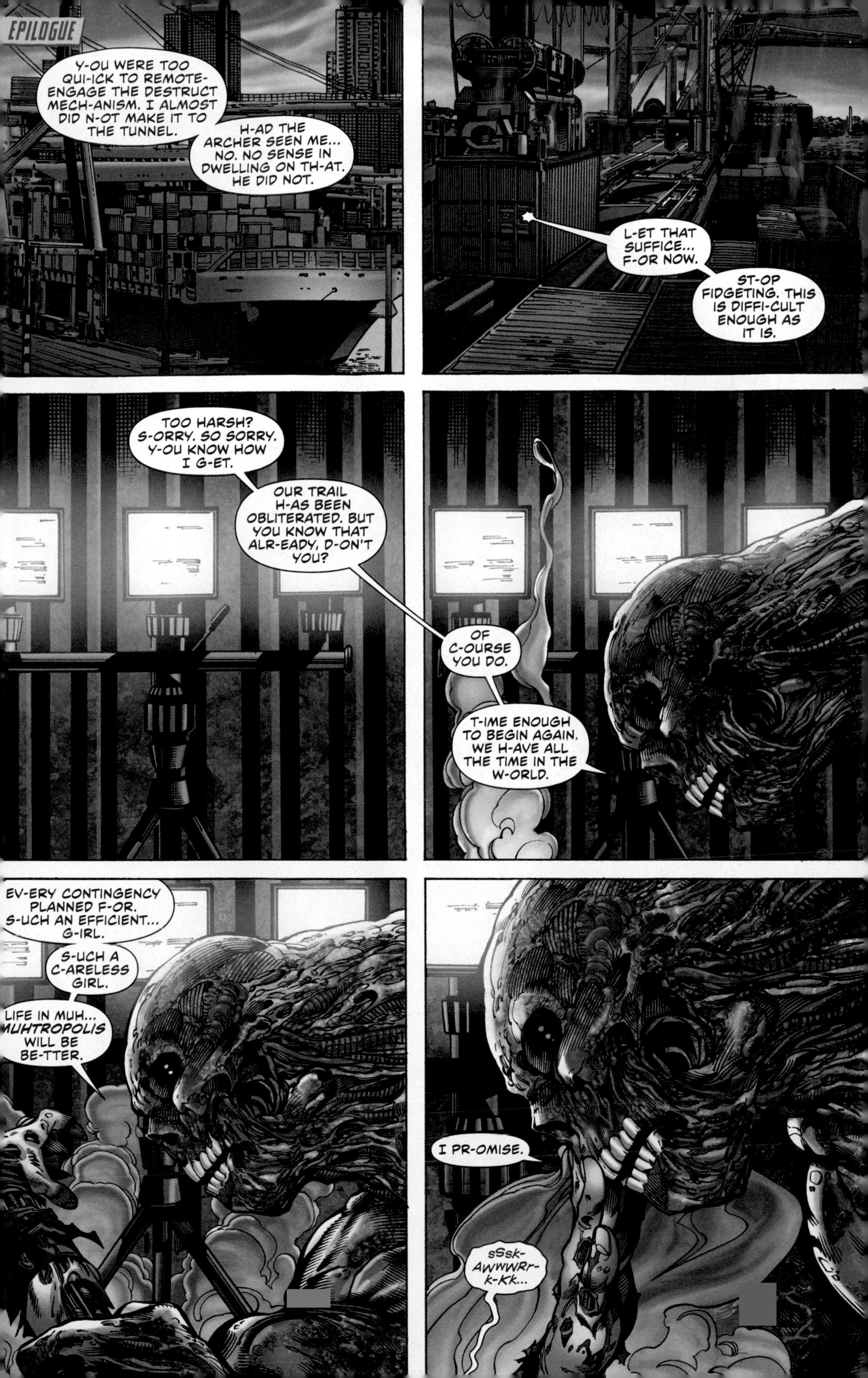
EPILOGUE
Y-OU WERE TOO QUI-ICK TO REMOTE-ENGAGE THE DESTRUCT MECH-ANISM. I ALMOST DID N-OT MAKE IT TO THE TUNNEL.
H-AD THE ARCHER SEEN ME... NO. NO SENSE IN DWELLING ON TH-AT. HE DID NOT.
L-ET THAT SUFFICE... F-OR NOW.
ST-OP FIDGETING. THIS IS DIFFI-CULT ENOUGH AS IT IS.
TOO HARSH? S-ORRY. SO SORRY. Y-OU KNOW HOW I G-ET.
OUR TRAIL H-AS BEEN OBLITERATED. BUT YOU KNOW THAT ALR-EADY, D-ON'T YOU?
OF C-OURSE YOU DO.
T-IME ENOUGH TO BEGIN AGAIN. WE H-AVE ALL THE TIME IN THE W-ORLD.
EV-ERY CONTINGENCY PLANNED F-OR. S-UCH AN EFFICIENT... G-IRL.
S-UCH A C-ARELESS GIRL.
LIFE IN MUH... MUHTROPOLIS WILL BE BE-TTER.
I PR-OMISE.
sSsk-AWWWRr-k-Kk...

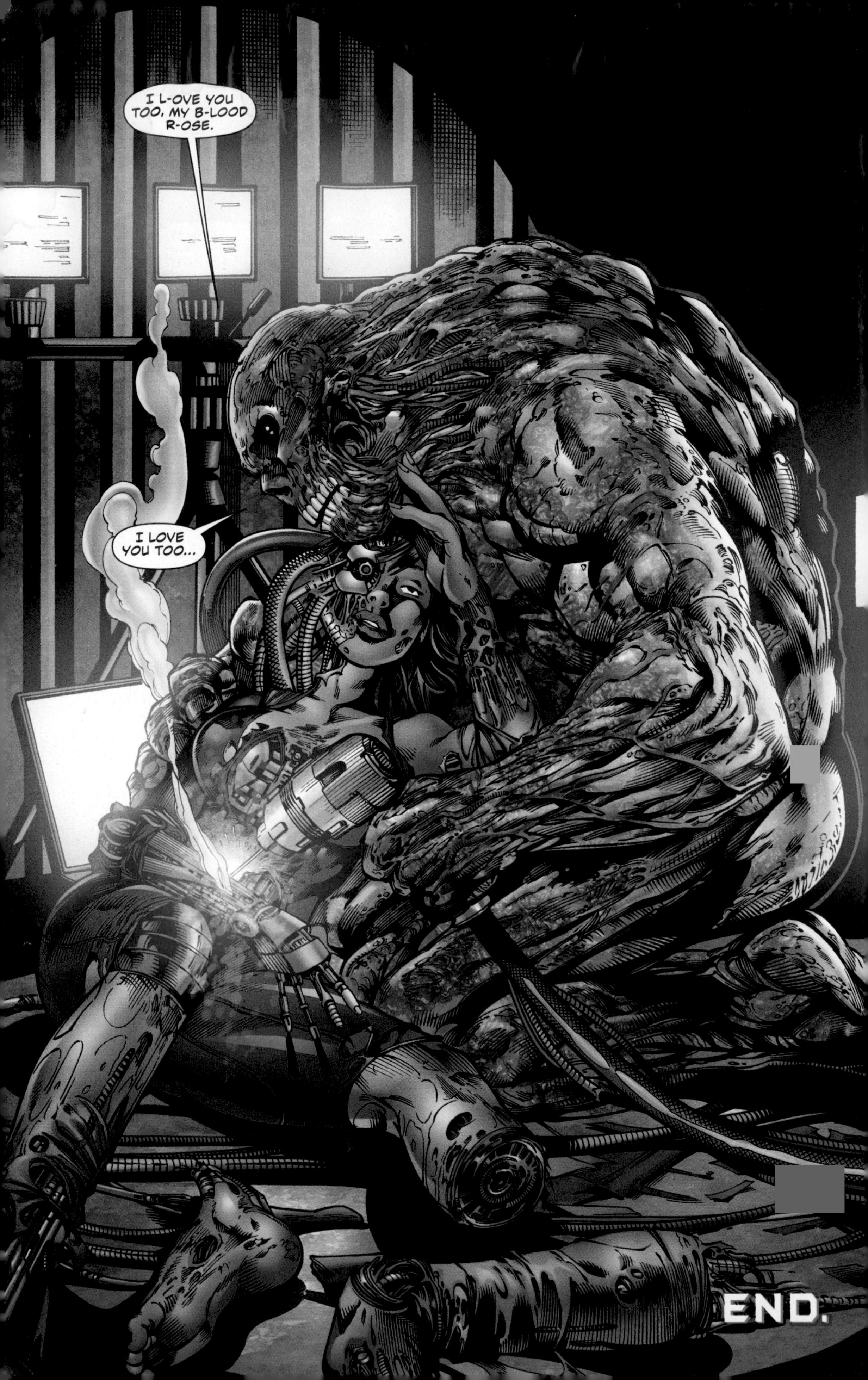
I L-OVE YOU TOO, MY B-LOOD R-OSE.
I LOVE YOU TOO...
END.

GREEN ARROW
CHARACTER DESIGNS

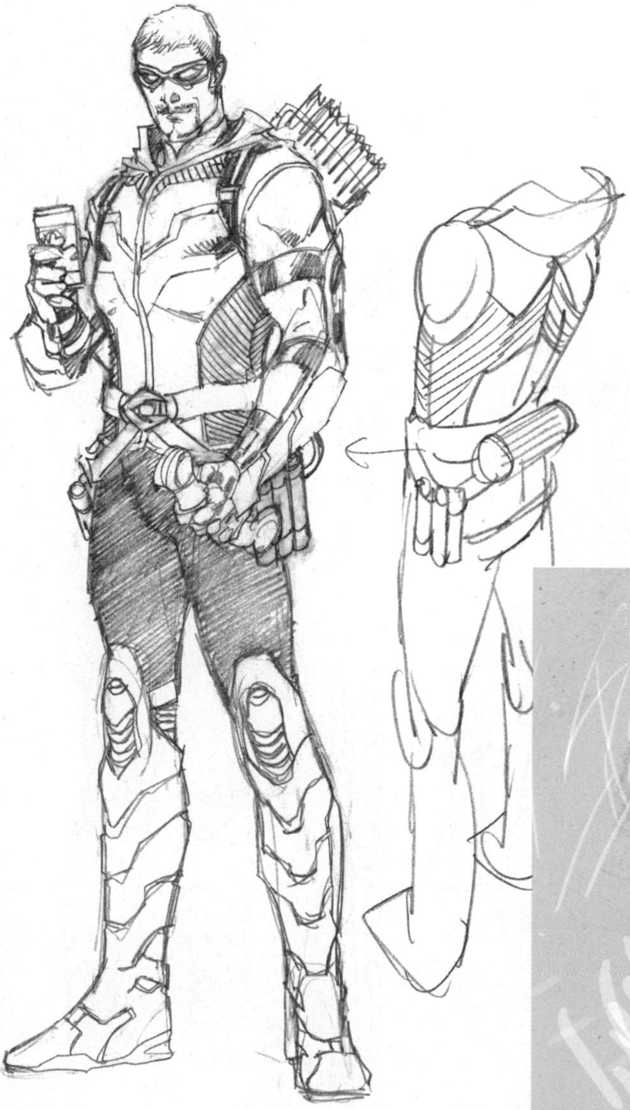

DC Co-Publisher JIM LEE nailed Green Arrow's new look right off the bat and may have secretly inspired Ollie's quitting-time drink at the end of GREEN ARROW #6.

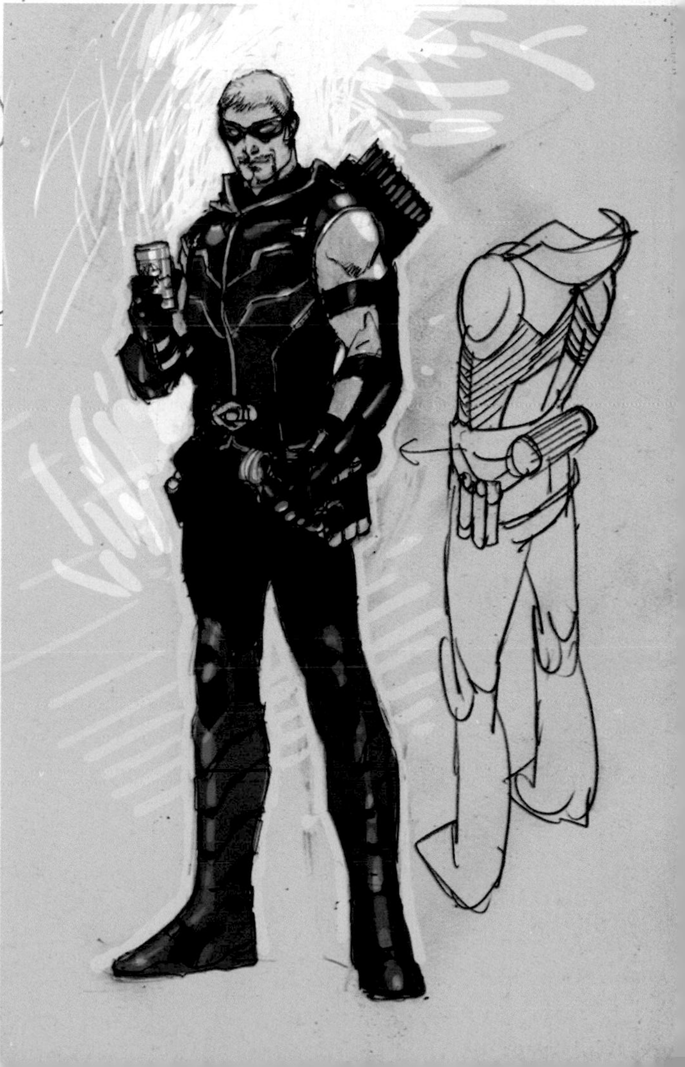

Artist CULLY HAMNER then stepped in for this character turnaround,
which would then be used to keep Green Arrow's look consistent across the
New 52 line. It even demonstrates how his bow telescopes.

GREEN
ARROW

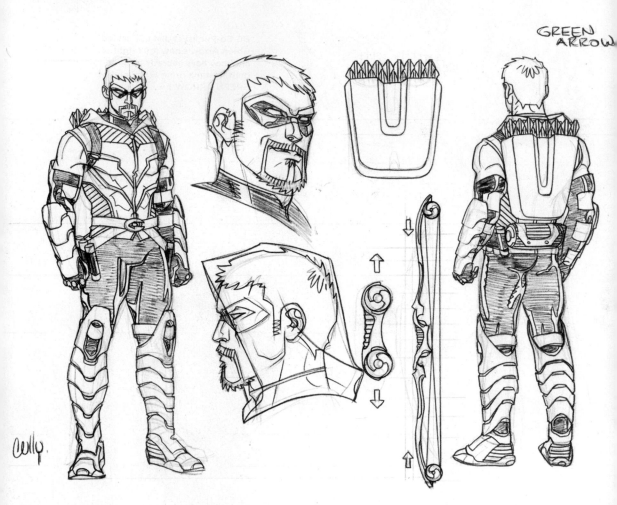

GREEN ARROW

In the final colored turnaround, Cully adjusted the size of Ollie's lenses and has him sporting stubble instead of his traditional goatee.

Here are artist DAN JURGENS's early takes on the gruesome, tragic Midas.

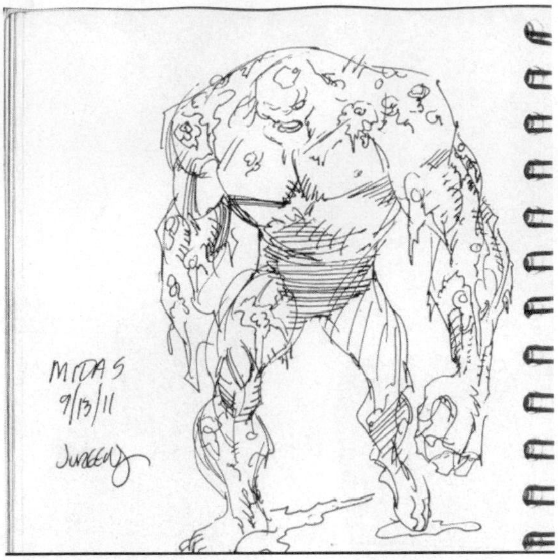
MIDAS
9/13/11
JURGENS

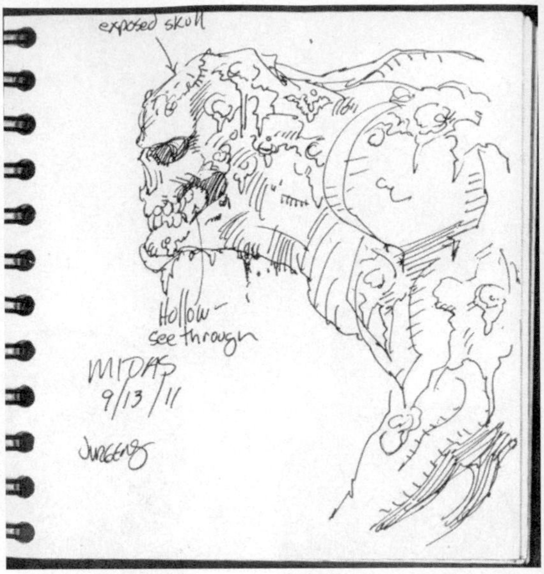
exposed skull
Hollow-
see through
MIDAS
9/13/11
JURGENS

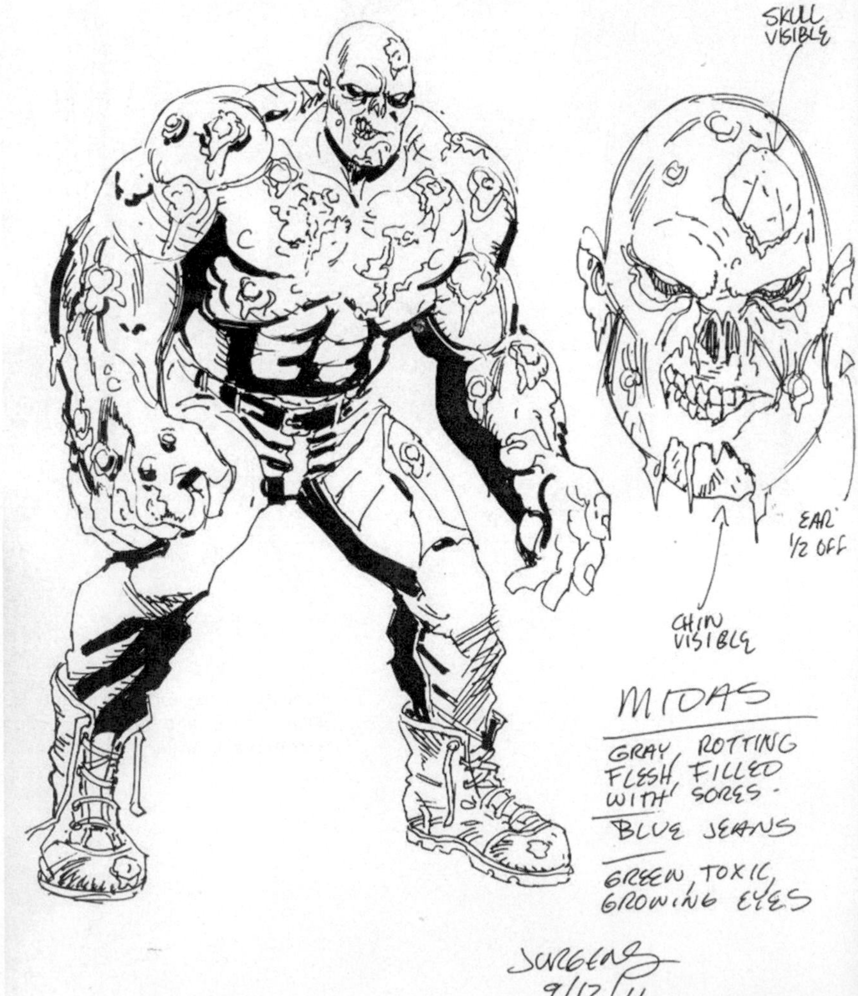
SKULL VISIBLE
EAR 1/2 OFF
CHIN VISIBLE
MIDAS
GRAY, ROTTING FLESH, FILLED WITH SORES -
BLUE JEANS
GREEN, TOXIC, GROWING EYES
JURGENS
9/12/11

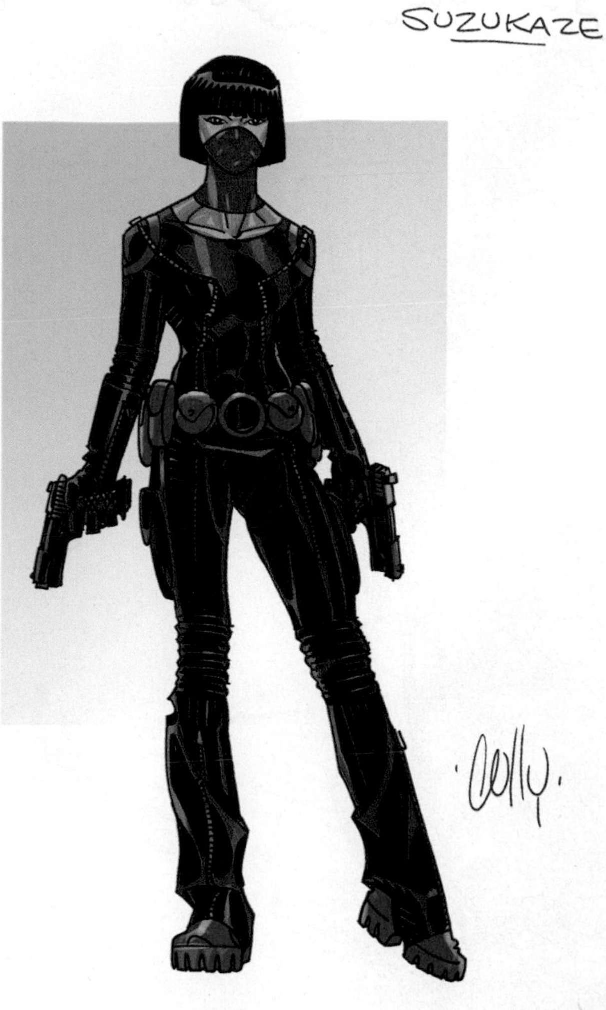
SUZUKAZE

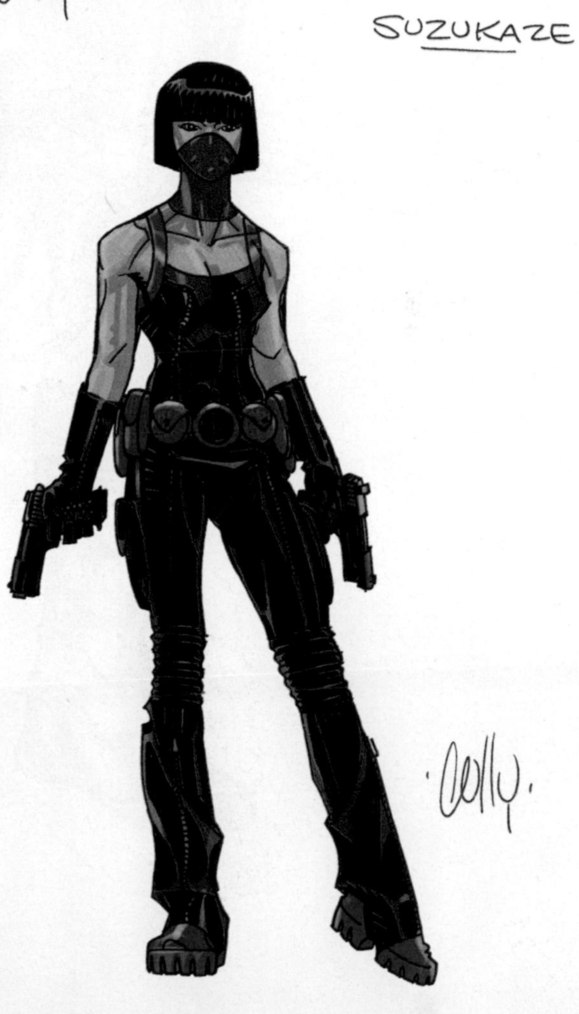
SUZUKAZE

Midas's partner in crime — and love — Blood Rose was designed by CULLY HAMNER.

Artist IGNACIO CALERO stepped in for the last issue of the collection. Here's his first attempt at drawing the Emerald Archer.

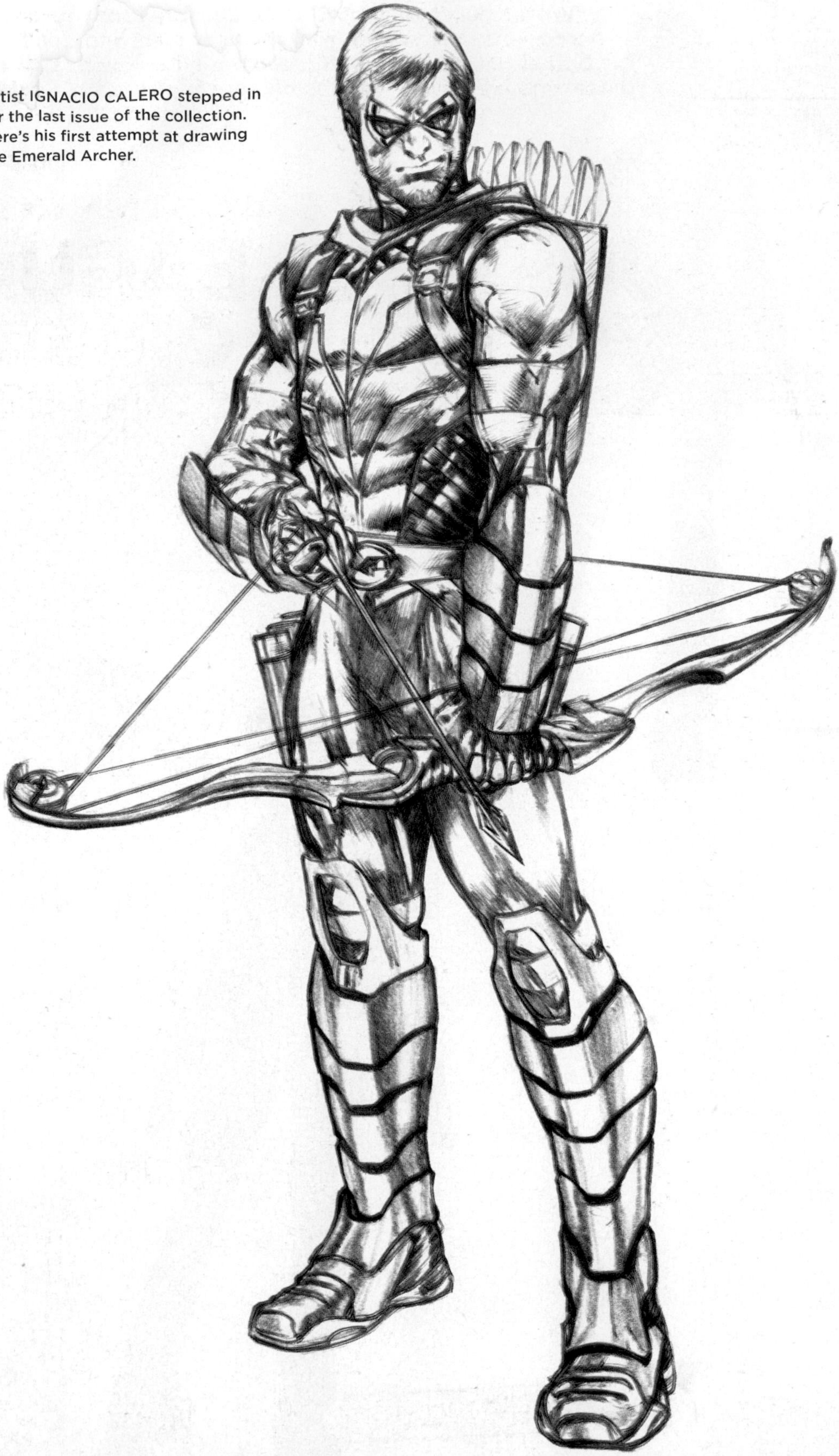

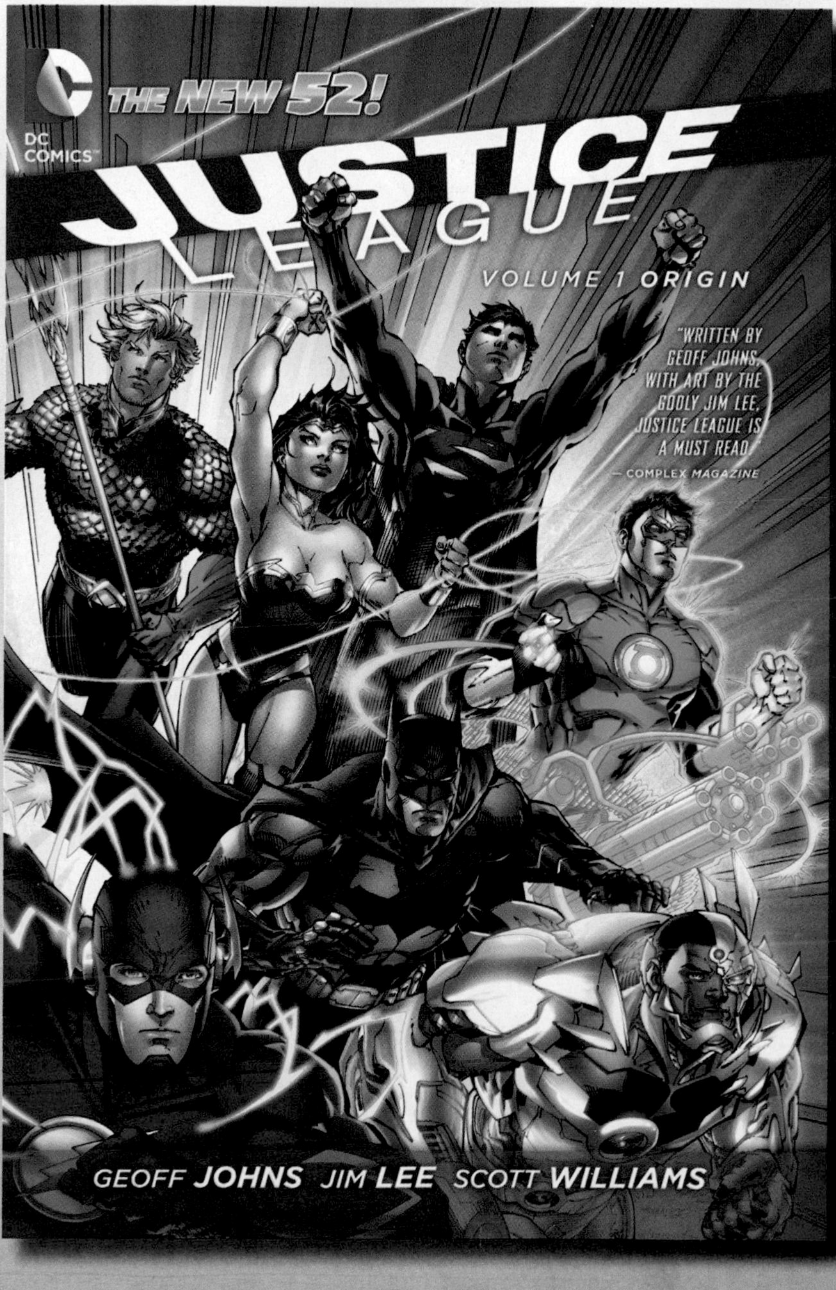
DC COMICS
THE NEW 52!
JUSTICE LEAGUE
VOLUME 1 ORIGIN
"WRITTEN BY GEOFF JOHNS, WITH ART BY THE GODLY JIM LEE, JUSTICE LEAGUE IS A MUST READ."
— COMPLEX MAGAZINE
GEOFF JOHNS JIM LEE SCOTT WILLIAMS

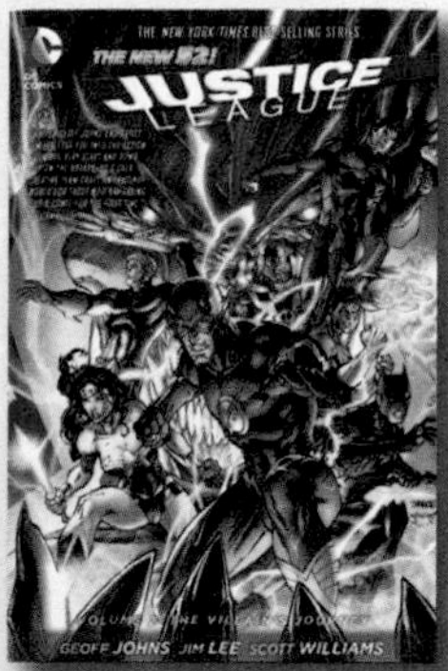
THE NEW 52!
JUSTICE LEAGUE
GEOFF JOHNS JIM LEE SCOTT WILLIAMS

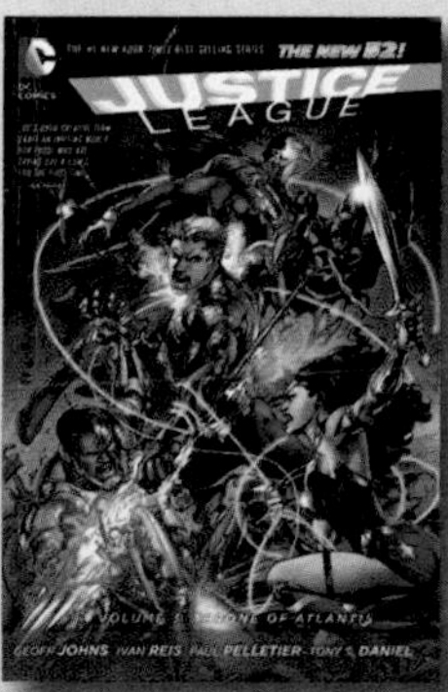
THE NEW 52!
JUSTICE LEAGUE
GEOFF JOHNS IVAN REIS PAUL PELLETIER TONY S. DANIEL

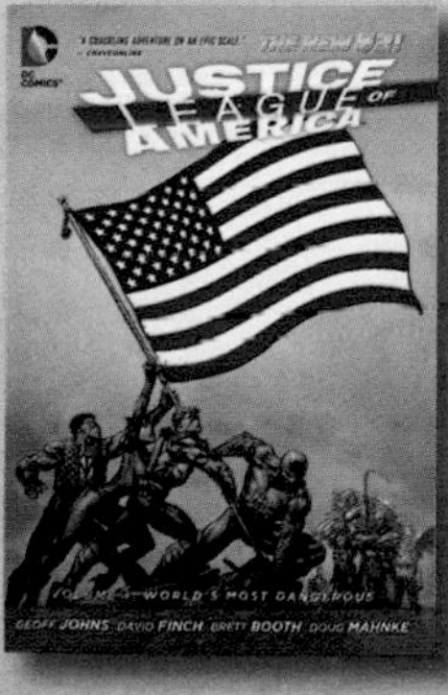
THE NEW 52!
JUSTICE LEAGUE OF AMERICA
GEOFF JOHNS DAVID FINCH BRETT BOOTH DOUG MAHNKE